SATURDAY AT M.I.9

This is the first inside story of the underground
escape lines in occupied North-West Europe
which brought back to Britain over 4,000 Allied
servicemen during the Second World War. It is not
an official history. Many details will remain
secret for a long time but Airey Neave who, in
the last two years of war, was the chief
organiser at M.I.9, gives his own unique
account. He describes how the escape lines
began in the first dark hours of German occupation and how thousands of ordinary people made
their own contribution to Allied victory by
hiding, feeding and guiding the men to safety.

The book covers the whole range of escape
operations by land, sea and air. It shows how
the leaders in occupied territory established
routes over the Spanish frontier after Dunkirk
and how they were reinforced and extended
despite the Gestapo. Over 500 people were
executed or died in concentration camps for this
work. Some lines were broken and mended many
many times after mass arrest but still
continued in operation. Altogether 3,000 Allied
airmen shot down in occupied territory, of
whom half were Americans, reached safety
before the Allied invasion of Normandy. This
astonishing result had an enormous impact on
the morale of the Air Forces and restored
trained men to the battle. The book closes with
the rescue of hundreds of airmen from the
Germans after the invasion, in which the author
himself took part.

Saturday at M.I.9.

A history of underground escape lines in
North-West Europe in 1940–5 by a leading
organiser at M.I.9.

Airey Neave

HODDER PAPERBACKS

Copyright © 1969 by Airey Neave
First published 1969 by Hodder & Stoughton Ltd
Hodder Paperback edition 1971
Second Impression 1971

Printed and bound in Great Britain for
Hodder Paperbacks Ltd,
St. Paul's House, Warwick Lane,
London, E.C.4
by Hazell Watson & Viney Ltd,
Aylesbury, Bucks

ISBN 0 340 12749 X

PREFACE

No official history of M.I.9 or its top secret section I.S.9(d), better known as Room 900 at the War Office, can be written for many years. This book is based on my personal experience at Room 900 in the Second World War. It is the first to be written about its escape organisation from the inside.

Ours was a comparatively small intelligence service so far as the number of principal agents was concerned, and we have kept in touch since the war. While writing the book, I have visited France, Belgium and Holland and talked to many of those still living. My wife did much of the research. Without her help I could not, in the midst of many other activities, have obtained valuable private information.

Nearly all the people whose story is told here have read the chapters concerning them, or have otherwise helped me to make the record as accurate as possible. I owe much to my conversations after the war with Major-General Albert-Marie Guérisse, G.C., D.S.O., Mlle. Andrée De Jongh, G.M., Mrs. Mary Lindell, O.B.E., the late Louis Nouveau, G.M., Baron Jean de Blommaert, D.S.O., and many others. Mrs. Beatrix Scholte-Terwindt, Capitaine Lucien Dumais, M.C., Lieutenant-Colonel R. M. Labrosse, M.C., Dignus Kragt, the late Val Williams, René and Raymonde Coache, François le Cornec and his Breton group, Leoni Savinos, and Comte Georges d'Oultremont kindly gave me personal reports on their missions.

Among those who lent photographs or supplied important details were: Madame Elvire de Greef, G.M., Madame Pierre Ugeux, G.M., Baronne Jean Greindl, Mrs. J. M. Langley, Madame Renée Nouveau, Major R. M. Crockatt, Georges Broussine, M.C., Omer Jubault and Jean-Pierre Mallet. I should also like to thank The Rt. Hon. Hugh Fraser, M.P., for reading the chapters about our operations after Arnhem, Jack Bottenheim and my son Patrick, for their study of the river crossings in Holland in 1944 and 1945; and Whitney Straight and F. W. Higginson for discussing their own escape stories.

I am especially grateful for the trouble taken by my former colleagues in M.I.9, Lieutenant-Colonel J. M. Langley, M.B.E., M.C., Ian Garrow, D.S.O., Donald Darling, H. B. A. de Bruyne, Susan Broomhall and Cecil Rait, M.C., in checking the manuscript. I had great assistance from the House of Commons Library, the Imperial War Museum, the Royal Air Forces Escaping Society, the B.B.C., Joy Robilliard, Mrs. Ann Arnold-Forster, Mrs. Mattha Lavington and Mrs. Joan St. George Saunders (of Writers and Speakers Research). The advice I received on revising the text from Mrs. Venetia Pollock and David Tutaev was invaluable. It was typed at various stages by Joan Hall, Pamela Plumb and Christine Prentice and the maps were drawn by Mr. A. Spark.

Compared with the large amount of published material on S.O.E. and the number of individual escape stories written since the Second World War, the literature on organised escape lines for Allied Servicemen is limited. My own books, *They Have Their Exits* and *Little Cyclone*, like the others, do not describe Room 900, for reasons which appear in the first chapter. To confirm my recollections and those of my friends I have studied:

Pantaraxia by Nubar Gulbenkian.
The Way Back by Vincent Brome.
No Drums No Trumpets by Barry Wynne.
The Great Detective by Iain Adamson.
Reseau Comète, *La Ligne de Démarcation* and
    La Maison d'Alphonse by Rémy.
Inside S.O.E. by E. H. Cookridge.
S.O.E. in France by M. R. D. Foot.
Travel by Dark after Arnhem by Graeme Warrack.
Cockleshell Heroes by C. E. Lucas-Phillips.
In Trust and Treason by Gordon Young.

I have acknowledged the use of material from some of these elsewhere. For Chapter 25 and the 'Commando Order' I have been able to draw on my own report in Volume XLII of the *Trial of the Major War Criminals* at Nuremburg.

My only regret is that in the complex history of the escape lines for which thousands of people in occupied north-west Europe risked their lives, I have not been able to include the names of many who deserve our recognition and gratitude.

AIREY NEAVE

CONTENTS

			Page
PART I	AFTER COLDITZ		
	1.	Background to the Escape Lines	15
	2.	Prisoner of War	26
	3.	Switzerland 1942	38
	4.	Louis Nouveau's flat	46
	5.	The Great Central Hotel	56
	6.	Saturday at M.I.9	64
PART II	THE O'LEARY LINE		
	7.	The Pioneers	75
	8.	The Return of Whitney Straight	82
	9.	Sea Operations	94
	10.	The Price	110
PART III	THE COMET LINE		
	11.	Dédée	127
	12.	The Maréchal Affair	140
	13.	A Winter of Disaster	151
	14.	Gibraltar Meeting	166
PART IV	WOMEN AGENTS		
	15.	Mary Lindell	183
	16.	The Commandos	194
	17.	Trix	205
PART V	BRITTANY		
	18.	Val Williams	217
	19.	'Shelburne'	226

PART VI   'MARATHON'

              20. Before the Bombardment   241
              21. The 'Sherwood' Plan   249
              22. The Race to the Forest   261

PART VII   OCCUPIED HOLLAND

              23. After Arnhem   275
              24. Pegasus I and II   289

PART VIII   AFTERMATH

              25. The Traitors   303
              26. In Retrospect   312

LIST OF MAPS

page.

Map showing Fort de la Revère, scene of escape operations
by O'Leary, 1942 — 101

Map of Spanish frontier zone showing Perpignan and Canet-
Plage where crossings to Barcelona and *Tarana* sea operations took place — 105

Map of the Spanish frontier zone used by Dédée and the
Comet escape line, 1941–1944 — 130

Map to illustrate Shelburne Naval operations in Brittany,
1943 and 1944 — 228

Map showing the site of the camp for airmen in the Forêt de
Fréteval, 1944 — 251

Area of rescue operations for First Airborne Division survivors, 1944 — 282

PART I

AFTER COLDITZ

CHAPTER I

Background to the Escape Lines

FIFTEEN years ago, I described how, disguised as a German officer, I escaped from Colditz castle near Leipzig, and reached neutral Switzerland in January 1942.[1] I wrote of my own reaction to this experience and the vivid contrast of the former prisoner-of-war set in authority over Goering and other Nazi leaders at Nuremburg three years later. Of what happened to me during those three years I said little. I devoted only two cryptic pages to my part in the organisation of secret escape routes by M.I.9 in Europe during the Second World War.

There were two reasons for this gap in my story. In war, the very young are often exposed to violent tensions and only in middle age do these subside. I could not banish from my thoughts the intense emotion of my successful escape from Colditz to England. With the years, this personal adventure became less important to me, and it was easier to write objectively of operations to save others from German prison camps.

The second reason for my veiled references to the escape lines, was the belief, when *They Have Their Exits* was published, that their structure and techniques might be used again. I wrote the book during a period of extreme hostility between the Soviet Union and the Western world. In the early nineteen-fifties war in Europe seemed possible over the same ground where the Allies had fought Hitler. It was assumed that men and women in countries occupied by the Nazis, who had served us so well, would volunteer a second time and, though stories of individual heroism had appeared in print, that true details of the organisations should remain unpublished.[2]

---

[1] *They Have Their Exits*, Hodder and Stoughton, 1953.
[2] In *They Have Their Exits* the real names of those who helped me to escape to Spain and other details were not disclosed.

Official reticence may be exasperating to those who assert that the secrets of the last war need no longer be kept. But in 1953, it was obvious that the nature of the system in London by which the escape lines were operated should not be disclosed. Even to⁻ᵈ .y, all documents and many particulars of M.I.9, the War Office branch concerned with Allied prisoners-of-war, remain subject to the Official Secrets Acts. But with the passage of time I am able, as one of those who took part, to give my personal account of its work in organising the return of Allied Servicemen.

My three years with M.I.9 were concerned with secret escape operations in France, Belgium and Holland and they are the subject of this book. I played no part in similar activities in Italy and the Middle and Far East. I seek to record how these lines were assisted from London and the courage and sacrifice of ordinary people who volunteered to help fighting men return to action against the enemy. Those who took part in this perilous work were of every age, from the very young who acted as guides, to the old and poor who hid men on the run in defiance of the Gestapo.

By the end of the war this form of clandestine service had become a popular movement in which large numbers of men and women of different backgrounds and political beliefs made their contribution to victory. Harbouring men shot down in air combat or cut off from their regiments, appealed to their humanity. They did not regard themselves as spies, nor were the escape organisations, except rarely, concerned with military intelligence or sabotage. Until the end of the war, there were few trained agents of M.I.9 in the field. The organisation depended on several thousand volunteers to contact the men and hide them till they could be brought to safety. The function of M.I.9 was to supply money, radio communications, the dropping of supplies, 'pickups' by aircraft and naval evacuations from the coasts of France.

The escape lines had few of the political complications which beset other secret services. Communists and priests could combine in what they believed to be a great human cause. It inspired doctors and nurses, artists and poets, to risk their lives. The characters in this story were their leaders but the majority came from lowly cafés, farms and working-class homes in all corners of occupied North-West Europe. At the end of the war M.I.9 estimated that there were over 12,000 survivors of this movement, but few realise the value and significance of their work today. Those who never experienced Nazi occupation may find it difficult to understand their enthusiasm, their mistakes and their extraordinary persistence in the face of treachery and the Gestapo. The survivors of that terror seek neither publicity nor to point a moral to a younger generation. They hated Nazi tyranny and acted in the name of charity and freedom. They wished, too, to play their part, however humble, in the Allied struggle.

The post-Dunkirk period in North-West Europe set the scene for future underground escape operations. By the Armistice of June 1940, France was divided by a demarcation line. All the country north and west of the line was occupied by German Troops. South of it was the Free or Unoccupied Zone administered by the Government of eighty-five-year-old Marshal Petain from Vichy. It was known, and is referred to here, as the Vichy Government. Though hostile to Britain and her allies, it lacked the authority to prevent the establishment of large-scale escape activities after Dunkirk until the Occupation by the Germans of the whole of France in November 1942.

In Occupied France, the rule of the Gestapo and other German counter-espionage services, made the running of escape routes a dangerous operation from the start, and there were early casualties. In the Unoccupied Zone, the security forces consisted of the gendarmes of French civilian police who frequently co-operated with escape workers and the hated Milice, a group of thugs recruited by the Vichy Government who often betrayed and arrested their own countrymen. They have been described as sadists drawn from the scum of the jails and a constant threat to the French Resistance Movement.[1]

The first escape organisations were formed by small groups of patriots in 1940, without money or outside aid, to enable survivors of the British Army and Air Force to avoid being taken prisoner by the Germans after Dunkirk. Several hundred drifted through France in groups or as individuals. Those who were not rounded up by the Germans crossed the demarcation line to the Unoccupied Zone and waited at Marseille for someone to take charge of them.

[1] M.R.D. Foot: S.O.E. in France, H.M. Stationery Office, 1966; and see Chapter 25 for an account of the Nazi Security system which confronted the escape lines.

Many of those who helped were nurses who spirited them out of hospital in northern France, hid them with friends and sent them on their way to Paris. For a few weeks after the armistice, many got through to the relative security of the south coast without papers or speaking a word of French, and sometimes in uniform. Soon such journeys became almost impossible without guides. French and Belgians determined to resist Hitler, began to organise themselves into teams to hide and shelter them, but it was not until 1941 that regular escape lines from Brussels, Paris and Marseille to neutral Spain were fully established. By then, the Gestapo had gained full control in occupied France and infiltrated their agents in civilian clothes south of the demarcation line.

June and July 1940 were romantic months in the history of escape. Soldiers who had lost touch with their units but were still free, settled down with French families in the north of France and were reluctant to leave. A few married, and remained there till the war was over. Others, accompanied by French and Belgian girls, walked or bicycled in the fine weather, from village to village, till they reached the Unoccupied Zone. The Germans, busy with the problems of occupation and the projected assault on England, caught few of them. Several weeks after the fall of France, bewildered figures in khaki battle dress could still be seen in the streets of Paris. On the French Riviera a committee of British residents, with the Duke of Westminster as Chairman, was formed to raise funds for those who were assembling on the coast with few ideas of how to rejoin their lines. The more determined, led by their officers, crossed the Spanish frontier, and, after experiencing the squalor of Spanish prisons, were released to the British Embassy in Madrid. A private soldier, on arrival in diplomatic hands, anxiously explained:

"I've lost me bloody rifle, sir!"

Throughout 1940 and 1941, organised escape routes took shape under leaders whose names were to become famous in the history of underground war. They have been portrayed in a number of books published in the last twenty years. The story of Captain Ian Garrow and Pat O'Leary at Marseille has been told by Vincent Brome in *The Way Back*.[1] 'Rémy' the great French Resistance leader, has compiled three volumes of interviews with the survivors of the Comet line founded by Andrée De Jongh (Dédée) and her father

[1] Cassell, 1957.

in 1941.[1] I have written an account of her and the Comet escape line in *Little Cyclone*.[2] To this period also belongs the story of Mary Lindell in *No Drums No Trumpets* by Barry Wynne.[3] These books reveal the atmosphere in which early escapes from the Germans were organised, and they are stories of splendid personal exploits, suffering and triumph. They convey only a shadowy impression of the organisation in London which kept in contact with their leaders. This was the top-secret section of M.I.9 at Room 900 in the War Office known as I.S.9(d).[4] This book is the first to be published about it. I was a member of its tiny staff from May 1942 until the defeat of Germany three years later, and I have tried to explain the nature of its duties and operations and to give a picture of the complex network of escape organisations in France, Belgium and Holland.

In 1939 the War Office held consultations with selected escapers from the First World War to decide how help could be given to prisoners. Shortly before the invasion of France, M.I.9 was formed, under Brigadier Norman Crockatt, to study this problem in the light of their advice.[5] In June, 1940, they were presented with the unforeseen and unprecedented problem of hundreds of troops cut off from their units after the defeat in the west. It necessitated the creation of an entirely novel form of secret service to maintain regular lines to neutral territory in Spain or Portugal and sometimes Switzerland. This broke fresh ground in the field of military intelligence. There were few examples of such activities in the First World War when static conditions in the trenches gave less opportunity for an underground escape system. The most inspiring was that of Nurse Edith Cavell shot in Brussels for helping British soldiers to escape to Holland in 1915.

The situation in 1940 required a new approach to organised escape, but despite the enthusiasm of M.I.9 and the urgency of the problem, I.S.9(d) was not in operation till 1941.[6] Another development, hitherto unknown, was the training of hundreds of thousands of

---

[1] *Réseau Comète*, Vols. I, II and III, Librairie Academique Perrin, 1966.

[2] Hodder and Stoughton, 1954.

[3] Arthur Barker, 1961.

[4] i.e. Intelligence School No. 9 (D).

[5] See Chapter 5. I.S.9(d) was largely Crockatt's creation. His staff included A. J. Evans, author of *The Escaping Club*.

[6] Though a War Office section to organise escape lines existed from the summer of 1940. See Chapter 7.

servicemen in the art of escape and the avoidance of capture known
as 'evasion', in which M.I.9 achieved remarkable success. The return
of trained soldiers and airmen to continue the fight became a notable
contribution to the Allied effort in war, and a source of anxiety to
the Germans.

The majority of those who returned by land, sea or air from
North-West Europe were from the Allied Air Forces. They were
highly trained and valuable aircrew. The miracle of their re-
appearance at Air Force bases and stations in Britain had a marvellous
effect, as I was able to witness, on the morale of all who flew against
Germany. It led to an undying legend among airmen of the genero-
sity and devotion of those who helped them to get back. This
feeling of gratitude and mutual sympathy in danger lives on in the
work of the Royal Air Forces Escaping Society which still maintains
contact with over 4,000 helpers.

The total number who escaped from enemy hands or evaded
capture was remarkable, but the form in which the figures were
presented by M.I.9 makes them difficult to interpret. In western
Europe, including Italy, the total number of Servicemen from
Britain and the Commonwealth *who reached the Allied front line*
(*including Russian*), between the outbreak of war and June 1945, was
3,631. For the same period, the number of Americans was 3,415
making a grand total of 7,046. These figures include those who
escaped from prison camps or in the battle zone, were brought
down escape lines to neutral territory, were evacuated by sea or air,
and by operational rescue during the Allied invasion of Europe.

There is no separate total for those who reached safety from
occupied France, Belgium and Holland, the territories with which
the work of I.S.9(d) was solely concerned. The fairest estimate
which can be made is that over 4,000, including Americans, returned
to England from these occupied countries, before the Allied landing
in Normandy in June 1944. This approximate figure is based on
reports from the main escape organisations after the war and on the
results of specific underground operations described in this book.
It incorporates about 1,000 soldiers who were not captured after
Dunkirk in 1940 and about 3,000 airmen shot down over occupied
territory before D-Day, of whom the majority reached neutral
Spain. After D-Day, between 500 and 600 were liberated by Allied
Forces including the special rescue units improvised by M.I.9

before our troops invaded Germany, making a grand total of approximately, 4,600 in north-west Europe.

The rest of the 7,046 in western Europe were those who got away at the collapse of Italy and in confused conditions at the time of the German surrender. A small number made their own way into Russian hands. All remaining prisoners-of-war were liberated from their camps or on the march. Another 5,413 took refuge in Switzerland, 227 of them Americans, mainly at the end of hostilities. Very few of them were regarded by M.I.9 as having escaped and they were recorded separately from those who reached the Allied front line.

M.I.9 divided the men who came back into two categories: escapers and evaders. To be classified as an 'escaper', it was sufficient to have been in enemy hands for only a few minutes. The circumstances ranged from an escape from a temporary cage in the battle zone to a breakout from a prison camp in the heart of Germany or Italy; 1,248 men from British and Commonwealth units were classified as escapers from these two countries during the war. Most of them came from prison camps at the time of the Allied advance, and only a very small number were in the hands of secret organisations.

Before Italy and Germany were entered, successful escapes from prison camps were few. Prisoners in Italy were better guarded than in Germany and only a handful reached Switzerland before the period of Italian surrender. Out of 135,009 British and Commonwealth prisoners-of-war in Nazi Germany, about 150 escaped to Sweden, Russia, Switzerland or Spain before the Allies converged on Hitler's forces and chaos ensued.[1] American escapers numbered 713 and, in most cases, reached the Allied lines during the last stages of the war. The majority of all genuine escapers came from Army units, though the Air Forces and Navy had their distinguished representatives. Only a few are the subject of this account of the evasion network in Occupied countries.

The position was different for those who were at no time captured by the enemy. They were known as 'evaders' and, except for several hundred survivors of the British Expeditionary Force at Dunkirk and St. Valery in 1940, came almost entirely from the Air

---

[1] Eleven British escaped from the special camp for escapers at Colditz in 1942 and 1943. The total captured by Germany and Italy was 142,319 of whom 7,310 were killed or died in captivity.

Forces. The distinction is important and from their approximate numbers, the real work of I.S.9(d) in occupied north-west Europe can be assessed, though the existence only of total numbers for western Europe, including Italy, makes it difficult to be more precise. *At least 3,000 airmen were shot down and avoided imprisonment before D-Day in occupied north-west Europe.* Ninety per cent of these arrived in Spain. Most of the 500 or 600 who were the subject of operational rescues in the battle zone after D-Day were from the Allied Air Forces. The largest proportion of all Air Force evaders were Americans.[1]

These men were aircrew, shot down on diverse flying operations, who had not suffered the rigours of a prisoner-of-war camp. They were often able to continue flying and many lost their lives afterwards, but they represent a significant renewal of manpower. They also demonstrate the value of training in escape and evasion. Their numbers account for the desperate efforts by the Germans in occupied territory to crush the escape organisations. A newly returned evader, especially a trained pilot, was of far more operational value than a man who had spent several months 'behind the wire', though most escapers from prison camps rejoined the battle and several were killed. A terrible price had to be paid by underground escape workers for this achievement. Over 500 civilians from France, Belgium and Holland were arrested and shot or died in concentration camps. A far greater number succumbed to their treatment after the war.

It is impossible to say how many servicemen were assisted by established escape organisations between 1940 and 1945. In 1940 there were many individual journeys over the Spanish frontier. Some lines began without aid but subsequently became absorbed or linked to those in contact with London. In M.I.9 interrogation reports, names frequently appeared of people who had hidden men and sent them on their way but belonged to no identifiable group. These were the good Samaritans who never failed to help. There were also a few independent and even eccentric men among the evaders who refused all assistance and miraculously got home, even as late as 1944. But, after 1941 the large majority of those who never became prisoners returned by organised escape lines. Most of

---

[1] The actual M.I.9 figures for Air Force evaders in Western Europe as a whole, were: 1,975 R.A.F. and Commonwealth and 2,962 United States Air Force.

them crossed the Pyrenees to San Sebastian in the west and to Barcelona in the east of Spain where, if not detained by the police, they were sheltered by the British Consulates and transferred to the British Embassy in Madrid.

By 1941, the method of evasion was well defined especially for an airman. If he could get away undetected from his aircraft, he entered a system of 'safe houses' whose owners hid and fed him, then sent him to a collecting point in the Hague, Amsterdam, Liège, Brussels, Paris, Marseille, Toulouse, or St. Jean-de-Luz. Supplied with false papers and suitable clothes, he was taken by train to a frontier zone and led by guides over the mountains to Spain. Later in the war, over 200 were recovered by naval operations from the South of France and Brittany for which I.S.9(d) were responsible. Air operations by Lysander or Hudson aircraft to pick up men at night from central France accounted for no more than fifty. Those extricated from behind the enemy lines after the Normandy invasion especially in France and Holland, were the subject of operations in which Special Air Service and American paratroops also played a part.

It is difficult to apportion the numbers to particular routes referred to in this book, though the O'Leary line was responsible for about 600 and the Comet line about 1,000. Many small groups which were known to exist, especially in rural districts, are not mentioned. Attempts by the Gestapo, and the traitors who served them, to infiltrate the lines, caused them to be broken many times and the men were transferred from one group to another. The Gestapo and other German secret police and security services behaved with great brutality to ordinary people caught with British or American airmen in their homes. It was their practice to dispose of those whom they considered humble and unimportant to their enquiries. The real organisers, if captured, were kept alive and submitted to torture. Nearly all the agents of I.S.9(d) who received training in England survived the war despite their ghastly experiences.

Over the escape lines hung the shadow of treachery. Of the 500 or more who died in this cause, at least 150 people, of all ages, were betrayed by the Englishman Harold Cole, and Belgian and French traitors who sold themselves to the Gestapo. This was the balance of sacrifice, which no one who worked in underground escape can ever forget. But as a contribution to the war in the air, their devotion had a profound influence. It was not only that, in those days, a bomber pilot cost £10,000 to train, and a fighter pilot £15,000. It was the encouraging impact on the Air Force who, in the later stages, had more than an even chance of return if they were shot down.

I do not attempt to conceal or defend the early amateurishness and the grave mistakes which were made in London and in the field. In underground war some errors are inevitable, but chairborne criticism is not enough. No one who has not been put to the test should keenly sit in judgement on those who faced the Gestapo. A generation after, I have tried to recapture their gaiety and courage.

Since the war, I have kept in touch with many of those who served us so well. The Royal Air Forces Escaping Society, which gives financial aid to those in need, has made me one of their trustees. I am also privileged to be a councillor of the Sue Ryder Foundation. The homes for victims of Nazi barbarism established by Sue Ryder and her husband Group Captain Leonard Cheshire V.C. are among the great humane achievements of our time. Many in these homes lost their health and sometimes their reason for their work in the escape lines. They are not forgotten by those they saved.

The struggle to achieve justice for British victims of Nazi brutality was a long one. For many years, with other Members of the House of Commons, I reproached the Foreign Office for their failure to make a financial settlement with the Germans. The campaign ended in June 1964 with an Agreement by the Federal German Republic to pay £1,000,000 in compensation, but for many it came twenty years too late. It is a sad reflection on our sense of priorities that the fear of embarrassing our former enemies, for reasons of foreign policy, should take precedence over the fate of those they mal-treated.

Two and a half years after the signing of this Agreement, came a scandal for which the Germans had no responsibility. This was the refusal of the Foreign Office to compensate a handful of British inmates of Sachsenhausen concentration camp. Among them were the great escapers, Group Captain 'Wings' Day, Mr. Sydney Dowse and Lt.-Colonel Jack Churchill. That justice prevailed in the end was due to the support which I received from all parties in the

House of Commons and to the Parliamentary Commissioner for Administration, Sir Edmund Compton.[1]

If my own experiences have influenced my actions in the last twenty-five years, they have also helped me to write this book. When I arrived in London after my escape from Colditz, I was appointed to I.S.9(d) at Room 900 in the War Office under the pseudonym of 'Saturday'. Before I tell the story of my life there and discuss the escape network, I shall briefly describe my own escape and the striking difference between being alone in enemy territory and of being a mere 'parcel' in an escape line. My adventure coloured much of what came after. It gave me the insight and comprehension which led to my service in M.I.9 and the desire to help those who had helped me. I had been a prisoner of the Gestapo and I understood the courage and resource which our agents would need. I used this knowledge when selecting them and devising their training.

I have tried to catch some of the tension and excitement, the sorrow and elation, which agents, escapers and evaders and my colleagues at I.S.9(d) continually underwent. This is not an official history but a story based mainly on my own knowledge and personal accounts given to me by many friends in the great escape fraternity. For me it is a moving chapter in the history of war and my own part in it began when frostbitten, hungry and exhausted I escaped over the Swiss frontier early in the morning of January 9th, 1942.

---

[1] Third Report of the Parliamentary Commissioner for Administration, December 20th, 1967, on claims by Group Captain Day and others for detention in Sachsenhausen.

CHAPTER 2

Prisoner of War

MY own escape story began at Calais. On the afternoon of May 24th, 1940, I was struck in the side by a machine-gun bullet as I raced across the Boulevard Léon Gambetta. It was a painful but not dangerous wound and I was able to crawl away from the stream of tracer bullets fired up the boulevard by tanks of 10th German Panzer Division which had encircled the town. All next day and night I lay in the cellars of a French hospital under heavy shellfire and dive-bombing till the morning of May 26th. As the Germans moved into the Old Town, and cornered the garrison, I made my first escape. The hospital staff tried to restrain me but I could not bear the thought of capture. It was not the only time I bore a charmed existence, for I staggered, half-conscious, through a minefield laid by the Queen Victoria's Rifles and collapsed on Platform One of the Gare Maritime. But there was no hope for the defenders and that evening, I was a prisoner-of-war.

The defence of Calais by the 30th Infantry Brigade which had landed from England on May 23rd and units, like my own, withdrawn from Arras, was one of the bloodiest of the war. The town was defended to the last round to delay the German attack on Dunkirk where the British Army was already embarking. Hitler was much impressed by the heavy casualties and stubborn resistance. An official historian has described the evening of May 26th when the survivors were forced to surrender. "Gradually the fighting ceased and the noise of battle died away as darkness shrouded the scene of devastation and death."[1] I remained in hospital at Calais until the end of July, and anxiously reflected upon my fate at the hands of the Germans. It was the Nazis I dreaded, not the front-line troops who behaved well to the wounded. As a reader of escape stories of the First World War, my thoughts turned quickly to the chances of

[1] *The War in France and Flanders 1939–40*, p. 168.

avoiding the inevitable journey to a prison camp. But I was more seriously wounded than my suicidal walk to the Gare Maritime had suggested, and too weak to escape from the hospital without help. In June a French soldier with a Red Cross arm band appeared in the ward which I shared with four officers and suggested a plan which caught my imagination. It would be possible, he said, to substitute me for the corpse of one of the prisoners who had died, and drive me out of the hospital in an ambulance. There were certain difficulties; the Germans inspected the bodies before they were taken to the Citadel of Calais to be buried but the driver was a loyal Frenchman and it might be possible to conceal me before the ambulance left the hospital. We also discussed our chances of sailing a boat across the Channel and other romantic schemes. The French soldier was Pierre d'Harcourt. He had avoided being taken prisoner with a tank regiment by disguising himself as a medical orderly. Before his sensational escape projects could be realised, he heard that British wounded were to be moved from Calais and thought it best to disappear to Paris. For many months he acted as a guide to British soldiers whom the Germans had failed to capture after Dunkirk, taking them across the demarcation line to the Unoccupied Zone of France.[1] In July 1941 he was arrested by the Gestapo in Paris and spent four terrible years in Fresnes prison and Buchenwald concentration camp which he has described in *The Real Enemy*.[2]

The influence of d'Harcourt and our discussions on the possibility of organising escape had a profound effect on me. But it was nearly two years before I could put my thoughts into action. With other wounded, I was moved to Lille by German lorry and there were several opportunities to escape at Bailleul where it broke down. Despite hair-raising accounts of imprisonment by a Catholic Chaplain attached to the Rifle Brigade, who had been captured in 1918 at Bailleul and was about to undergo this fate a second time, I had neither the nerve nor the physical strength to make the attempt. My vacillation cost me dear, but at this time there was no military training in such matters. While the lorry was repaired in Bailleul, I wandered unguarded through the streets with other wounded survivors of Calais. We were welcomed at every door, food and wine

[1] A group led by André Postel-Vinay, had begun to take men from Paris to Marseille in the summer of 1940.
[2] Longmans, 1967.

was pressed on us, and many offered to hide us from the Germans. Only a month after the fall of France, the spirit of Resistance and humanity was there. Why did I not take advantage of these generous offers? Though my thoughts had already turned to escape and its organisation, the weeks in hospital seemed to deprive me of all initiative. At sunset, as crowds waved and threw flowers in the main square of Bailleul, I suffered myself, to my shame, to be driven off to hospital in Lille.

This was not a heroic episode in my life, but had it not happened, I might never have escaped from Colditz to England and gained the experience which enabled me to plan the escape of others. At Lille, with the restoration of my strength, I determined to show more spirit. A pretty young French girl who brought flowers and food to the wounded was ready to help an officer of the Rifle Brigade,[1] Corporal Dowling of the Durham Light Infantry, and myself to disappear from the hospital. We planned to get civilian clothes in Lille, take the train to Paris and live in some Left Bank hotel. We had no papers and very little money. A quixotic adventure, but typical of France in 1940, when escape did not seem too dangerous. We were lectured severely on the reprisals which might be visited on other wounded, and within a week were bustled out of the hospital to Germany.

After a grim march through Belgium, I reached German territory at Emmerich in a coal barge in August 1940. As the barge moved slowly up the Scheldt and into the river Waal, it passed beneath the bridge at Nijmegen in Holland, four years later to be the scene of rescue operations by M.I.9 for men of the First Airborne Division after the battle of Arnhem. On German soil, for the first time as a prisoner, I was overcome by despair. I could admire but not always feel the dogged cheerfulness with which the British soldier greeted his predicament. He never seemed beaten even under the worst conditions in prison camps. He never believed the war was lost and derided the Germans to the end. A captured Gestapo report showed their anxiety at the effect of this unquenchable optimism on German civilians who came in contact with British prisoners working in factories and on farms. Their indestructible good humour, their mischievous propaganda and sabotage of war production, was a serious threat to the Nazi regime. It is deplorable that British

[1] John Surtees, M.C.

Governments have not extracted some compensation from the Germans for those who were starved, beaten, and tortured in contravention of the laws of war.[1]

Resigned as it seemed to many years of imprisonment at Oflag IXa at Spangenburg near Kassel, I settled down to writing and meditation. I produced half a novel about the life after death of an eighteenth century peer, a superficial study of Shakespeare's sonnets, and an essay on Eccentrics in the camp magazine. By December 1940, I was overcome by frustration and boredom and again became interested in escape. Already several brave attempts had been made to break out of Spangenburg. The escapers were beaten up by drunken German civilians, but the few who had caught the fever continued to plan new methods.

These pioneer escapers in German prison camps were often unpopular with British senior officers. They were, in rare instances, threatened with court-martial, though how this was to be achieved did not seem very clear. They were considered a disturbing influence in the orderly life of the camp where the pre-war British military and class system was applied from the day of arrival. More important reasons for this discouraging attitude were the low morale among officers and the meagre rations. Non-commissioned officers and men in separate camps (Stalags) went on working parties outside and their rations were supplemented. I soon discovered that this gave them a better chance of escape and planned to transfer myself to a Stalag.

With the arrival of the first Red Cross parcels in the autumn of 1940, health and spirits improved, and with it the attitude of senior officers who no longer claimed that escape was hopeless and would bring severe reprisals on others. But the early escapers were those who refused to conform to the idea of a settled existence; reading, talking and waiting for Red Cross parcels. At Spangenburg they were viewed with a certain reserve until the news of successful escapes began to inspire others. In the next few years several hundred attempts were made in all parts of Germany. The treatment of those recaptured varied and after Himmler took control of political and military prisoners in 1944, the penalty was often death. Many were beaten up especially in the Stalags and several were killed or wounded

[1] Detention in a prisoner-of-war camp was not included in the Anglo-German Agreement of 1964 to compensate victims of Nazi persecution.

in the attempt, though nothing exceeded the cold-blooded execution of fifty-two Royal Air Force officers arrested after the mass
escape from Stalag Luft III at Sagan in the spring of 1944.

In February 1941, the Spangenburg prisoners were moved by
train to a fortress on the River Vistula at Thorn in Poland, as a
reprisal for the alleged ill-treatment of enemy prisoners-of-war in
Canada. Met at the station by tanks, searchlights, and Field Police
with Alsatian dogs, they were marched to their new 'camp'. Conditions were harsh. The officers were housed in damp underground
rooms in the antiquated fort and allowed little exercise. Nor did
Poland, an unknown country to them, offer many prospects for
escape. It was the existence of Stalag XXa, a camp for several hundred British N.C.O.s and men, three miles from the fort, that
gave me my first opportunity. Among them were survivors of
Calais from my own battery and we were soon in communication
through working parties which came daily to the fort. All escape
plans needed the approval of the senior British officer. Mine consisted of escaping from the surgery of a captured Army dentist
which adjoined Stalag XXa, and secreting myself inside the hut
reserved for warrant officers. These men agreed to hide me with
Flying Officer Norman Forbes until we could escape from one of
the daily working parties outside. They had obtained civilian clothes
for us from the Poles. They risked much harsher penalties than
officer-prisoners and there were many stories of brutality by German
guards. In *They Have Their Exits* I have already paid tribute to their
generous help.

On April 16th, 1941, I marched with Forbes and other patients
to the dentist a distance of two miles from the Fort. His surgery
adjoined the Kommandantur of the Stalag, and lay opposite its
main gate. Our escape was well planned and took the Germans by
surprise. We received permission from our guards to go to the
'abort', removed our officers' uniforms, and collected bundles of
wood placed there by British soldiers. A tall sergeant whistled softly,
while others kept the German guards in conversation, and we walked
calmly into the main compound of the Stalag. We stayed there for
five days while the Germans searched for us. We even watched
S.S. men with machine-pistols receiving their orders for the man-
hunt while we stood a few feet from them inside the wire. During
rollcalls we hid under beds in the warrant officers' hut, When the

hue and cry seemed to have died down, we left the camp early one morning with a party of prisoners to fill palliasses with hay in a large barn. The men seemed to enjoy their secret especially when the Germans informed them that we had been captured and mauled by the Alsatians. They organised our escape from the barn with great thoroughness, smuggling in two extra men in a ration lorry to make the same number when they returned to the Stalag at night. They left us hidden, high up in the hay, after loosening the wire which held one of the doors of the barn.

At ten o'clock at night, dressed as 'German Nationals' or Volks-deutscher resettled in eastern Poland by the Nazis, we crept from the barn and set off in the direction of Warsaw. We had two alternative proposals. One, with a sketch plan of the German aerodrome at Graudenz, north of Warsaw, was to fly to Sweden. But this was soon abandoned. Forbes was a pilot, I was not even a navigator but an artillery officer. The other alternative was the Russian armistice line at Brest-Litovsk which we hoped to reach by making contact with the Polish Resistance in Warsaw. By the fourth day, after struggling through huge, dark, forests and along rough tracks, we were twenty miles from the city near the town of Sochaczew. Blistered, hungry and exhausted, we were arrested at a control point and driven to Gestapo headquarters in Plock, a grim town on the Vistula.

I was to learn many lessons from this first escape. The most important was not to be caught with incriminating documents. I was able to destroy a piece of paper bearing an address in Warsaw which another escaper had given us and which I should not have been so thoughtless as to carry. Lectures and training by M.I.9 later in the war strongly stressed this danger and averted many tragedies. As Forbes and I were taken to the Gestapo I tore up undetected one copy of the sketch of Graudenz aerodrome, but when we were searched another was found on me in a matchbox. The faces of the Gestapo officers grew fierce as they studied it. Graudenz was a bomber station and the German attack which began the war with the Soviet Union was only two months away. For a while, the Gestapo were convinced that Forbes and I were taking information to the Russians. We were taken before a man in civilian clothes with blond hair and a pale, cruel face, I was in great terror though I tried to appear calm and innocent.

"So you are from the British Secret Service, my friends."

He looked at us with murder in his eyes. We explained that we needed the map to fly to Sweden but finding this impossible, were making for Warsaw. The veins showed in his cheek and in a savage outburst he shouted:

"You are lying. You are spies. You were taking this to the Russians."

We were untrained for such interrogation but its very violence helped us to keep our heads. An S.S. officer in uniform continued the questions. Had we obtained the sketch of the aerodrome from the Poles? No, we replied politely, from other prisoners. This was true. Three Canadian pilots had escaped from the Fort at Thorn a month before in home-made German Air Force uniforms and had been arrested as they were about to take off. This impressed him. Stalag XXa was telephoned, and our identities confirmed but our interrogator was still not satisfied. We were taken to the civil prison nearby and the word 'spion' fixed to the door of our cells. My heart sank as I paced the stone floor. I now knew what it was to be in the hands of the dreaded Gestapo. I did not doubt that their jealousy of the German Armed Forces would make them keep us as long as possible, even if we were genuine prisoners-of-war, and that we would suffer further interrogation.

Next day, we were questioned separately and my heart sank as I saw the words 'Geheime Staatspolizei' beside the door. But the atmosphere had changed surprisingly. I was even referred to as 'Herr Leutnant' and offered a cigarette and coffee, as I sat before a sinister dark creature in civilian clothes. He was almost affable and explained why he was not in uniform. He had taken part in the attack on Poland in September 1939 but had been transferred to the Gestapo and was now concerned that I should not suppose that he had never been a soldier. What was the reason for this volte-face? At first, I thought that knowing that Forbes and I were genuine prisoners-of-war, he was anxious to appear a 'gentleman', a word well-known to the Germans to express affinity with the British. Such protestations caused hearty laughter in prison camps and were considered pathetic. He told me he admired my 'Teutonic' appearance and nearly put me off my guard. Suddenly, he began to press me once more about the sketch of Graudenz. Why were we walking to Warsaw and the Russian frontier? Had we made contact with the Polish underground? I was determined not to betray the Polish

farmer near Wlocawek who had hidden us for the night in his barn,
and claimed that we had travelled unaided with our supply of Red
Cross chocolate, sardines and condensed milk. I denied having
hidden in Stalag XXa. We had escaped directly from the dentist's
surgery. The man from the Gestapo seemed half-satisfied; perhaps
the German army were demanding our return to Stalag XXa at
Thorn. I was returned to my cell, but I still trembled at the thought
of further interrogation. How should I react if I were beaten up?
I felt sure that I should admit more of the truth under pressure, for
if we had succeeded in reaching the Russian lines we would certainly
have given them the sketch of Graudenz.[1] On it were clearly marked
important details of the aerodrome. In after years I was always to
remember this incident when I was responsible for training others
who might have to face the Gestapo. Fortunately, Forbes and I had
agreed upon our story before we were captured and we never
allowed ourselves to be driven from it by the threats of being
treated as spies which were made to us on arrival at Plock. But
when I was back in my cell with my own thoughts and fears
the threat of execution seemed very real, and I felt defenceless and
alone.

After ten days, the Gestapo reluctantly decided to return us to
the Army and we were taken by train under heavy guard to Thorn.
On the journey, we spoke cheerfully in German to our embarrassed
sentries as they sat stiffly in the carriage holding their rifles. But the
Kommandant at Thorn had his revenge. We were put in solitary
confinement in cellars, without ventilation, which had been the
ammunition chambers of the fort. Despite this gross breach of the
Geneva Convention, I felt an enormous sense of relief, for a strange
thing had happened. When I collected and signed for my few belongings before leaving the prison at Plock I was handed back the matchbox. Inside it, through some error in administration, was my compass. I managed to hide this during our brutal reception at Thorn,
and memorise the details of Graudenz aerodrome which I passed
to the British Military Attaché in Switzerland when I made my
final escape from Colditz. This was one of a number of extraordinary
and unexplained incidents in my encounter with the Gestapo who
made similar mistakes with the agents of I.S.9(d). A second time I

---

[1] Few British soldiers who reached the Russian lines during this period were heard
of again.

might not be so lucky, but I knew that despite its terrible reputation the Gestapo had weaknesses, especially in its distrust of the German Army and a certain respect for 'officers'. This is one of the reasons why most secret agents, trained in Britain, were commissioned or able to describe themselves as officers. Though it did not prevent torture and degradation, it often saved their lives.

In May 1941 Forbes and I were transferred to Colditz, near Leipzig, a Sonderlager, or special camp, for persistent escapers and other 'enemies of the Reich' under the title of Oflag IVc. The prisoners from all the Allied forces were detained in the huge castle which towers above the rolling Saxon countryside and was once the palace of Augustus the Strong. It was heavily guarded and declared by the Kommandant to be 'impregnable'.[1] In this formidable place, the German High Command collected all the most determined escapers. This miscalculation had inevitable results, for half of all the successful escapes by British officers, before the Allies invaded Germany and confusion ensued, were made from Colditz.

At Colditz no one thought of anything but escape and a committee was formed to fix priorities for the plans with most chance of success. I had first been to Germany at the age of seventeen and I spoke German fairly well, but my first plan, though selected by the Committee, was more of a theatrical performance than an escape. In August 1941, after the evening parade in the inner courtyard of Colditz, I managed to march past the sentry at the gate dressed in a home-made German corporal's 'uniform' by showing a stolen metal disc. The 'uniform' was a Polish tunic to which I had applied scenery paint from the camp theatre. Under the arc-lights along the causeway outside, it appeared bright green instead of field grey. I was immediately surrounded by the guards, hustled off to the cells, and threatened with the death penalty for an insult to the Wehrmacht. My uniform was such a pantomime affair that I could hardly blame them.[2]

Next day I was photographed for German police records, and later, after pleading that under the Geneva Convention a prisoner was entitled to take all reasonable steps to escape, I was sentenced to a month in the town jail. To reach it, I was marched across a

[1] P. R. Reid, *The Colditz Story*, Hodder and Stoughton, 1953.
[2] Eggers, *Colditz. The German Story*, Robert Hale Ltd., 1961.

drawbridge over a dry moat, and so discovered a new method of escaping from the castle.

At nine o'clock on the evening of January 5th, 1942, with snow falling heavily outside, Lieutenant Luteyn of the Dutch East Indies Army[1] and I, dressed as 'German officers', broke into a loft above the guardhouse which adjoined the prisoners' quarters. Softly we descended a stone spiral staircase, past the door of the German Officers' Mess on the first floor. The strains of 'Lili Marlene' muffled our footsteps. On the ground floor we passed the guardroom itself where, though I did not know it until after the war, was pinned on the wall the police photograph taken after my first attempt. In bitter cold and driving snow, the sentries posted along the causeway mistook us for visiting German officers. We reached the drawbridge of the castle, opened the wicket gate which I had noticed on my way to the town jail, then climbed into the moat and up the far bank. Beyond was a high paling, bordering a park where the prisoners exercised, which we climbed, and sliding down a steep grass slope, reached the twelve foot outer wall of the castle.

It was difficult to get a foothold, until standing on Luteyn's shoulders, I was able to grasp the icy coping and hoist him beside me. We landed heavily on the frozen ground and buried our German officers' overcoats and caps made from Dutch Home Army uniforms, in the deep snow. Within ten minutes of our escape from the guard house we set forth in a curious mixture of converted uniform jackets and R.A.F. trousers with ski caps made from blankets to pass as Dutch electrical workers. Our papers, forged in the camp, permitted us as foreign workers to travel from Leipzig to the university town of Ulm, about one hundred miles from the Swiss frontier. At ten o'clock on the evening of January 6th, we took the express from Leipzig, paying for our tickets with money obtained by selling Red Cross chocolate and cigarettes to the sentries at Colditz. We reached Ulm on the morning of January 7th and attempted to buy tickets to Singen, a town near the frontier, but when asked to show our papers, we were promptly arrested by the railway police. Convinced that we were genuine Dutchmen, they escorted us to the office for foreign workers, from which we escaped within five minutes of our arrival.

Throughout January 7th, we travelled on local trains until late

[1] Now a Colonel in the Royal Dutch Army Engineers attached to N.A.T.O.

that evening we reached Stockach near Ludwigshafen. The snow-storm had ceased, and walking by moonlight, we made for the frontier town of Singen, surrounded by dense forests, where we knew that successful crossings had been made. Frozen, hungry and exhausted, we were stopped early next morning by woodcutters on their way to work. After our escape from Ulm, we had changed our identity to 'Polish workers' from a local labour camp. The woodcutters, in disbelief at this story, tried to arrest us but we broke away among the fir trees of the forest, while they went for the police in Singen.

An hour later, we could hear the sound of dogs barking and at dawn came upon a hut in a snow-driven copse. It was locked, but breaking a window, we found no one inside. We slept here undis-covered and ate a few bars of chocolate until dusk on January 8th. With a rough map, smuggled into Colditz by another prisoner, we now planned our route across the frontier at Singen. The owner of the hut kept bees whose hives were buried in snow, and each with one of his white coats and a heavy shovel, we marched towards Singen, pretending to be workmen returning from the forests. At five p.m., we were stopped on the road by two boys of the Hitler Jugend with bicycles and truncheons. Luteyn declared to them that we were Westphalian workers billeted in Singen since the Dutch accent resembles the Westphalian. Before we continued on our way, they said a little anxiously:

"We have been told to look for two British prisoners who are trying to cross the frontier tonight."

We both laughed but, afterwards, agreed that we should have had no choice but to silence these boys with our shovels. We could not know that Lieutenant John Hyde-Thompson[1] and another Dutch officer who had escaped by the same route had been recap-tured at Ulm twenty-four hours after we had been there. We had good compasses, and, marching on a bearing, went north of Signen into more forests, then swung due south across the railway, till we were close to the road to Schaffhausen which forms the frontier between Germany and Switzerland. A hundred yards away was the German control post and, to reach safety, we had to cross the road and an area of no-man's-land covered by very deep snow. The temperature was several degrees below zero as we crouched among

[1] M.C. died 1954.

the trees. Luteyn was suffering from frost-bite and both of us from severe exposure and hunger. We made ready for our final effort.

As the moon began to wane on the morning of January 9th, we flung away the shovels and put on our bee-keepers' coats. We could hear the voices of the Frontier Police and the tramp of sentries, dangerously close to us. Then the wind rose, and choosing our moment, we crawled across the road towards Switzerland. The frontier is formed at this point by a narrow appendix of land and on each flank there is grave risk of blundering back into Germany. It took us an hour to struggle through snow-drifts till we reached a road that led to the town of Ramsen in Swiss territory. With beating hearts, we waited in its main street until we were challenged by a Swiss frontier guard. We flung ourselves on him, shaking him by the hand and dancing with him in the snow. He was delighted that we had escaped the tyranny of Hitler and the street echoed with our cheering. Later that morning we were taken by Swiss police to Schaffhausen and placed under 'hotel arrest'. Eighty-four hours after my escape from Colditz, I was in the care of the British Military Attaché in Berne.

CHAPTER 3

Switzerland 1942

THOUGH I have criticised the postwar Foreign Office for its attitude to those who suffered under the Nazis, the conduct of its staff in 1942 was in the best tradition.

In Berne, the imperturbable British Legation was surrounded by enemies on every side. Germany, Austria, Italy and Vichy France exulted in the isolation of the staff and they were under a persistent barrage of Nazi propaganda and Vichy defeatism. Led by the British Minister, Sir David Kelly, and his wife, they bore these trials with elegant composure and courage, and like their colleagues in other neutral territories, made an important contribution to the work of M.I.9.

The arrival of escapers from Germany however was not particularly welcome to them. It was even an embarrassment, for the escapers were impatient, high-spirited and starved for months of feminine company. Nine of them had escaped from German prison camps since 1941. They had risked their lives at the hands of Nazis to continue the fight, and their principal interest lay in how to get out of Switzerland as soon as they had recovered from their adventures.

What was to be done with them?

By order of the Vichy Government, men of military age without diplomatic status could not travel legally through unoccupied France to neutral Spain or Portugal. Until some clandestine system of organising their escape from Switzerland could be found they must be removed as far away from the bright lights of Berne and Geneva as possible. The Gestapo had an active organisation in Switzerland. It was a perfect hunting ground for spies and *agents provocateurs*, as it had been in the First World War. A new generation of attractive girls were employed to trap the unwary in bars and bedrooms. One of their principal tasks was to discover whether the handful of

British prisoners-of-war who had escaped from Germany and Italy were being smuggled back to England.

When I reached Switzerland in January, I was little more than a refugee. I was dirty and frostbitten. At the Legation, I sat for half an hour in a small cold place like a dentist's waiting-room, reading the *Illustrated London News*. When officialdom receives the British citizen the joys of deliverance from the enemy are often refrigerated. But for several members of the Legation staff, my seven hundred mile escape from Colditz Castle was a matter for discreet celebration in strictly neutral surroundings, and they seemed to regard the event as out of the ordinary.

After a short interrogation and the delivery of my message about Graudenz aerodrome, I was led into a cellar beneath the Legation where a pile of second-hand men's suits was laid out as if for a village jumble sale. I selected a green tweed creation with baggy trousers. It was sad to see my 'Dutch electrical worker's' clothes, which had served me so well, added to this pile of cast-off garments. After a medical examination, I was exiled to Fribourg, where I lived for three months, waiting for the next phase of my adventure. I could only dimly imagine how I should ever reach England. Exulting in my new freedom, I spent these months in the pursuit of pleasure, drinking absinthe, and, for some reason, attending lectures on architecture at Fribourg University. After all, I was only twenty-six, and my escape from Nazi Germany after three attempts had been the great emotional event of my life. But it made me suspicious, restless and especially contemptuous of those who did not believe in an Allied victory.

I flung myself with enthusiasm into the frivolities of Fribourg under the genial surveillance of the Swiss security police who were openly on the side of Britain. In March 1942 I was sent for by Colonel Henry Cartwright,[1] the British Military Attaché in Berne, who cautioned me severely in his office at the Legation to be more careful of my girl friends. He said that the hotel where I was staying was full of 'unreliable' characters, anxious to gather information from me over the absinthe. He need not have worried; my previous experience of the Gestapo had taught me the art of telling misleading stories to their agents. Nonetheless, when I was sent for again on

[1] Colonel Henry Cartwright, C.M.G., D.S.O., M.C., British Military Attaché in Berne, 1939-45. Died 1957.

April 15th and invited to dinner in Berne I expected another lecture on security. I was astonished when he peered at me doubtfully over his spectacles and said:

"We're sending you back first, Neave. M.I.9 have asked for you."

After dinner in his flat, Cartwright and I watched each other over the indispensable port and nuts. I tried to imagine him twenty years before, for he had been a famous escaper in his time, and I greatly respected him. His book *Within Four Walls*[1] was a classic and had inspired a new generation of escapers. As a small boy, I had read it with romantic pleasure, and it played a great part in forming my philosophy of escape. He had made five attempts to escape from German prison camps after his capture in 1914 and had finally succeeded at the very end of the war.

As I smoked one of his excellent cigars, I wondered what effect these experiences had had on him in after years. Did he envy the young and their carefree attitudes? Was he afraid for them? There was no clue to his thoughts at this uneasy meal. I knew from his manner that something serious was coming, but I knew little or nothing of M.I.9. Nor could I understand why they should want me back.

Then suddenly his serious expression left him and, with a smile, he raised his glass:

"Here's to your safe journey to Spain tomorrow!"

I stared at him in total silence.

I had been waiting for the moment, but it came as a shock. I had supposed that any plans for my escape would be announced without emotion. I expected detailed regimental orders to proceed to the Unoccupied Zone of France.

Later Cartwright was still gruff, but his smile was encouraging.

"We are sending you out before the others although they escaped from Germany before you."

I knew he was referring to the eight other British officers still in Switzerland.

He paused and lit another cigar.

"There is a reason, you know."

He rose from his chair and walked over to the the the mantelpiece. In the silence I was trying to imagine how anyone could get across the Unoccupied Zone of France to Spain and Gibraltar without getting caught. I had heard grim stories of British officers returned

[1] Edward Arnold, London, 1930. Cartwright escaped to Holland in August 1918.

to German hands after capture by the Vichy police. I was appalled that our former allies should do this. But these fears were unimportant compared with the sheer excitement of starting on a new journey into the unknown.

An eternity passed before he spoke again, still standing before the mantelpiece.

"M.I.9 have sent orders for you and Hugh Woollatt[1] to cross the Swiss frontier as soon as possible.

"We have sent one or two people through before," said Cartwright calmly, "but you are still guinea pigs."

This was the usual way for the British army to explain that the journey would be dangerous.

I also had a sneaking feeling that Woollatt and I, who were inclined to be gay and uninhibited in our social adventures, would be given priority in any case. Perhaps M.I.9.'s like Cartwright's real fear was that we might become entangled with beautiful Gestapo spies. There was ground for his anxiety. Several efforts were made to discover how I had reached Switzerland. Sophisticated Fribourg might be fun, but it was dangerous too. It was time for me to leave.

Cartwright then told me to leave Berne by the early train to Geneva and go to a bookstall. Hugh Woollatt would be going separately from Lausanne and would meet me in Geneva. Hugh was brave, carefree and independent; his escape from Oflag Vc at Biberach in southern Germany had taken place a month or two before my own. He would make a lively and exuberant companion for an escape.

It was now nearly midnight as he continued his instructions. This was before the day of James Bond, and Phillips Oppenheim was my only guide to the situation.

Cartwright seemed to be enjoying himself; to be putting himself in my place. He smiled as he told me to meet a man at the station bookstall, reading a copy of the *Journal de Genève*. I was to approach him and give a password. He handed me a small typewritten piece of paper.

"Now read this and be sure you memorise it."

I held the paper in my hand. It was all very well to have read Phillips Oppenheim. This was the real thing, and it seemed dangerously amateur. I had read Somerset Maugham's *Ashenden*, the

[1] Captain Hugh Woollatt, M.C., Lancashire Fusiliers. Killed in action July 1944.

master British spy in Switzerland during the First World War. Surely he had been more professional?

Cartwright took back the note and with grave ceremony burnt it with his cigar lighter in the fireplace. He waited deliberately for a moment, then turned towards me.

"Any questions?"

"What clothes shall I need for this escape?"

The very question sounded ridiculous, as if I were going to a dance.

Cartwright replied that 'Victor' who represented him in Geneva would take charge of me. I would be given suitable clothes and I could leave my awful Legation suit in Geneva.

"You look like a Swiss bookmaker," he said. "Put yourself in Victor's hands."

I went to bed in a state of mystified excitement. More than twenty-five years afterwards I can still feel that strange mixture of pleasure and apprehension. Early next morning Cartwright said goodbye to me in his dressing gown, which, as a mere Lieutenant in the Royal Artillery, I reckoned a considerable honour. I could see that he secretly envied me. He could see himself setting off on such an adventure more than a generation before. He died in 1957 after playing an indispensable role in the wartime escape organisation of M.I.9.

In the train to Geneva I watched for signs that I was being trailed, but no one seemed to take the slightest notice. Even the two stout German businessmen with their hard blonde wives in the same compartment ignored me. They talked incessantly of food, then fell asleep, snoring.

I tried to imagine what lay before me. What powerful secret organisation now controlled my destiny? What would Victor be like? Would he be like Ashenden, the ace of the British Secret Service, a suave, thin old Etonian?

At Geneva, I hurried among the crowds to the bookstall. As I reached it, I felt a tap on my shoulder. I turned, expecting to see one of those grim-faced men of the Gestapo in long dark raincoats. A man, holding a copy of the *Journal de Genève*, gave me a reassuring smile as I stammered out the password. He shook hands and hurried me to a car outside the station. He drove me through the old part of Geneva and drew up outside a shabby hotel where Woollatt was waiting in high spirits. He was amused by the character of the hotel which was revealed by the arrival at the entrance of a couple of Swiss gentlemen with prostitutes. On our guide's whispered instructions, we signed the register with fictitious names. An old crone at the desk winked and handed him a key.

Customers were moving rapidly up and down the stairs, as we reached a small, sordid bedroom. Here we were told to wait until three o'clock in the afternoon. There was nothing else to do except smoke, drink champagne and make silly jokes about life in a brothel. If only I could paint like Toulouse-Lautrec, I thought, it might be rather fun to stay there.

At three, there was a knock on the door, and I walked over and cautiously opened it.

A slender Englishman in a pin-striped suit, and a green Homburg hat, as close as he could get to my picture of Ashenden, entered the room, carrying an enormous suitcase, which looked incongruous with his Foreign Office appearance. He laid it on the bed, and, opening it, revealed several crumpled men's suits. This was 'Victor'. He apologised in a quiet voice that the suits were not very smart, but our 'cover story' was that we were refugees from Czechoslovakia making for a reception centre at Marseille.

"But why Czechs?" I said.

"There are plenty of Czechs in unoccupied France at the moment who don't speak French. It is unlikely that the Vichy police speak Czech."

"But what happens," I asked, "if we meet someone who does speak Czech?"

"I'm sorry, you will have to risk that."

It seemed to me that we had a good many risks to take. The jumble sale at the Legation had had a far better selection than 'Victor's' suitcase. I was almost sorry to substitute my terrible green Swiss tweeds for the dirty old jacket and trousers which I now tried on.

I was more difficult to disguise than Woollatt, who was dark and slightly Latin. He looked excellent in a beret but with my boyish features and fair hair, I did not seem to be disguised at all. Victor pondered the problem for a moment and then produced an old green workman's cap which he claimed made me look 'Teutonic' and sufficiently Czech. He then gave us buff-coloured identity cards already filled in with unpronounceable Czech names. Passport photographs, taken secretly in Berne some weeks before, were attached to them. We spent a few hilarious minutes trying to get the correct pronunciation.

It seems extraordinary that we should have treated this adventure in such a lighthearted manner. But we were young and gay.

After dinner at a restaurant, we walked back to the hotel. In the evening shadows it seemed sinister and cut-throat. We regained our bedroom, where Victor gave us more advice.

He handed us ration cards and some French money. At five o'clock next morning there would be a knock on the door. The man who came would be an officer of the Swiss police in civilian clothes. We should follow him down to a car outside which would take us to the Swiss frontier, where we would be given all instructions.

"How shall we know," asked Woollatt, "that he is the right man?"

"He will say, 'Mr. Churchill expects you'."

Before he went, Victor reminded us to put our British Legation clothes into the suitcase and leave it on the bed. He shook hands politely and left the hotel. We watched him from the window, walking down the street, relaxed and informal, as if he were in Whitehall instead of organising a secret escape line for M.I.9.

The hours passed slowly. Waiting for the knock on the door, I could hardly sleep. By two o'clock, there was silence in the hotel and the customers seemed to have settled down for the night. I lay on the bed in my new Czech disguise and was awakened by a sharp rap on the door. There was a moment of panic.

The door opened, and revealed a tall man, a cross between Maigret and the Special Branch of Scotland Yard. He seemed entirely at his ease.

"Vive Winston Churchill!" he said excitedly. "He wants you back. Now hurry up, please, the car is waiting."

With a last check of our identity papers, ration cards and money, we followed him down the stairs. The old proprietress still sat at her post and gave us a twisted smile as we went into the chilly street. In the car which stood before the hotel I could see Swiss police uniforms. We were hustled inside and driven fast through the empty streets of Geneva. The policemen seemed delighted by the whole adventure.

Travelling westwards beyond the outskirts of the town, we came to a large cemetery surrounded by a high wall and, leaving the car, crouched among hideous family monuments. I could not help laughing. Surely this could not be the real thing?

As dawn began to rise, the plain clothes officer whispered instructions.

Beyond the cemetery wall there were two coils of barbed wire. We should cross them slowly to avoid getting entangled and climb up a grass bank on the French side. We peered with him over the wall and through the dawn light could see a small white house. At this point there was a cross-roads with a signpost to Annemasse, the frontier town. We were to wait for an elderly gentleman riding a bicycle. He would be dressed in blue workman's clothes with a beret and sabots. He would have a clay pipe in his mouth upside down.

The policeman looked at his watch.

"Three minutes to go."

Crouched among the tombstones, we shook hands.

"Regards to Mr. Churchill, and good luck.!"

We vaulted the cemetery wall and started to negotiate the barbed wire, half expecting a fusillade of shots from the French side. I tore my trousers on a strand of wire, but in a minute we were across and climbing up the grass bank.

I looked back for a moment to neutral Switzerland which had given me such generous help. Then walking smartly along the road towards the white house, we reached the signpost to Annemasse.

Soon large numbers of men on bicycles travelling to their work came past. All of them were dressed in berets, blue overalls and sabots, and most were smoking clay pipes.

Suddenly a distinguished-looking grey-haired man, with a clay pipe upside down, stopped before us and placed his bicycle against the signpost. There was something familiar about him as he bowed to us. It was as if he were about to take our orders for an expensive breakfast.

"Good morning, gentlemen," he said. "I am Louis Simon, formerly of the Ritz Hotel, London. Would you care to follow me to the frontier post?"

As rain began to fall, we walked with him along a tree-lined road towards Annemasse.

CHAPTER 4

Louis Nouveau's Flat

CARTWRIGHT and Victor had warned us that we had a long journey to safety in Gibraltar.

In April 1942 the Vichy authorities still held several hundred British soldiers, sailors and airmen prisoner. They were guarded in fortresses at St. Hippolyt, near Nîmes, and at Fort de la Revère at La Turbie, a few miles from Monte Carlo. Most of them were the survivors from Dunkirk, who had made their way over the demarcation line to be arrested by their former allies. Others, more fortunate, had been repatriated by the Vichy Armistice Commission or escaped to Spain. Vichy had also imprisoned a number of pilots of the Royal Air Force shot down on operations over France.

Over all these men hung the threat of being sent to German prison camps and interrogation by the Gestapo. The Vichy government had many times been threatened with the occupation of the whole of France south of the demarcation line. In November 1942, when German troops entered the Unoccupied Zone, the majority of these prisoners were sent to camps in Germany.

As grey-haired Louis Simon led us past the French frontier post at Annemasse, he engaged the French *douanier* in laughing conversation and the officer never glanced at us.

But it was a dangerous moment. I could see myself recaptured, beaten up perhaps, but, worst of all, returning over the seven hundred miles to Colditz. Whatever happened, I must make a run for it among the crowds of men and women walking and bicycling to work through the streets of Annemasse.

The rain which had been falling when we crossed the frontier gave way to sunshine, and with it the terrors of arrest. When one is young, such fears pass swiftly. The beauty of the distant mountains, the scent of spring flowers drenched with rain, restored my spirits. I would live to fight another day.

A mile beyond the frontier, Louis Simon led us up the pathway of a new brick villa where his wife had prepared us a splendid 'London' breakfast. The Ritz itself could have done no better.

But her handsome face was pale, and her voice faltered a little.

"I have not slept the whole night in case something should go wrong. Thank God you have got this far."

I was not the only one in danger. At least I had the chance of being treated as a prisoner-of-war. But for Madame Simon there would be the concentration camp and the single revolver shot in the back of the neck.

Throughout the day, we travelled through the Haute Savoie. A quiet, mystic young girl led us from Louis Simon's villa to the back streets of Annemasse, where she knocked on the door of a shabby home. Inside she led us along a dark passage to the kitchen.

She had said nothing until now. For the first time she smiled:

"All I ask is that you should send a message on the B.B.C. if you get back safely."[1]

She glanced at us shyly. She could not have been more than eighteen, but in her eyes there was a strange light. Nothing could have expressed more powerfully the spirit of resistance to Hitler. It inspired a respect which made our bawdy lives in neutral Switzerland seem insincere. We both fell silent as she left us without another word. I never forgot this first revelation of the courage of ordinary French men and women in helping us to escape. In the kitchen of the house, a frightened, sad-faced woman with two small children made us coffee. We listened for an hour to the loud ticking of the kitchen clock.

A plump Frenchman now entered the house and introduced himself. He was, he explained, ready to drive us to Annecy on the next stage of the journey.

"I am well known in the black market," he said, and took us to an ancient Citroën outside propelled by a charcoal burner or 'gazogène'.

The car, after many chokes and gasps, started off, and passing Ugines, we came to the shores of the Lake of Annecy. The sun shone on its blue waters.

[1] Messages on the French news service of the B.B.C. were a regular means of communication with agents in the field. See later chapters.

A treble horn sounded along the road. "Les flics!" said the driver, "Into these bushes. I will stay with the car."

We hid in the undergrowth beside the shore of the lake and listened.

The police car stopped, and there was the sound of loud French voices. After a minute the police moved off, still sounding their treble horn, and our escort, unconcerned and smiling broadly, recalled us to the car.

"I told the flics that the car had broken down."

He drove at reckless speed into a square in Annecy, to an old house where a magnificent lunch awaited us. Our host was a tough-looking young Frenchman.

"Messieurs, you will drive with us to Chambéry. Then we take the train for Marseille."

I was at first fascinated and bewildered. Despite all the leaks and rumours in Switzerland, I had never really believed that such an organised escape line existed. I had supposed that we would be directed from place to place and left to make our way by train without escort.

But it soon became clear that the two French guides considered us in their charge. In the evening, they drove us to Chambéry, and we waited with them in the twilight of the station.

The crowds surged round the train, so that we were nearly parted from our escorts. But having no luggage except two ancient brief-cases, we forced our way into a carriage. Through the night I slept fitfully and once went into the corridor for air.

A young cadet of the Vichy police organisation, the Milice,[1] stood beside me. He was a blond creature in a dark-blue uniform with suspicious, hard blue eyes. I had seen such eyes before in Nazi Germany.

I looked back towards our guides as they sat in the compartment. One of them elbowed his way into the corridor and engaged the young man in conversation. I breathed more freely, but those eyes were still watching me when at seven o'clock in the morning of April 17th we reached Marseille and swiftly vanished among the crowds.

I should not have liked to trust my 'Czech' cover story to questions from that young man.

We were frightened and walked through the streets seeking the

[1] See Chapter 25.

'safe' address where we were to be handed over to the chief of the escape line. But something had gone wrong. Our guides were unhappy.

It was past midday when, hungry and exhausted, we came to the Café Petit Poucet on the Boulevard Dugommier.

We sat anxiously at a table until a small, stout man appeared from double glass doors at the end of the café. He motioned us to a square, old-fashioned room and ordered drinks and coffee.

Our host was red-faced and angry.

"Why did you come here first? Wait here—I must be sure of your identity. This gentleman will see you remain."

He opened another door. There was a gendarme in uniform.

It was an uncomfortable position. Which side was he on? Were we in the right hands? The guides were silent. It dawned on me as the afternoon passed that they had taken us to the wrong place. The café was much too dangerous.

But our anxieties were quickly dispelled by the arrival of Louis Nouveau. Louis amazed me as soon as I saw him. He was slightly built and wore a light grey suit and suède shoes, a silk shirt and a dark red bow tie with white spots. He looked—and was—a successful merchant banker and stockbroker, well known in Marseille. He demanded from us the password and seemed satisfied. He then checked my false papers. My identity document gave my destination as the Cercle d'Accueil for Czech refugees at Banyuls-sur-Mer near the Spanish frontier.

Louis Nouveau's spare, humorous French face turned from astonishment to annoyance. He looked at me with his sharp, grey eyes.

"A Czech? The people in Geneva must be crazy! Why, you look positively British and public school!"

His English was perfect.

"Do you speak Czech?" he enquired.

"Not a word. I escaped from Germany as a Dutch electrical worker, although I don't speak one word of Dutch. When I was on the run in Poland, I was a German Volksdeutscher from Bessarabia. I have never been to Bessarabia," I said solemnly.

He laughed. "Well done. Congratulations. If we get you back to London, you'll have a wonderful tale to tell. They won't believe you, of course."

He was standing in the back room of the café. He began to look serious. He glanced at his wrist watch and then started humming softly to himself.

"Je t'attendrai, le jour et la nuit . . ."

The words took me back to Nazi Germany. Sous-Lieutenant Blum, nephew of Leon Blum, the French Socialist leader, used to play the tune on a rickety old piano in the French quarters at Colditz. I thought of my fellow-prisoners, longing for home.

Louis Nouveau turned to us.

"Follow me at thirty paces, stop when I stop."

Woollatt and I followed him from the café, down the Canebière and along the quayside of the Old Port. Through the cluster of masts we could see him approach a modern block of flats on the Quai Rive Neuve. Then he turned back, motioning us into a shop doorway.

"I think there's someone watching the flat. Hide here till I give the signal." he whispered.

He sauntered slowly to the door of his apartment house, studying a newspaper. A uniformed gendarme passed by. Louis lifted his hat, wiped his brow with a red silk handkerchief.

"False alarm," he said as we climbed the stairs to the fifth floor.

Next morning I went to the window of the flat and looked out over the Old Port of Marseille. An April breeze was blowing from the sea, where a steamer sounded its siren across the bay. The sky was an infinite blue, as I looked to the west and thought of what lay beyond.

Along the glowing Mediterranean shore, and the whole length of Spain, lay Gibraltar. I was already more than half way to British territory. To the north, I sensed the great expanse of France, with its unknown dangers. And eight hundred miles distant was embattled England.

I stood in nothing but a cheap French shirt, watching Hugh Woollatt as he slept. His thin face was troubled and his long, dark, untidy hair spread over the pillow. He murmured in his sleep.

I could see my old boots in the shadow. I had worn them since I landed in France in 1940. They were almost human, and showing signs of those restless, dangerous months. They had been with me in the battle of Calais, through dark, mysterious forests in Poland and in Gestapo cells.

There was a knock on the door of our bedroom. The Nouveaus' flat was on the fifth floor of the house in the Quai Rive Neuve. It was time for breakfast.

I began to shave, glanced without much attention at the round, unlined face which stared at me from the mirror, and dressed once more in the 'Czech' disguise. I was about to put my boots on when I remembered Louis Nouveau's orders. No boots or shoes. I put on the heavy felt slippers beside the bed and went into the living-room, where Madame Nouveau, slight and trim, was pouring coffee.

The slippers were hairy and too large for me. They made a soft, shuffling sound as I moved round the flat. They had amused me at first, until they became a symbol of my helplessness. Three years later I was to see a prisoner in his cell at Nuremburg wearing slippers like these. It was General-Fieldmarshal Keitel, Chief of the High Command of the German Armed Forces.[1] With a field-grey officer's tunic they looked ridiculous and unmilitary. I even felt slight sympathy for this broken martinet, whose war crimes and blunders ended on an improvised scaffold in the gymnasium at Nuremburg prison. At least we used a rope. Hitler, his master, preferred his victims to be strangled with piano wire.

As I came shambling up to the table, Louis Nouveau laughed. "How do you like your slippers?"

"They are very comfortable, thank you," I replied, without conviction.

"Everyone has to wear them. The people in the flat below may be pro-Vichy. They could become suspicious and report us to the Gestapo if they hear too many people tramping around."

I understood. Gestapo agents were well established in Marseille and I had been on the run long enough to know the need for these precautions. But somehow the slippers made me feel afraid. If the police should raid the block, it would be hard to escape from the fifth floor.

But I did not show my irritation. I was in the hands of the 'Pat O'Leary' escape line. Who they really were, or how they worked, I did not know. And who was their legendary chief Pat O'Leary? Perhaps it was best not to know too much. I was merely a 'parcel', as they described the men they hid and sent across the Spanish frontier.

[1] The author served the Nuremberg indictment on Keitel in October 1945.

But being a parcel made me feel claustrophobic. It was very different from my escape in Germany and its glorious sense of individual achievement.

As I drank my coffee, I looked at the large, comfortable sitting-room. There were long rows of books, many of them in English, and some modern paintings. The room had large bay windows with a seat from which one could look down on the crowded quays and the blue sea beyond.

"That window is our sentry-box," said Louis Nouveau. "Keep it manned."

Marseille! The day had grown warm and the windows were open, bringing the smell of the sea, tarred ropes and fish. After Madame Nouveau had cleared away the breakfast things, she left the flat with Louis, saying to us: "You must stay in the flat and keep your slippers on. Don't open the door to anyone unless they ring three times. We will be back for lunch."

When they had gone, there was silence in the flat. Woollatt picked up a novel and began to read. The morning passed slowly, as I trudged in my clumsy slippers from our bedroom and back to the living-room.

What was the next stage of this adventure? The Nouveaus had told us nothing of the future except that they would try to get us into Spain. But I felt caged and restless.

I could look back on nineteen months of high adventure.

I had been wounded and captured at Calais, escaped from a reprisal camp at Thorn in Poland, recaptured by the Gestapo and after making two attempts to get out of Colditz in fake German uniform, had finally succeeded at the third attempt. Then, I had been an independent individual, a fugitive in enemy territory, pitting my luck and endurance against the Nazis. Now, I felt myself to be entirely in the hands of a secret organisation over which I had no control. Should I make a break for it now on my own, away from the flat, get a boat from Marseille and sail all the way to Gibraltar? But I had only the few francs Victor had given me and I had never sailed a boat.

I blew a plume of blue smoke in Woollatt's face by accident.

He waved it away and looked up from his novel.

"For God's sake, stop pacing about and sit down."

He got up from the window seat.

"It's your turn to man the sentry box," he added.

I sat down.

What had really made me so keen to escape, to get home? Everyone in Colditz, where the German High Command had foolishly assembled all the most determined escapers, had their own reasons for wanting to escape. These ranged from a desire to rejoin their regiments, or the more prosaic, but nonetheless real, urge for sex.

But my strongest motive was the overwhelming, almost animal desire to be free from any form of imprisonment; to rid myself of the atmosphere of a prisoner-of-war camp and the society of those who endlessly reminisced about their last stand before the enemy.

Even at Colditz, where some of the finest and most adventurous officers were detained, the atmosphere was often like a badly conducted school. A school in some grim autobiographical novel, with our drunken Camp Captain, Hauptmann Priem, as headmaster.

My attitude was more romantic than practical. Once out of the camp and in enemy territory, though aided by maps and compasses, I left a great deal to chance, believing that somehow a kindly fate would protect me. At no time did I fully appreciate my danger. My life as a prisoner had divorced me from such reality.

But now after my experience of the last few days, I began to remember my talks with Pierre d'Harcourt at Calais, to realise that escape could be organised, and this fascinated me. I began to think about the problems and needs of an escape line. The more I thought about it, the more it intrigued me and I began to take an even deeper interest in the people who were planning my escape to Spain. Who were they? Why did they do it? How would I best be able to repay them when I reached England?

There was a sound of a key in the door. We started and shuffled off into our bedroom as quietly as we could. The prospect of jumping out of a fifth floor window did not appeal to me. I armed myself with heavy stool.

"Don't be an ass," said Woollatt. "If it's the police, we'll try to bluff it out. You talk French, don't you?"

"Of a sort," I replied. I spoke reasonably good French.

It was Madame Nouveau returning with her husband and a bag marked 'alimentation' and a bottle of wine. I put down the stool and looked admiringly at this petite, soft-voiced, woman, with her ironic smile.

Known to the organisation as 'Marquisette', her devotion to the
Allied cause and to de Gaulle had led to this trying existence of
housing dangerous visitors in her flat. For this she had gladly given
up her intellectual life. She considered us helpless, which indeed we
were, and managed us with politeness and French sophistication.

"We will have a tea party this afternoon. You will meet some of
our colleagues," said Louis Nouveau.

Later, there were three rings at the door and a short, middle-aged
man in the smartest business clothes, carrying a black hat and cane,
like a character from some pre-war film set on the French Riviera,
entered, bowed low over Madame Nouveau's hand and introduced
himself with care and elegance.

"Mario Prassinos, at your service," he said.

He laid his hat and cane carefully on a chair and, turning to
Louis, he asked:

"Have the others arrived?"

We had not long to wait for another three rings. The next visitor
was a young, dark, strongly built man. He had an air of confident
determination, a certain aloofness.

He was introduced as Francis Blanchain, the chief guide, who
took parcels from Marseille to the Spanish frontier.

We sat in the window seat, drank tea and talked about the war.
The photograph (in the group following p. 120) today shows us as
we sat there on that April afternoon twenty-six years ago. Only
Francis Blanchain and I survive.

Prassinos was evidently in charge as we took our places at the
Nouveaus' dining-table, like a board of directors.

"Pat, our chief, has reached Gibraltar for his conference with
M.I.9. He will tell them of our need for money, a new wireless
operator and arms. Pat should be back from Spain in a fortnight."[1]

Woollatt and I made no enquiry. We sat as quiet as 'parcels'. I
did not then realise how dangerous it was for Prassinos to talk in
front of us. More than one agent died after a captured evader had
been made to talk.

A week later, Francis Blanchain collected Woollatt and me and
took us by train to Toulouse. From Port Vendres, where we met
our Spanish guide, we crossed the Pyrenees on foot into Spain and

[1] Prassinos had been informed of this by M.I.9 through a prearranged B.B.C.
message.

reached the British Consulate at Barcelona. We were then passed onto Gibraltar, the first British territory I reached after my escape. Here we were interrogated by Mr. Donald Darling, the listening post of M.I.9 on the Rock. Early in May, we left from Gibraltar on a troopship and, a few days later, sailed into the Clyde as the first American troops arrived on the *Queen Mary*.

On May 13th, 1942, I stood among them at Gourock, uncomfortable in a rough off-the-peg battledress issued to me in Gibraltar, as they offered me cigarettes and whisky.

The Americans were friendly and eager to hear my story. I tried to explain my forlorn and scruffy appearance. In the years to come, hundreds of Americans were to make this same journey in the hands of the great escape organisations.

The news of my arrival in England was radioed to the headquarters of M.I.9 at Beaconsfield as the pink gins circulated in the mess before lunch. An elderly staff officer rushed in:

"We've got Neave out of Colditz!" he exclaimed.

When I heard this, after my 1,500 mile journey across Europe from Colditz, I could not help laughing.

But I knew that it was more than half the truth.

CHAPTER 5

The Great Central Hotel

WHEN Woollatt and I reached Glasgow, no one seemed to believe we had really escaped from Germany. Our scruffy uniforms did not inspire confidence, and our attitude to authority was irreverent. We were constantly interrogated by the Military Police, who could not understand who we were. That evening they took us before a sallow, drooping, full Colonel dressed in a 'British Warm', from whom we demanded passes for the train to London.

"How do I know you are not enemy agents?" he said. "Where are your papers?"

I produced a document signed by Donald Darling in Gibraltar and was grudgingly released.

When we reached Euston next morning it was raining hard. At the Station Hotel we breakfasted off toast with the consistency of flannel and the weakest tea.

Oh for the flat on the Quai Rive Neuve at Marseille and the cuisine of Madame Nouveau!

What was happening to these gallant people? And the girl in Annemasse who looked like Joan of Arc?

Our orders were to go to the Great Central Hotel at Marylebone for interrogation. So we took a taxi and found more Red Caps, sandbags and even bayonets. Had we really escaped? Or was I still dreaming in my two-tiered wooden bed at Colditz?

Before the war, the Great Central Hotel held a strong attraction for me. Not that there was any romantic experience to record—a drink or two, a hilarious bath at four o'clock in the morning before taking a milk train from Marylebone in white-tie and tails.

I was drawn to the magnificent dullness and solidity of the hotel. I liked the brass bedsteads, the marble figures on the stairs and the massive afternoon tea. Outside this refuge my young world was threatened by Hitler. Inside, I could pretend that I belonged to a safer age.

We were directed to the reception desk where two years before a splendid blonde in black had been on guard.

Now there was a sergeant at the desk.

"What is this place, sergeant?"

"The London Transit Camp, sir." He studied me politely. "Where are you from, sir?"

"Germany."

He did not bat an eyelid.

"Quite so, sir. Then it will be M.I.9 you want. They are on the second floor."

I climbed the wide stairs, with my cheap suitcase, still feeling I was a prisoner arriving at a new camp. The corridors were stripped and bleak. Everywhere I could hear the sound of typewriters and the bustle of troops in transit.

I entered what had been a large double-bedroom, which now served as an office for the interrogation of returned escapers by M.I.9. In place of the brass bedsteads were trestle tables and wire baskets. For half an hour, I gloomily watched the rain falling in Marylebone Road, and the mist obscuring the distant barrage balloons.

I wanted to get home. I had telephoned my father from Euston. He was shaving at the time and could think of little to say.

An earnest captain in the Intelligence Corps began to interrogate me. He was vastly interested in my 'Colditz story' and he would have kept me there much longer had I not shown my impatience. My adventures were taken down and reduced to War Office language. I could hardly recognise them. The account was far less exciting than a report by the C.I.D. on their observation of a public convenience.

He showed me the report he had written of my first escape from Stalag XXa at Thorn in April 1941 and my arrest and interrogation by the Gestapo.

It read as if I had been summoned for riding a bicycle without a rear light.

How the British glory in understatement!

Only the reference to a 'rubber truncheon' suggested something out of the ordinary.

I pretended not to care. I was young and lucky. The rubber

truncheon had remained on the wall of the Gestapo office. But there was nothing to convey the sheer terror of being in their hands.

Then came a bald account of my escape from Colditz. How I 'entrained' at Leipzig and crossed the Swiss frontier. Luteyn and I had 'entrained' with a senior S.S. officer who offered us a place in his reserved compartment as 'Dutch allies' and 'detrained' at Ulm when we escaped from the German Railway police. These M.I.9 reports gave to high adventure the style of a Government circular.

The interrogation officer wanted me to continue with my story. Slowly he dragged the information out of me. Later I was to interrogate many returned prisoners myself and it was often very difficult to make them talk.

Writing of Charles II of England and his six weeks on the run after the battle of Worcester in 1651, Richard Ollard remarks that this great adventure became the central episode in the King's career.[1]

It was his principal topic of conversation in after years.

In a modern comparison, Mr. Ollard writes:

"People who have worked in resistance movements or prisoners-of-war do not care to dwell on their experiences. What is thrilling to the reader was frightening to the man he is reading about."

This is profoundly true. The men, often very young, had been exposed to the feeling of being hunted, sometimes for several months. They hated this cross-questioning and a desire to sublimate their anxiety, added to the rather soulless War Office system, did not allay their fears. The shock of arrival, after weeks of danger and excitement, at the hideous Great Central Hotel increased their reticence.

Like King Charles too, in his flight from Boscobel to France, no man escapes without helpers and like the King, they never forgot the people who hid them at certain risk of execution. But in one's gratitude one was often afraid to give them away or to compromise them.

I was asked for the names of Pat O'Leary's organisation.

"They told me not to give their names."

"Oh, we know them. We just want to confirm them for our records," said the Intelligence Officer unconvincingly.

Reluctantly I gave him the names, not knowing which were code-names and which were real. For that May morning I knew

[1] *The Escape of Charles II*, Hodder and Stoughton, 1966. The King was dark, over six feet in height, and difficult to disguise.

nothing of the problems of M.I.9, of the need to learn more about the escape lines and to check the stories of suspicious arrivals.

"Captain Langley is waiting downstairs," said the Intelligence Officer. "He says you know him."

I picked up my shabby suitcase, impatient to be gone, and went to the ground floor of the hotel in time to see Hugh Woollatt wave goodbye. I never saw him again.

A man was sitting in the lounge, now described as an Officers' Mess. It had awful brown armchairs and a coloured photograph of the King on the wall. I looked at my watch. It was eleven o'clock and the bar was still closed. When should I be allowed home to my family at Ingatestone in Essex?

I wanted to get the homecoming over and done with and then get back to London to make up for time lost. Besides the pleasures of the city, I had a list of relatives of fellow-prisoners to visit. In a moment of supreme confidence, I had collected them the night before my escape from Colditz.

The officer got up from his armchair, a small, moustached Captain in Coldstream Guards uniform with two decorations. He had lost his left arm, and the empty sleeve was sewn neatly to his tunic.

Jimmy Langley![1] Surely he was still in France?

Twenty months before, in the summer of 1940, I had been brought with other wounded from Calais to the Faculté Catholique, a school in Lille, converted into a hospital for British prisoners-of-war. A sombre, red-brick affair with stone floors and a smell of wounds and disinfectant.

I could see Langley, pale and strained, playing cards in one of the wards. I remembered his high forehead and bright eyes as he sat on his bed dressed in a tattered shirt and trousers. Three months after our capture we were still in our bloodstained uniforms.

It astonished me that after the amputation of his arm, Langley had been able to escape from Lille. He had been put in touch with a shadowy organisation called the 'Institut Mozart' late in 1940 who aided his flight from the hospital and took him to Paris. He was then escorted over the demarcation line to unoccupied France. In the spring of 1941, the Vichy Armistice Commission declared him unfit for "all future military service" and he was repatriated over the Spanish frontier by train.

[1] Lieut.-Colonel J. M. Langley, M.B.E., M.C.

The Vichy authorities would have been surprised to see him in the Great Central, for he was now in charge of that section of M.I.9 known as I.S.9(d).

"You made it," he said to me. "Congratulations."

"I'm not supposed to discuss it."

He laughed, and asked me to lunch with 'someone important'. I was furious for I wanted to get home, but fortunately the bar opened, and a pink gin improved my temper.

Cartwright had said that M.I.9 wanted me back. For the first time I began to feel interested; my anger at not seeing my family faded.

"Who am I going to meet at lunch?"

"Brigadier Crockatt, Head of M.I.9 and Deputy Director of Military Intelligence (Prisoners of War) to give his full title.[1] D.D.M.I./P.W. we call him."

I have always hated Army abbreviations, and I frowned, but grudgingly agreed.

While Langley went to telephone, I was left alone in my ill-fitting battledress in the brown club chair. Officers came and stood by the bar. They glanced at me severely. I wondered with secret pleasure what they were thinking.

It was twenty-four months since the capture of Calais and there had been little news of me. On January 15th, 1942, came the War Office telegram:

"Important. Information received that Lieutenant Airey Neave is in British hands in a neutral country. Under-Secretary of State for War."

That was all. Was I in Sweden, or Switzerland?

People on the station platform at Ingatestone came and silently shook my father by the hand. The news of my escape from Germany had leaked. The writ of M.I.9 did not run at Ingatestone.

Our neighbours were astounded. They did not believe I was the 'type'. What was the 'type'? I have never since found out. What one needs is confidence, plenty of luck and a powerful motive. Escape is open to everyone.

Langley re-appeared and we were off to Rule's Restaurant in Maiden Lane.

Crockatt was sitting beside the bar. He was unlike the father-

[1] Brigadier Norman R. Crockatt, C.B.E., D.S.O., M.C. Died 1956.

figure of the standard spy story, but youngish and military. He shook hands, beckoned us to chairs and ordered us his 'specials' in one elegant gesture.

He had a handsome, kind, intelligent face. Dark hair, with a neat moustache, slim and smart. He was wearing the uniform of the Royal Scots with the D.S.O. and M.C. He must have been forty-five, with features of distinction. In red tabs and tartan he stood out among the chairborne officers who crowded at Rule's.

I had half expected the chief of M.I.9 to be another Ashenden and I was relieved. This man was a real soldier and I liked him immediately.

Crockatt was friendly and relaxed. I could imagine him twenty years earlier. He was of the generation of 1914 and Mons. Behind his smile, there was a look of resignation I had seen before.

He asked me for stories of life in prisoner-of-war camps.

I told him eagerly that in one camp, so it was said, the prisoners tunnelled and emerged by mistake in the Kommandant's wine cellar, which was full of rare and expensive wines. The Kommandant was a connoisseur and often asked the local nobility to dinner.

The prisoners managed to extricate over a hundred bottles, drank them, put back the corks and labels after refilling them—I paused—with an unmentionable liquid.

Crockatt laughed. "We must tell that to Winston".

Then he was suddenly serious, looking at me intently.

"You've seen the people who work for us behind the lines. They need money and communications. Do you want to help them?"

Of course I did. I thought of Louis Nouveau and the felt slippers.

Crockatt talked in a pleasant unhurried voice. He said that until the end of 1941 most of those who evaded capture were the remnants of the British Army after Dunkirk. Since then, R.A.F. raids on Germany and occupied France had increased and the problem was to recover aircrew who baled out after being shot down.

Apart from human considerations, it cost money to train pilots. Then there would be the Americans, who would soon be flying in large numbers. M.I.9 had the assignment to organise the return of all Allied aircrew whatever their nationality.

He explained how I.S.9(d) had been begun to train agents and establish new routes to Spain.

More men like Pat O'Leary were needed who were good

organisers of underground escape.[1] Already the Gestapo were on the track of the Marseille organisation and they would not last much longer.

Crockatt sighed.

"And now, Neave, subject to your being cleared by the Security Service, I'm going to offer you a job. Would you like to work in our secret escape section with Langley?"

"I think, at the moment," I said, "that it's the one job I should like to do. I have become used to the atmosphere of escape, and I would do anything to help the people over there. I am very pleased, sir, that you think I am suitable."

"Don't be modest," said Crockatt sharply. "You are one of the very few who has had such experience—not only of escape from Germany but of the Resistance as well." Compared with others, I was far from modest about my exploit but it seemed a remarkable offer to an escaped prisoner-of-war on the day of his return.

"All right then," said Crockatt. "Langley's section is here in London at Room 900 in the War Office—I.S.9(d). You will be posted to it next week as a captain. You will work here in London. I shan't see you often because my headquarters are at Beaconsfield.

"You will look after secret communications with occupied Europe and training of agents. I cannot say more at present. Except this. It won't be a bed of roses."

Langley intervened to say that he wanted me to build up an organisation in Belgium and Holland, 'in case anything happens to Dédée.'

"Who is Dédée?" I asked.

"Dédée is a Belgian girl aged twenty-six," he said abruptly.

Crockatt rose without another word, and we followed him through the tables of the restaurant into Maiden Lane. We stood outside for a moment and shook hands.

"Now go on leave for a week and see your family, and then start work. Not a word to anyone. You and Langley will be on your own. Remember that many lives will depend on you. For God's sake, keep your mouth shut and get results."

It was the only time he spoke with real vehemence. He looked a fine soldier. I saluted him as he and Langley turned away.

When they were gone, I stood in Maiden Lane to absorb the

[1] O'Leary was actually trained by S.O.E.

emotions of this extraordinary day. In the last few hours, I had savoured all the anticlimax of my homecoming. Now I had before me the prospect of another great adventure.

I tried to cast from my tired mind these fascinating thoughts of secret intelligence.

It was time to make a brief contact with my earlier life.

On my way to take the train home, I turned into the Temple. I was following the same road as in my prisoner's dream some months before in far-off Colditz. I walked to the barristers' chambers at Farrar's Building close to the Temple Church where before the war I had been a pupil.

War had come this way. The ruin of the church was padlocked, and ugly Farrar's building had a wounded look.

It must have been a terrible night when the bombs came. On the stairs of the Chambers, the walls were grimy from the smoke and the windows broken and boarded.

The room where I had sat as a pupil was empty. The high shelves of legal authorities, sombre desks and chairs, eminently fit for the Victorian disciplines of the the law, had disappeared. Through the cracked windows I saw the pigeons flutter inside the roofless walls of the church.

I opened the door of the clerk's room in silence and shyly looked in.

Charles Hiscocks, clerk to John Morris, K.C.,[1] sat before a table piled high with fee books and briefs. He was a large, round-faced man who seemed unchanged since I had gone away. He appeared never to have moved from this small room, the centre of power in Farrar's Building. A genial authority, presiding over the fortunes of the Chambers, into whose presence young barristers entered with awe and respect.

He looked up and started. Then turning pale, he found a frightened voice at last.

"You can't come in here, sir! You're supposed to be dead!"

[1] Lord Morris of Borth-y-Guest.

CHAPTER 6

Saturday at M.I.9

ON May 26th, 1942 I presented myself in a new uniform at the War Office. The day seemed appropriate for it was the second anniversary of my capture by the Germans at Calais.

I.S.9(d) had two rooms in London for their clandestine operations in North-West Europe and their official address was c/o Room 900, War Office. For the rest of the book I shall therefore refer to I.S.9(d) by the much more convenient name of Room 900.

The rest of the M.I.9 staff, apart from the Interrogation Centre in Marylebone, was housed at Beaconsfield. There they collected intelligence about Allied prisoners-of-war. From interrogation of escapers and other sources, they built up an excellent system of briefing the three services on how to avoid capture. This became the basis of modern military training in escape and survival.

Information for briefing lectures on evasion, especially for air-crew on operations, was also provided by Room 900. Reports from our agents in occupied territory contained much useful advice on what to do when shot down. We were also able to give details of German controls in frontier or coastal zones and their methods of checking passengers on trains.

Room 900 placed emphasis on the security of their agents and helpers. On no account were airmen to put names and addresses of those who hid them in writing. If captured by the Gestapo in the hands of an organisation, they were to give only their names and numbers as they would be obliged to do if captured in combat.

At the end of 1942, it became necessary to order the airmen to disclose more details, not to the Germans, but to the escape lines. Determined efforts were made by the Gestapo to penetrate the lines with their own agents posing as Allied airmen. In 1943, a system of interrogation was devised in London to assist our helpers in checking the men who came into their hands.

The briefing system of M.I.9 extended during the war, to over 600,000 British and Commonwealth servicemen. Lectures were often given by returned escapers or evaders who were able to emphasise the problems by their personal experiences. They tended to concentrate on how to evade capture, rather than escape from prison camps, since in North-West Europe the main objective was to secure the return of trained men by underground means. Until the invasion of Normandy, most were Allied aircrew who risked capture when they were shot down.

From 1942 the American forces formed a fully integrated staff—known as M.I.S.X.—with M.I.9 at Beaconsfield, which carried out the same functions. The effectiveness of the system can be judged by the numbers of escapers and evaders given in Chapter 1. Not only did the information and advice give the men confidence in their ability to avoid arrest in occupied territory, but the emphasis on security prevented many tragedies among those who helped them.

The principal instruction which they received was not to be captured and, if they were, to escape at the earliest opportunity. If they landed by parachute or were cut off from their own troops, they should cautiously approach a house or farm but not enter till the owner appeared to be alone and there were no German troops in sight. Whether it was possible to bury their parachutes on landing depended on the circumstances. It was usually necessary to lie under cover until they were sure that search-parties were no longer looking for them. In some cases it might be better to make off across country as soon as possible. School teachers, doctors, and priests were invariably helpful, as they often spoke English. The latter could safely be approached at the confessional.

Once the initial approach had been made, civilian clothes provided and their wounds, if any, treated, it was essential to wait patiently in hiding. It might take several days for those who sheltered them to contact an escape organisation. On no account were they to attempt, through boredom and frustration, to make their own way to safety. Those who did, speaking no French and without authentic documents, were invariably arrested. When the organisation took charge of them, it must be implicitly obeyed. A few cases occurred of men whose behaviour led to quarrels with their helpers but those were rare and drew a shamefaced apology after a night of drinking and making love. Considering the number of occasions where these fighting men were looked after and guided from place to place by attractive girls, the number of such incidents was not high. But organisers of escape lines were well aware of this danger and sought to enforce discipline.

The instructions for 'foreign travel' were as precise as possible. If they were in the hands of an organisation they had nothing to do but obey orders till they reached neutral territory. But if it was necessary to travel alone, moving perhaps from one 'safe house' to another in occupied territory, it was best to move by day and observe the curfew at night. Bicycles must not be stolen as this could easily lead to detection. They must keep to the right-hand side of the road, as failure to do this had more than once led to arrest by the local police.

The British tendency to start friendly and unnecessary conversation was dangerous and on no account should cigarettes[1] —especially Players, Gold Flake, or American brands—be offered to anyone on the journey. Nor should chocolate—unknown in most places in wartime—be eaten in public.[2] In Germany, before the Allied invasion, there was no prospect of help from the population for those who escaped from prison camps. The recommendations for travel were the opposite to those for occupied territory. By day, walking in Germany was extremely dangerous though several, like myself, escaped by train. On foot, it was best to move always by night avoiding military installations with sentries and the streets of large towns.

The reaction of the men to these lectures was unpredictable. Most followed their instructions and some took them sufficiently seriously to learn languages and study the countries where they were due to go on operations. Others assumed that nothing would happen to them. To enliven the lecture period true and sometimes amusing, stories were told of the adventures of others. One, which may be apocryphal, was always a success. A sergeant pilot in the R.A.F. was shot down close to a French convent. Before the Germans

[1] Nicotine stains on the fingers betrayed several escapers.
[2] The author was nearly recaptured through eating a bar of Red Cross chocolate at Leipzig station.

could catch him, a number of nuns appeared and spirited him inside. Walking in the convent garden, the sergeant, dressed in the habit of the Order, found himself beside a beautiful nun. After he had made shy advances, she turned and replied in masculine English:

"Don't be a bloody fool, I've been here since Dunkirk."

As part of this 'preventive training' M.I.9 provided various 'escape aids' to operational troops, especially R.A.F. flying personnel. They were also issued to submarine crews on special tasks, Commandos, the United States 'Rangers', airborne and armoured units. Among them were 'escape packs' containing silk maps, twelve pounds in foreign currency, a small compass, and a hacksaw. Another type of aid box contained nourishing food for twenty-four hours, a compass, a water bottle, desalination tablets and such helpful items as a fishing line and hook. A phenomenal number of these aids were designed at M.I.9 headquarters in Beaconsfield. In Europe, North Africa, and the Middle East alone, 760,757 maps and 1,700,241 compasses were distributed.

M.I.9 was staffed by all three services but for a long time it failed to gain co-operation of senior officers. This has always been something of a mystery, since its aim was to help men either evade capture or escape from prison camps. In part, this indifference was due to the distrust with which Regular officers regarded what they chose to call 'Cloak and dagger' work. To them, secret operations seemed somehow civilian in character, nor did they encourage their men to ponder overmuch the possibilities of capture. I well remember the natural disgust with which surrender to the enemy, even in the most desperate circumstances, was regarded in the 1940 campaign in France. This attitude changed after the retreat of the British Army to Dunkirk and the return of many of its survivors through Spain. But even in 1944, there were many whose background made them reluctant to accept the need for escape and evasion training. This was all the more surprising in the case of the Air Ministry. All their crews received lectures and escape equipment, yet they showed little enthusiasm for the provision of aircraft for clandestine escape operations, and the parachuting of Room 900 agents. But they were at all times subjected to persistent pressure from S.O.E. and other secret intelligence organisations which claimed priority.

A full history of M.I.9 and its different functions must await the

appointed day under the Official Secrets Act. It carried out similar
operations in Italy, the Middle East and the Far East with which I
had no concern. In these areas, it experienced considerable success.
Intelligence School Number 9 or I.S.9 was the more secret and
executive branch of M.I.9. It was concerned with facilitating escape
and evasion and was the personal achievement of Crockatt. Starting
with a handful of staff officers and his able assistant, Susan Broomhall, he created this special section. Room 900 to which I reported
on that May morning in 1942 was his top secret staff, consisting of
Langley and myself. Its work was kept separate from the rest of
M.I.9 and was practically unknown at Beaconsfield.

Langley's diminutive office, on the second floor at the War
Office, was a room reserved for making tea in peacetime. I was with
some difficulty seated opposite him at an extra table. Two large
filing cabinets obscured the light from a single window. It was
obvious that, in the world of military intelligence, we were extremely small beer.

An even smaller room was provided for our two secretaries.

Could this really be the nerve centre of that remote, powerful
system referred to by Prassinos in Marseille as 'l'Intelligence Service'?

All such romantic images were instantly dispelled. A cup of War
Office tea was set before me as I took my place.

I sat before my blank sheet of official blotting-paper listening to
Langley.

He announced that I had been cleared for 'Security'. There was
nothing known against me by "those people who hover round at
cocktail parties—mostly dons and barristers—but we have good
friends there."

"And this place?"

"We just work here and leave them alone. They leave us alone,
thank God."

He then explained the relationship between Room 900 and other
secret organisations. Room 900's task was to bring Allied servicemen
back to the fight. It was not to collect military information or conduct sabotage. The wires must never be crossed.

"And who does the sabotage?"

"S.O.E. or Special Operations Executive, commonly known as
'Baker Street'. They are a new organisation and not popular."

S.O.E., it appeared, had trodden on many distinguished toes in secret intelligence. But I was far too dedicated to helping the escape lines to interest myself in this domestic warfare, and except for one sad affair, I had much co-operation from the French, Belgian, and Dutch sections of S.O.E.

The main event of the morning was a meeting with our chief at the War Office, a veteran intelligence officer. We finished our tea, and walked down endless corridors. A fierce, iron-jawed figure sat writing at a long table.

"Sit down," he grunted.

There was only the scratching of his broad-nibbed pen. We waited in total silence.

The transformation from a German prison camp to the War Office was proving a strain on my emotions. Perchance I was only dreaming that I had escaped. I glanced nervously round the room.

The old man suddenly looked up at me with a glare of appraisal. He watched me for a few moments. There were years of shrewd experience and cunning behind his glance.

But then he smiled, his pale grey eyes softened, and he said:

"Many congratulations. The best escape—so far. But your next job will be much harder."

"Thank you, sir."

He continued to gaze at me.

"These escape lines run by Langley and Darling are dangerous. They may get mixed up with other operations which have priority."

I had every reason to know they were dangerous. The real risks were not taken in London, but in Marseille, Brussels and Paris.

Our chief now embarked on a favourite War Office theme. Nurse Edith Cavell had mixed help to British escapers in the First World War with sending out military information. Though he often used this example to demonstrate his point, I believe that he did Edith Cavell an injustice.

She was shot for hiding Allied soldiers in her clinic in Brussels in 1915, the year before I was born. She made a full confession of her actions which she believed to be morally right. She sacrificed herself in the cause which she had made her own, that of mercy to helpless British soldiers. At no time did the Germans charge her with espionage. Nor was she a spy.

Her legend was of great significance in the Second World War especially to the Belgians and many young women risked their lives for her example. She was to be an inspiration for those heroes and heroines of the escape lines who felt the humanitarian importance of their work. Of them, it can surely be said, that mere patriotism was not enough.[1]

There was something distasteful about these remarks. It was one of many sarcasms about those who, perhaps through errors of judgement, were caught by the enemy but died gloriously. The urge to help men escape, as I had seen at first hand, had no relation to the motives of a professional spy. Perhaps this is why, by the end of the war, Room 900 recruited agents of such high quality.

But in one sense the old man was right. Secret organisations should keep separate from each other. Evidently he feared that escape lines to Spain would be used by the Germans to send their own spies to England. He had every reason for his caution.

He began to talk of Dédée, the young Belgian girl of whom Crockatt had spoken briefly at our first meeting. He claimed to be doubtful about her though she had already delivered thirty soldiers and R.A.F. at San Sebastian. I was later to know her as one of our greatest agents.

He talked of training organisers, of wireless sets, codes and couriers, which meant little to me. It seemed that if there were such facilities to spare, Room 900 would not be allowed many of them. All these things, he said, were 'extremely risky'. I wondered how we should be able to carry out Crockatt's orders to 'get results'.

He concluded with this admonition: "This is a tough game and you must learn the rules."

Then he grimaced and we were out in the bleak corridor, returning to our small office. I was silent and dismayed. All the enthusiasm to work in M.I.9 had evaporated. Would it be possible to get anything done for Pat O'Leary and his friends in this extraordinary place?

It was different when you had been in the field. You felt these things very deeply. The War Office was just as crazy as Colditz but a lot less human.

Was I too sensitive? Later I saw men and women arriving in London from the dangers of occupied territory experience this same sad deflation.

[1] Several nurses trained by Nurse Cavell in Brussels worked for the escape lines in the Second World War.

In war and peace, one cannot be too careful about security. But there are many courageous and loyal people who have their moments of weakness behind the lines. It may be a moment of terror, a sexual indiscretion. Whatever may be the defect, chairborne intelligence officers should exercise imagination and, if possible, humility.

Once back in Room 900, Langley explained to me about cover names.

I found the system of names amusing. There was 'Horse' at the British Consulate at Barcelona. 'Monday' was at the British Embassy Madrid. I had met him when I passed through Spain. Donald Darling at Gibraltar was 'Sunday'. Langley appeared to be 'Jimmy' to M.I.9 and even to our agents in enemy territory.

"Now what are we going to call you?" said Langley. "You will need a nom de guerre."

"What about Saturday?"

So 'Saturday' I became for my next three years at Room 900 though I had other strange names as well, as I soon found out that the War Office also expected me to meet agents under the name of 'Anthony Newton'. But I abandoned this idiotic arrangement for a few weeks when I interviewed an Air Force officer I had known before the war.

I did however sign with the name 'Albert Hall' a number of microphotographed messages which went by courier to Brussels. An airman arriving in Gibraltar told Donald Darling that his orders from Brussels were to report to the Albert Hall. M.I.9 were not amused. The pseudonym became known to the Gestapo and no doubt caused them similar confusion.

I used my own name except in telegrams and letters to 'Monday' and Darling for the rest of the war. Were these 'cover names' necessary for intelligence officers in wartime London? People outside this dream world often saw through them. In the case of agents, however, they were essential, especially for those whose real names were known in occupied territory.

'Cover names' were often designed to protect intelligence departments against the curiosity of their rivals. If more time had been spent on the security of agents in the field than on internecine squabbles, fewer tragedies would have occurred.

Since Room 900 did not conduct espionage, and consisted of only two or three officers and a handful of trained agents at any time during the war, it could afford a less neurotic attitude to itself and concentrate on actual operations. But we made our fair share of blunders nonetheless.

PART II

THE O'LEARY LINE

CHAPTER 7

The Pioneers

IN my first week at Room 900, Langley showed me files on the escape lines and their leaders. The first which I studied concerned the origin of the line to Barcelona used by Woollatt and myself a month before. It disclosed a story as subtle and entertaining as any that Somerset Maugham could have written. Indeed, with his own experience of secret intelligence work, he would have greatly enjoyed it.

In July 1940, Donald Darling, our man in Gibraltar, was sent by M.I.9 to Lisbon and Barcelona to create underground links with France. M.I.9 had been quick off the mark, for this was only a fortnight after the surrender of the French Army and the occupation of northern France. Darling, who had just left France, was well qualified, for he knew the Spanish frontier region intimately. One of the results of his work was the line from France to Barcelona later used by Pat O'Leary.

Darling made a great contribution to the successes of Room 900. He was dark-haired and well-built—a younger version of the actor Herbert Marshall—and possessed of a remarkable memory for faces and names. His witty and ingenious correspondence signed 'Sunday' was always eagerly awaited.

During the long, hot summer of 1940, he busied himself in Lisbon and Barcelona making the first links in the chain to France. Though his communications were limited and insecure, he had many contacts on the French side of the frontier who might, if paid, be willing to guide escapers over the Pyrenees. But to set up a two-way traffic required a personal visit by someone of influence able to travel in Vichy France, for there were financial bargains to be struck. Smugglers and 'passeurs' were not likely to risk execution by the Germans or General Franco without substantial rewards. As the Dunkirk evaders flowed over the demarcation line, a solution to the problem became urgent. Darling himself seemed the obvious man for M.I.9 to send across the frontier from Barcelona. He understood the complex political world of the Pyrénées Orientales, but it was not only guides who were needed. Contacts were required at the heart of the Vichy government. Apart from the soldiers congregating at Marseille, numerous British residents remained on the Riviera, who could not leave without exit permits. From the beginning there existed officials in the Vichy administration who were pro-British and willing to render under-cover services to the Allies. For several months after the Armistice, visas and exit permits were issued to British subjects, some of whom were secret agents. Others including escapers from Dunkirk arrived at Lisbon equipped with Irish passports.

In July 1940, the War Office found the ideal agent to make the necessary contacts at Vichy and negotiate a system of guides with the underworld in Spanish frontier zone. This was Mr. Nubar Gulbenkian who had the double advantage of being an official of the neutral Iranian Legation and the son of Calouste Gulbenkian. Calouste Gulbenkian, immensely rich and powerful, and known as 'Mr. Five per cent' for his share of Middle East oil production, had left Paris after the Occupation and was temporarily settled at Vichy. These circumstances gave Nubar Gulbenkian an excellent cover-story for an exploratory visit.

He has described it in his remarkable autobiography: *Pantaraxia*.[1] Accompanied by his English valet, he flew to Lisbon, where he was given instructions by Darling, crossed to Barcelona, and, by train and taxi, reached Perpignan on the French side of the frontier. France was in chaos, the trains and roads choked with returning refugees and defeated soldiers. There was little security, and the mail remained uncensored. After an exhausting journey he at last arrived at Vichy and stayed at the Hotel des Ambassadeurs where he was reunited with his parents. The following morning his English valet, named Bailey, went to the Hotel Majestic where Calouste Gulbenkian was staying, to borrow an iron for pressing his master's clothes. The hotel was also the administrative headquarters of the Vichy regime and on leaving it, Bailey was suddenly confronted by a group of visiting German officers. Alarmed at the sight of their uniforms, he dropped the iron on the toes of Field-

[1] Hutchinson, 1965.

marshal von Brauchitsch, then Commander-in-Chief of the German Army. Fortunately, the Germans took him for a neutral American and the incident passed off amicably[1]. The unreal world of Vichy, where everyone seems to have listened to the B.B.C., included such personalities as Mrs. Corrigan, an American society hostess in London between the wars, and it had rapidly become a hive of rumour and espionage. After making a number of useful diplomatic contacts, Nubar Gulbenkian then returned safely to England.

It was his second mission, a few weeks later, that became of supreme importance to M.I.9 and the whole organisation of escape from unoccupied France. He received his instructions at the official flat, later occupied by Langley, at 5 St. James's Street. These were to make contact with a garage proprietor in Perpignan known as 'Parker'[2] and arrange for the payment of guides to take British servicemen to Spain. The terms were to be forty pounds for an officer and twenty pounds for 'other ranks'. These amounts, typically enough, had first to be authorised by the Treasury. In Lisbon, he met Darling, who after an exchange of passwords gave him the address of Parker in Perpignan. Parker was to be responsible for the collection of the men at his garage and passing them to smugglers and guides who would take them to Spain, where they would be liberated from internment by diplomatic means.

The meeting between Nubar Gulbenkian and Parker took place at a café in Perpignan. Parker was, in accordance with Darling's instructions, reading the French newspaper L'Indépendent upside down. After asking the test question; "Have you a Parker pen? A Parker Duo-fold?", Gulbenkian commenced negotiations which were completed in twenty minutes. He informed Parker that payment would be strictly by results and the transaction completed when each man was across the frontier. The money would accumulate in England for the benefit of Parker at the end of the war. His work done, Gulbenkian returned to Barcelona still accompanied by his valet, Bailey. He paid yet another visit to Perpignan and Vichy, this time without Bailey, where he established further contacts and recrossed the Spanish frontier on October 10th, 1940.

Although the guides to Spain later increased their prices with the tightening of control on the frontier, it was the Gulbenkian mission,

[1] He later found himself pressing German officers' trousers.
[2] A contact of Darling named Michel Pareyre.

aided by Darling's knowledge of the situation, which tied together the two ends of the original escape line.

At the French end was Captain Ian Garrow of the Seaforth Highlanders.[1] Garrow was the first real chief of the escape organisation in the South of France. With a party of soldiers he escaped from St. Valery on the north coast of France after the surrender of the 51st (Highland) Division at the end of May 1940. He was a tall, commanding Scotsman; quiet and deliberate in speech and thought. He knew little French and his Highland features made disguise impossible among the population of Marseille. But he exercised a great fascination for his early helpers to whom he became a symbol of British defiance. They were attracted by his earnestness and soft Scottish voice. A generation after, he still remains an endearing figure to them.

Garrow's decision to remain in France instead of seeking escape was in itself heroic. His height and appearance put him in constant danger of arrest by the Vichy police. It is remarkable that he was able to remain free until as late as October 1941, when he was arrested, court-martialled, and sentenced to imprisonment at Fort Meauzac in the Dordogne. Judging that he would be more useful to the British Army if he were to stay and organise an escape route, he began to collect funds to hide those men who had not been interned in Vichy camps. Among his first helpers were Louis Nouveau of the flat on the Quai Rive Neuve, his wife, and Mario Prassinos.

In the first ten months of 1941, Garrow set the pattern for future escape operations over the Spanish frontier. He organised a chain of guides from Paris and northern France over the demarcation line and a system of reception in Marseille and Toulouse. The administrative problems were great. The strict rationing of food, increasing controls, and general disillusionment, made his position precarious. But his determination was rewarded and at the time of his arrest, regular parties were reaching the British consulate at Barcelona.

The creation of the special section at Room 900 in the summer of 1941, to communicate with escape lines, was a great encouragement to Garrow, though it came too late to save him many anxieties. Moved by stories of this courageous figure with little money and primitive communications, M.I.9 attempted to give him more assistance. Money was sent to him over the frontier to supplement

[1] Lieut.-Colonel Ian Garrow, D.S.O.

what he received privately, but he was, throughout his career as an organiser, without any radio links with London. He had to depend on couriers from Barcelona and Gibraltar who brought him instructions and had often to wait for a fortnight or more to receive an answer to his requests through messages on the French news service of the B.B.C. In the face of these obstacles, his achievement was extraordinary. It was due to his persistence that the system of reception of evaders and escapers in Spain at the British consulate at Barcelona, had become firmly established by the time of my arrival at Room 900. From Marseille and Toulouse, the men were brought by guides, financed by Parker and Darling, over the mountains to a wayside station on the Spanish side, and taken by train, through police controls, to the consulate at Barcelona.

Barcelona, Madrid and Gibraltar all served as listening posts and reporting centres for M.I.9. At the British Embassy in Madrid the men were briefly interrogated by 'Monday' after their long, dusty journey in a car, frequently driven by 'Horse', who had served a short apprenticeship at Room 900 before joining the consulate at Barcelona. 'Monday' would telegraph their names and urgent information to Room 900, and make arrangements for their transport to Gibraltar, usually by motorcoach as a party of 'students' or 'French-Canadians'.

Once I had grasped the outline of this fascinating organisation, I became eager to know more of O'Leary, the successor to Garrow as leader of the group in Marseille. What was his nationality? The face in his passport photograph was of a man of about thirty. I judged him to be energetic and intelligent, with bold, clear eyes. He wore a Royal Naval officer's uniform and cap but his face was not English. There was something about the eyelids and mouth which puzzled me. The expression was half-smiling and yet a little ruthless. Even in this small photograph, he was clearly a formidable man. And how did he come to be described in the file as 'Lieut.-Commander Patrick Albert O'Leary R.N.'? I could not wait to ask Langley his true identity.

"His name is Albert-Marie Guérisse[1] and he is Médecin-Capitaine in the Belgian Army."

Langley insisted that this information was to be kept secret even from M.I.9 at Beaconsfield. He described how O'Leary had been a

[1] Major-General A.-M. Guérisse, G.C., D.S.O.

medical officer in a Belgian cavalry unit in 1940 and had then escaped to England. He had volunteered for the special section later known as S.O.E. and his first assignment was that of second in command in H.M.S. *Fidelity*, a 'Q' ship conducting clandestine sabotage operations on the south coast of France. The captain, a Frenchman, and O'Leary both insisted on wearing Royal Naval uniforms. The Admiralty, after some shuffling permitted the enterprising Belgian doctor to be commissioned as a Lieut.-Commander R.N. and, as he showed a strong preference for an Irish name, was known as Pat O'Leary.

My opinion of the Admiralty soared when I was told that they had also agreed to *Fidelity* carrying a woman first officer, but there was hell to pay when it was discovered that she was a Wren. The director of the W.R.N.S. protested vehemently. I never saw the correspondence at Room 900 but it appears that the Admiralty quoted Nelson and Lady Hamilton as a precedent. The director is supposed to have replied that to 'the best of her belief' Lady Hamilton was not a Wren. Sometime after O'Leary started work for Garrow's escape line, *Fidelity* was torpedoed in the South Atlantic and lost.

How did O'Leary arrive in Marseille? The file showed that in April 1941 he was left behind in error from *Fidelity* during a night landing operation at Collioure and nearly drowned. French coastguards arrested him, to whom he maintained that he was a French-Canadian officer trying to escape to Spain. He was interned at the camp for British prisoners at St. Hippolyte du Fort near Nîmes. Ian Garrow discovered his presence there that summer and engineered his escape. In St. Hippolyte, his cover story was at first suspect until he was able to prove his identity as an officer of the Royal Navy. Even then the Marseille organisation was at first unwilling to believe him.

By this time, Garrow had regular couriers to Barcelona and sent a message to M.I.9 and the Admiralty to confirm O'Leary's story. He requested a reply on the French news service of the B.B.C., for O'Leary seemed an excellent recruit. He had already been trained in secret service work and was a man of exceptional character. He was cool and ingenious and spoke excellent English. If permission was granted for him to remain in France, the reply should be:

"Adolphe doit rester."

A fortnight later, when O'Leary, waiting anxiously, had almost given up hope, he heard the sentence on the B.B.C. at nine p.m.

This was the beginning of his glittering service to the Allied cause which won him the George Cross, the D.S.O. and over twenty other decorations.

CHAPTER 8

The Return of Whitney Straight

I WAS conscious that Langley, alone and one-armed, had, since 1941, carried the full burden at Room 900. 'Monday' and Donald Darling were brilliant operators but he badly needed help in London. We were very much on our own with little influence among the giants of Military Intelligence. To them, prisoners-of-war or 'P.O.W.s' were of slight importance to the war effort. It was not until two years had gone by that our work was taken seriously.

In June, I had taken a flat not far from Langley's. It was fit for Bertie Wooster with twentyish furniture and here I lived for six months until I married. Langley and I would sit in the masculine armchairs, drinking whisky in the evening, and discuss the state of our two-man organisation. We were always on duty. Often the telephone rang, to announce the arrival of an excited telegram from Darling or from 'Monday' which sent us rushing back to the War Office. It did not seem a soldier's life. Sometimes I felt, thinking of those I had left behind in Colditz, that I had no right to this luxury. But there were great plans and decisions to be made that summer. In April, O'Leary, Langley and Darling had all met in Gibraltar for a conference, while I was in hiding in Louis Nouveau's flat in Marseille. They had discussed the possibility of using wireless operators, of sea evacuations, of the need for more money and finally the most pressing and menacing of all anxious problems, that of Cole.[1] Langley felt as a result of these talks that the man was definitely a traitor. Hitherto, the authorities in London had been inclined to give him the benefit of the doubt, in spite of a warning from Darling in 1941 which was unfortunately ignored.

One day Langley said: "When I was repatriated on account of losing this arm, Cole was a trusted operator. In 1941 he was bring-

[1] See Chapter 25.

ing regular parties from Lille and Paris over the demarcation line.

"O'Leary had never liked him, but he brought results. Have a look at this photograph. I thought you should see it."

It was a photograph of a man with light hair brushed across his forehead. There was a faint smile on his face, and his close-set eyes gave him a cunning expression. The note attached to it described his hair as red.

"He is very attractive to women,"said Langley, "with mistresses all over France. He also loves money and this may be the clue to his actions. To the French he describes himself as a Captain."

The photograph was entitled:

"Cole, Harold, alias Paul, born London June 24, 1906. See correspondence with Special Branch."

Langley continued in a worried voice:

"Scotland Yard say he has a string of minor convictions for housebreaking and fraud. He is a big talker and con man. He makes constant use of the expression 'old man'."

Since my arrival, Special Branch had made more enquiries. There was no Captain Harold Cole of this description serving in the Army at the time of Dunkirk, but a Sergeant Cole had disappeared before the battle began, taking with him the funds of the Sergeants' Mess.

The outline of this dreadful story had now reached Room 900 but it was still hard to believe. In September 1941, Ian Garrow found Cole at a party in Marseille, with a mistress, when he was supposed to be in northern France. This was overlooked. But O'Leary, still suspicious, decided to check on him with a helper named Duprez in Lille, who hid airmen. Lille had been Cole's first headquarters and he had been given large sums of money for Duprez, who denied receiving a sou. O'Leary had therefore taken Duprez back with him over the demarcation line to report to Garrow. As soon as they reached Marseille in October, they heard of Garrow's arrest by the Vichy French. O'Leary's suspicions soared, but there is no evidence that this was the work of Cole.

O'Leary arranged to meet Cole in the flat of Dr. Rodocanachi, a most trusted agent, where he accused the Englishman of spending the money intended for Duprez on women. Cole flatly denied this and assured him that Duprez had been paid. O'Leary then opened the door of the next room. Suddenly confronted with Duprez,

Cole went white and moved towards O'Leary, who hit him hard in the mouth. He fell, and lay bleeding and moaning on the floor. He then confessed to having done 'something terrible' in a moment of weakness.

With O'Leary at Dr. Rodocanachi's flat were Prassinos and their friend Bruce Dowding, an Australian who worked for the line. While they debated what to do with Cole, they locked him in the bathroom. Bruce Dowding was for killing him, but Prassinos, a gentler character, was horrified. O'Leary, too, was undecided, wondering whether he should send him back to England. He did not realise, at this time, that Cole was known to Scotland Yard. There was a noise from the bathroom. Dowding opened the door in time to see Cole escape through the window into a corridor of the block of flats. He raced downstairs after him, but Cole escaped in the crowded streets of Marseille.

There was not a minute to lose. O'Leary and Bruce Dowding hurried to occupied France to warn their chief agent in Abbeville, the Abbé Carpentier, who supplied false identity papers on his own printing press. This heroic priest, knowing the danger, refused to leave his post, forging passes for the forbidden zones and cards for the demarcation line. O'Leary urged Duprez to change his name and leave Lille for the South of France. But he refused, unwilling to leave his family and business. In spite of what had happened in Dr. Rodocanachi's flat, it was difficult to persuade French people that any Englishman could really turn traitor. This was also the feeling in London before Cole's record and identity was confirmed.

On December 8th, 1941 Cole arrived at the Abbé Carpentier's house with three airmen. Two were spies of the German military counter-espionage service known as the Abwehr, one was genuine. Dowding, who was hiding in the house, overheard Cole's voice, and escaped by the back door to warn other agents. But Cole had given the Germans the addresses of at least ten people. At the third address where Dowding called, the Germans were waiting for him. This was the first Abwehr operation using the traitor Cole and bogus British airmen. There were to be several more. Within a week, poor trusting Monsieur Duprez was arrested in the same manner at Lille. All three were brutally treated and later executed, victims of treason. The gentle Abbé, the earnest businessman Duprez, and the gallant Australian, Bruce Dowding, died at Cole's hands. Cole was later to

betray his mistresses and even his French wife and her elderly relatives for money. We did not hear the full story until the end of the
war.[1] His treachery cost the lives of fifty of the escape organisation's
bravest helpers. Yet there are many alive today whom he helped
to safety.

While O'Leary was at Gibraltar in April 1942, it was agreed that
not only should all addresses, 'post-boxes' and cover names, known
to Cole, be changed, but orders be sent to all underground groups in
France that he was a traitor and should be shot on sight. M.I.9 in
London warned S.O.E. and other intelligence services. In May, Cole
was arrested with his young French wife by Vichy detectives. He
was court-martialled for spying for 'a foreign power' and sentenced
to ten years' fortress detention. The circumstances of this trial were a
mystery to us for a long time.[2] Looking back on this tragedy, I
have always felt that the possession of a radio link might have
avoided the doubts and hesitations about his treachery and the
arrests which followed. O'Leary was still relying, at the time of the
arrests in Paris, on a shaky system of messages in toothpaste tubes
brought by couriers over the Pyrenees. It was extraordinary that
his magnificent team was allowed to continue for so long without
a radio operator, but the explanation lay in the lack of influence
of M.I.9 with other organisations who could provide recruits for
secret wireless training. Until the summer of 1942 and even afterwards, organised evasion had the lowest possible priority with the
Air Ministry and without their help it was impossible to drop agents
and wireless sets by parachute.

If the plans to evacuate people by sea from southern France to
Gibraltar were to succeed a direct radio link with Room 900 was
essential. A trained radio operator called 'Ferière' was found and
flown to Gibraltar. After the conference in April, he returned with
O'Leary to Perpignan. O'Leary did not think much of him. He was
very nervous but managed to get his wireless set to Marseille. After
that Ferière completely lost his nerve. He never came up on the air
and vanished. It appeared later that he had volunteered for the
mission for the sole purpose of rejoining his wife whom he had left
behind in France. O'Leary then found another operator for Ferière's
set, a Frenchman who worked on the aerodrome at Nîmes. Though

[1] See Chapter 25.
[2] See Chapter 25.

this man had no special training, O'Leary was at last in contact with us by May 1942. In June, Langley decided to send Jean Nitelet, a Belgian in the R.A.F., to the O'Leary organisation. Shot down in France several months earlier, he had passed through the line to Spain. He lost an eye in combat and, no longer fit for flying duties, volunteered to return as a wireless operator for O'Leary.

Money was the other most important problem discussed at the Gibraltar meeting between O'Leary, Langley and Darling. Growing numbers of men hidden by the escape line had to be fed and the proposed expansion into northern France financed. O'Leary and Louis Nouveau made frequent journeys to their helpers in Lille and Paris, to get further news of Cole, and their expenses were increasing.[1] Nouveau had already contributed some of his considerable private fortune to Garrow. In the summer of 1941, he discovered a further source of funds. A Mr. Gosling, formerly manager of the French factory of J. and P. Coates in the Perigord district, was reported to be hiding there with six million French francs belonging to the company. Nouveau persuaded Gosling to transfer French francs to him in instalments in exchange for an equivalent sum to be credited by M.I.9 to J. and P. Coates in England. The deal was successfully concluded by secret correspondence between Nouveau and 'Monday' in Madrid.

A year later, the 'Gosling millions' were exhausted, and O'Leary faced a crisis. M.I.9 funds he was receiving by courier from Madrid and Barcelona were inadequate to sustain his growing escape network. To add to these anxieties, the security of the organisation was now threatened by the number of Gestapo agents, in raincoats and pork pie hats, who appeared in the Unoccupied Zone. The Vichy Government, prompted by the Germans, also administered savage sentences to ordinary people for hiding Allied soldiers and airmen.

The arrival of Jean Nitelet, the one-eyed radio-operator, nearly ended in disaster. Returning at night in an R.A.F. Lysander, he narrowly escaped arrest. The aircraft landed near Chateauroux but the pilot was unable to take off again. All efforts failed to get the wheels out of the soft ground of the field, and the plane had to be

---

[1] After the arrests in Paris, the organisation in northern France was led by Jean de la Olla who later showed conspicuous courage under torture by the Gestapo.

[2] Nouveau was assisted in this transaction by Lieut.-Col. Richard Broad, M.C., who later escaped to Spain.

abandoned. Nitelet struggled with his radio set to Louis Nouveau's flat in Marseille, but the Lysander pilot, Flight Lieutenant Mott, R.A.F., was caught and sent to the Vichy camp at Fort de la Revère. Nitelet was told to operate his set with the utmost caution, moving from flat to flat, for German wireless detector vans were already active in Marseille. Without him we had no means of mounting the sea operations from the south coast to Gibraltar.

Langley explained to me the plans which he had discussed with O'Leary in April. Two operations had already succeeded from beaches at Port Miou near Cassis and St. Pierre Plage near Narbonne. The trawler *Tarana* with a British crew, and secretly armed, was to sail from Gibraltar to a new beach at Canet-Plage near Perpignan and take off parties of evaders in small boats. On leaving Gibraltar, the crew would paint her in neutral colours, sometimes flying the green Moroccan, sometimes the Portuguese flag till her return. Similar missions were carried out by fishing boats manned by Poles.

This was not information for the 'cold feet' department, I thought. This usually meant, quite unfairly, the Foreign Office, though the activities in Spain of their brave representative, 'Monday', did not suggest that he would worry over much.

The plans to use *Tarana* on these clandestine voyages coincided with the presence in Forts de la Revère and St. Hippolyte of several important R.A.F. pilots whose return was badly wanted by the Air Ministry. Among them was Squadron Leader Whitney Straight, R.A.F.[1] With other pilots, he was the subject of a direct order from Crockatt that all possible steps were to be taken to prevent their falling into German hands. Whitney Straight was one of the most dashing airmen who evaded capture at this time. American by birth, he was a racing driver of international repute. He was also an exceptional pilot with a distinguished record before he was shot down while attacking E-boats near Le Havre on July 31st, 1941. I had heard of his adventures while I was still in France. He was a romantic figure in the world of escaping. During the few weeks I had spent at Room 900 hardly a day passed without a call from the Air Ministry or Crockatt. What news? What were we doing about him?

It was therefore with intense, if top secret, excitement that we received on July 24th, 1942, a message from Donald Darling which

[1] Later Air Commodore, C.B.E., M.C., D.F.C.

began as usual, "Gibraltar: Room 900 from Sunday." *Tarana* had arrived with Whitney Straight and Leoni Savinos and his German wife. The Savinoses had been sent out by O'Leary after an attempt by the Gestapo to turn Savinos into a double agent after his arrest in Paris in April. The message ended "Sending by air and should arrive Hendon tomorrow 25 July stop Please remind Saturday Madame Savinos is German repeat German.'

The rescue of Whitney Straight and other airmen from the beach at Canet-Plage, near Perpignan, was a landmark in the history of Room 900. It showed that we could mount such special sea operations with success.[1]

It was also with real relief that I knew that Leoni Savinos and his wife had got away. Savinos was a Greek friend of Mario Prassinos in Marseille and had worked for O'Leary for several months. I had met him with his wife in Louis Nouveau's flat in April. It seemed from Darling's message that he had important information about the Gestapo, but I did not at first recall the significance of Darling's reminder that Madame Savinos was German.

Langley and Darling, who had organised the reception of the passengers in Gibraltar, were both entitled to celebrate. It was a triumph for their efforts, even if the real heroes of this affair were the O'Leary organisation and Whitney Straight himself. Two evenings later, the telephone rang at No. 5 St. James's Street. Whitney Straight had arrived at Hendon and would soon be with us.

He was dark and strongly-built, with an air of authority, and about thirty at this time. There was a businesslike determination in his manner. He spoke of his escape without great emphasis on the dangers, but with restrained amusement and valuable detail. He had throughout displayed remarkable coolness and resource. His was one of many exciting escapes in the history of Room 900 and a story with dramatic quality.

He sat before us, relaxed in smart civilian clothes.

"I landed wheels-up," he said in his quiet voice, "in a field beside a French farmer who looked rather surprised. I got out and tried to blow up the aircraft, but I failed. So I set off on a zig-zag course across country."

It was clear that Straight had given more thought than most to the subject of evasion. He had, for instance, equipped himself with

[1] Including Whitney Straight, thirty-five airmen were rescued on this operation.

passport photographs and a leather jacket to hide his R.A.F. uniform. Like most aircrew, he had been briefed by M.I.9 and he spoke excellent French. He decided that a hat was needed to go with his jacket and he went to a farm where he made good use of his French money by buying one from the farmer's wife, who told him to disappear as the farm was surrounded by German troops who had seen his aircraft land.

He hurried on towards the town of Bolbec and approached another farmhouse. It was curfew time and dangerous to be abroad in the countryside. There was nowhere to sleep but the barn.

"The only disadvantage," said Straight, with the genuine nonchalance of the period, "was that German soldiers were billeted in this barn. But I was in a desperate position, so I tunnelled under the hay and soon heard the tramp of German boots all round me."

The Germans settled down for the night a few feet from where he lay. They began to snore loudly, as he dozed. Suddenly he became aware of the dawn, and crawling softly from the hay without waking the Germans, he slipped out of the barn. He took the train for Rouen undetected in his hat and leather jacket. At Rouen, he had to change, and while waiting for the train to Paris, wandered round the town.

This is always a risky moment for escapers. I remembered the hours I spent in the cinemas of Leipzig after I was safely out of Colditz, waiting for the express to the Swiss frontier.

Whitney Straight sat back in his chair.

"What do you think I did?"

"Went to the cinema," I said.

"Not at that hour. I saw that various houses in Rouen had notices on them saying they were requisitioned by the Germans, so I spent an hour dropping British pennies in the letter-boxes."

He got safely to Paris and here, despite the Germans in the streets, felt that all would be well. With his American connections, he had only to go to the United States Embassy and he would be repatriated. America was not yet at war with Germany, but he was sadly disappointed.

"I rang the bell. Then suddenly I saw a notice on the door saying: 'This Embassy is closed. Enquiries should be addressed to the United States Embassy, Berlin'."

We laughed a little. Straight was still talking with attractive understatement, but I could see from his face what a shock this must have been to him.

At first there was no answer to the bell. Then the door opened a few inches and the frightened face of a man appeared.

"I am Whitney Straight, you must help me," he said.

"The man replied, 'I heard on the radio you had been shot down. You must go immediately—the S.S. are across the street!' "[1]

There was nothing for it. He left the Embassy and sat down at a café nearby, disappointed and angry. Surely the American Embassy could do something for him? He got up and telephoned.

The same Embassy official who had peeped round the door answered.

Straight told him to bring some money to the café immediately and waited in the gents' lavatory until he heard someone whisper. The man from the Embassy handed him 10,000 francs, and vanished.[2]

"I was delighted. This would be enough for a train fare to the south. I had heard about escape organisations, but I thought that, speaking good French, I could make my way over the frontier. And I did not know who to contact in Paris or anywhere else."

Whitney Straight paused in his story, which he recalled to me in 1968 when I was writing this book. He had the great advantage over many evaders of knowing France. For others, such situations presented greater difficulties, especially with the language. But his adventure was interesting for its combination of initiative and, later, the activities of O'Leary. He called at Hotel Vendôme in the Place Vendôme where he was known before the war. But it was full of senior German officers. So he stayed at the Hotel de Moscou in Montparnasse, where no questions were asked.

He bought a map next morning and decided to cross the demarcation line at Chenonceaux in the valley of the Loire, where the river Cher marked the boundary. It was a hot Sunday afternoon in July as he reached the river near the Château given by François I, King of France, to Diane de Poitiers. German sentries paced the bank as he timed them with a stop watch to judge the moment when they would be furthest from him.

"I calculated," he said, "that if I swam underwater and got half-

---

[1] *The Way Back*, page 171.
[2] The American consul-general was still in Paris and later declared *persona non grata* by the Germans for helping British servicemen.

way across, then came up for air, they would not see me. A few Sunday fishermen sat on the bank, but they were far too occupied to notice as I slipped into the water."

"I had a good deal of training as an underwater swimmer. I had to break water for air only once—halfway. I reached the opposite bank without being seen, crawled among some bushes and lay drying in the sun."

He walked 100 kilometres to Chateauroux and twice changing trains, reached Pau in the Spanish frontier zone where he spent the night. Next day he was questioned in the train not far from the frontier. Leaving the train at the next station he walked towards the foothills of the Pyrenees. Within sight of the frontier, he was betrayed, while eating a meal in a café, to the French police. It was the end of a daring effort and he had deserved to succeed. I had heard many stories of evasion but few which displayed such individuality and panache.

By August 9th, he was at St. Hippolyte du Fort, under the name of 'Captain Whitney' of the R.A.S.C. Had his true identity become known, the chances of getting him back would have been remote. News of his presence in the fort reached Pat O'Leary, and later Room 900 through the Reverend Donald Caskie of the Seamen's Mission in Marseille. Caskie, pastor of the Scottish Church in Paris, had escaped the German occupation in 1940. He reopened the Mission and for some months hid British soldiers in his cellars for Garrow's early organisation. After Garrow's arrest, he worked for O'Leary visiting the camps in the capacity of spiritual adviser and entered Fort St. Hippolyte. He combined these duties with passing information and identity cards to potential escapers. He was later imprisoned by the Gestapo for his services to the line.

The first attempt to recover Whitney Straight was a scheme for 'repatriation' by the Medical Board of the Vichy Armistice Commission. The Board included German and French doctors and as 'American representative', Dr. Rodocanachi in whose flat the famous scene with Cole occurred in November 1941. Already Langley and a large number of wounded had been examined and sent home by them. The case of Straight presented few problems except his real identity. He had been wounded in Norway and now pleaded that he was 'unfit for further service'. His skull had been fractured, his eardrums damaged, and he had received a severe wound in the back. On instructions from O'Leary, Dr. Rodocanachi had little difficulty in persuading his colleagues on September 9th that 'Captain Whitney should be repatriated'. M.I.9 and the R.A.F. owe much to the brave doctor. We shall never know how many 're-patriations' he organised, for had the German representatives known that 'Captain Whitney' was the famous Whitney Straight the story would have been different. He died in a concentration camp in 1944 and the Boulevard Dr. Rodocanachi in the centre of Marseille commemorates another victim of the traitor, Cole.

But Straight was unlucky. When he reached Perpignan with eight other 'repatriates', the plan was cancelled, in reprisal for a devastating R.A.F. raid on the Citroën works at Boulogne-Billan-court, the night before. This set-back made necessary an entirely new plan of escape.

Straight himself continued: "I was sent to the Pasteur hospital at Nice under close guard. It was some time before O'Leary could make contact with me. This he did through Francis Blanchain."

This was the guide who had taken Woollatt and me to the frontier in April. Blanchain knew a nurse in the hospital who worked in the ward where the British 'repatriates' were kept. She gave him the layout and the position of the guards. Escape was only possible if the guards—two of them—could be 'neutralised'. This had to be done at lunch-time, when they could be drugged. The nurse gave Whitney Straight powerful sedatives to slip into their wine for they used to lunch and play cards in the ward. While one of the prisoners created a diversion, they looked away, and he dropped the tablets into their glasses.

"I was not quite sure how much to put in," he said calmly. "It seemed ages before they fell asleep. They were not unconscious, but dozing heavily.

"I had to take the chance that they would not wake. I slipped through the door onto the flat roof of the hospital, through a gate of which the lock had been fixed.

"Francis Blanchain was sitting on a hill outside the hospital. He had papers for me as a Czech agricultural worker."

Surely not Czech again!

"What date was this?" asked Langley.

"June 22nd."

Part of this story had already reached us on Jean Nitelet's radio, part in correspondence sent by courier from O'Leary over the Spanish frontier. There had been some discussion in M.I.9 about the priority to be given to particular prisoners. Why should one merit more risks by O'Leary's helpers and sub-agents than another? Whatever we decided would never be popular with those who stayed behind. Crockatt ordered that special steps should be taken where the prisoner:

1. was of exceptional value to the war effort because of his training and record of service;

2. had already shown initiative and resource in evading capture or had worked for one of the escape lines.

This was Room 900 policy for the rest of the war. It applied to special prisoners in camps where an elaborate escape operation was required and later to a full-scale raid by Special Air Service or other forces. Generally, where a man was shot down or otherwise evaded capture and was hidden by the organisation, he took his chance with others. But Whitney Straight and other highly qualified pilots justified these risks. So, for another reason, did Ian Garrow, pioneer of escape lines, still in Vichy Government hands at Fort Meauzac.

The telephone rang, and I answered it.

I turned to Langley:

"Two messages: A Belgian called Louis Rémy[1] has swum from Algeçiras across the bay into Gibraltar harbour and has told them that he knows me well. They want me to identify him."

"He must be crazy."

"The second message is more important," I said. "Nitelet has come on the air from Marseille with a message from O'Leary. It reads:

"Escape of Higginson and others from Fort de la Revère planned for six August."

[1] General Louis Rémy of the Belgian Air Force.

CHAPTER 9

Sea Operations

THE next three months of 1942 brought new successes for O'Leary with his sea operations—two more followed on September 13th and October 12th, rescuing over a hundred servicemen—and more evidence of Gestapo attempts to destroy his organisation. I learned of this when Leoni Savinos and his wife reached London. After arriving with Whitney Straight at Gibraltar, they were both detained at the Royal Victoria Patriotic School at Clapham. This was the forbidding interrogation centre known at the R.V.P.S. for all non-British arrivals in the United Kingdom.

The foundation stone of this vast, disturbing edifice was laid by Queen Victoria in 1857. It was named the Royal Victoria Patriotic Asylum for the Orphan Daughters of Soldiers and Sailors killed in the Crimean War. In 1939 the girls were evacuated to make way for the interrogation teams. Its workhouse atmosphere gave a harsh welcome to England for genuine volunteers for the forces and escaped Resistance workers. But for the primary purpose, of catching enemy spies, this hideous place was effective. I studied it with sympathetic interest, comparing the methods employed with those of the Gestapo.

In Poland, the Germans had tried to frighten me by unnecessary drama and shouting. They would point to a leather-thonged whip hanging on the wall, sometimes brandish it, and put on ferocious expressions.

Throughout the war, they frequently threatened both escapers and their helpers with execution. They accompanied interrogation with long statements of Nazi propaganda and, in more serious cases, used methods of torture for which they must never be forgiven. As a system for obtaining information, this was probably less successful than that of the R.V.P.S. There is plenty of evidence that, even when tortured, the bravest continued to mislead them.[1] After the first feeling of terror was past, German threats began to lack subtlety. The will to resist returned. One's brain began to work more clearly, the cover story became more convincing. But the circumstances of the two counter espionage services were different. The R.V.P.S. was trying to 'break' professional German agents who had entered Britain. Many victims of the Gestapo were humble volunteers with no intelligence training whatever.

I never experienced a fraction of the horrible treatment to which they subjected men and women who worked for the escape lines. No one has any right to claim that they would not talk under torture or even under threat of it. The real heroes and heroines were those who despite the barbarities of the Germans gave no useful information.

In contrast, the R.V.P.S. system seemed deliberately soulless. It wore down the suspect by patience, suspense and boredom, mixed with cigarettes and endless cups of official tea. When not under interrogation, the inmate was allowed to roam the stone-flagged corridors and school-rooms, like an orphan of the Crimea, to ponder on the future. The very dreariness of the place, and the taste of that Government tea, would, I thought, be enough to break the stoutest German agent.

Room 900 were often permitted to extract their accredited agents after interrogation and rush them to 'safe' flats, warm baths and dinners. However sure we might be of their loyalty, the ultimate responsibility for their release was with the R.V.P.S. who maintained a high standard of detection throughout the war.

I went there to identify Louis Rémy, subject of the telephone message, who had swum from Algeçiras to Gibraltar. He was a young Belgian Air Force officer with bright red hair who had escaped from Colditz. For some reason, he had been unable to join a party from the British Embassy and cross the frontier at La Linea, and had thought fit to swim across Algeçiras Bay. He was nearly drowned, but was rescued by the Navy in the nick of time. Darling reported in a humorous letter that this method of entry had greatly annoyed the Governor and his staff. In view of Italian attempts to blow up ships in the harbour, this was not surprising. Rémy was fortunate that I could identify him as an ex-inmate of Colditz.

[1] See M. R. D. Foot, *S.O.E. in France.*

Leoni[1] and Madame Savinos were soon released from the R.V.P.S. I remember them at Louis Nouveau's flat in April. Madame Savinos had straight, blonde hair and fierce blue eyes. She had seemed silent and thoughtful. As soon as I saw her, I understood Darling's reminder that she was German. One evening, when the sun had set over the Old Port of Marseille, I sat talking with members of the O'Leary line. On the morrow, Woollatt and I would take the train for the Spanish frontier and freedom.

When I spoke of my treatment by the Germans, I declared with unfortunate emphasis:

"Only we who have been their prisoners really understand what swine they can be."

Madame Savinos eyed me sharply and then she smiled:

"No, Monsieur. I must tell you that I am a German. The Germans you saw were Nazis. I am a communist, but I love my country."

It was a distressing moment. I looked wildly at the others.

Louis Nouveau nodded.

"Yes, it's true. Do not drop the heavy brick."

I went miserably to bed in my carpet slippers. It was a terrible gaffe. That Germans could be in the service of the O'Leary line had not occurred to me. The incident taught me a lesson. This woman had been prepared to face the most terrible price for her hatred of Hitler. She was not merely a political opponent in exile. She was actively helping enemy combatants to freedom. Since she was a well-known communist, she would certainly have been executed, but it helped to secure her early liberation from a reformatory life at the R.V.P.S. I took her with her husband to dine in London. At first, I felt a sense of bewilderment, then I realised the logic of dining with a German in London. This underground rescue movement defied all idealogical barriers. There were no politics in this humane form of warfare.

Savinos was a tall Greek with strong, dark features, and I understood why O'Leary had valued him for he seemed loyal and courageous. I studied him as we ate fricassee of rabbit disguised as chicken and drank harsh red Algerian wine. This was the best that London could manage in 1942. But it took from my guests some of the strain of their escape and their regret at giving up their dangerous work.

"Why did Pat send you out?" I asked Leoni.

[1] O.B.E.

"You will remember," said Leoni, "I told you in Marseille that the Gestapo arrested me in Paris last April."

His story gave me serious cause for anxiety. He had acted as interpreter for General Plastiras, the Greek statesman who was then living in the South of France. The Germans had sent S.S. Gruppenführer Nosek to win Plastiras over to their side and Savinos took part in the negotiations. For his services he received an official Gestapo pass, which enabled him to travel freely between Marseille and Paris. Thus armed he went on a number of missions for O'Leary and Louis Nouveau as their courier to Paris and contact with other organisations. In April 1942 he had arranged to meet another agent at the Gare Montparnasse in Paris when he was arrested by plain-clothes Gestapo. They demanded to know the identity of his contact, who promptly disappeared.

Savinos told me the story calmly. He was very sure of himself, with a broad smile. He shrugged his shoulders:

"I told them the truth. I did not know this man. I had never seen him before. They took me off to Fresnes prison.

"I was in a spot, I can tell you. I had on me the key of Mario Prassinos' flat, the plan of a factory making parts for German fighters, and £1,500 in francs!

"But I also had my Gestapo official pass from Nosek."

Savinos must have had extraordinary presence of mind. He had explained away the latch key, but the factory plans were 'more awkward.'

Puzzled, the Gestapo had sent for Nosek, the S.S. officer who had tried to win over General Plastiras.

"Nosek questioned me at length, and I had to use all my skill. He did not believe my story that I was engaged in trading between the occupied and unoccupied zones. But he knew me well over the Plastiras affair, and I explained away the key of the flat and the French money."

"He knew that I spoke French and German. So he began to hint that I should work for the Gestapo. I was to go back to Marseille as a spy for them then report to Paris."

Savinos' only chance was to agree with this proposal, then disappear. The Gestapo knew little at this time about O'Leary. They may have learned his description from Cole, at the end of 1941 but seemed unwilling, said Savinos, to carry out wholesale arrests in unoccupied France. They were biding their time until they had complete control, and they needed a stool pigeon.

Savinos grinned and showed a gold front tooth. His wife listened quietly. Once, out of courtesy to her, I broke into German and a hornrimmed young officer at the next table looked startled.

Savinos continued:

"Nosek said I could work for them if they held a hostage to make sure I was loyal."

"And who was that to be?"

"My wife."

We were all silent. I pictured the dilemma Savinos had faced. I could imagine the Gestapo file on his wife.

"I told Nosek," he continued, still smiling broadly, "That the line would suspect me if I was released but my wife was arrested."

He had argued that he could not work for the Gestapo under such conditions and Nosek seemed to see sense in this, but the S.S. officer might have felt differently had he known who Madame Savinos was. After much bargaining, Savinos agreed to act as a double agent in O'Leary's line. The report from the R.V.P.S. confirmed this extraordinary story. But it was disturbing, for no one knew if the Gestapo had followed Savinos from Paris when he was released from Fresnes prison.

When Savinos returned to Marseille, Woollatt and I had just arrived and he was lying low until O'Leary came back from Gibraltar. As soon as O'Leary returned, he ordered both husband and wife to leave on the first possible sea operation.[1]

We walked in the warm August night in Piccadilly, so far and yet so near to the dangers. Why had we three, Madame Savinos most of all, been saved? A line of Rupert Brooke's ran through my mind—

'Safe though all safety's lost;[2]

We were safe. But why? And Dowding, Duprez and the Abbé Carpentier victims of Cole? Reports of Cole's court-martial by the Vichy authorities and his sentence of imprisonment still came

---

[1] Savinos went back to France for S.O.E. in 1943.
[2] Sonnet: *Safety*.
    War knows no power. Safe shall be my going,
    Secretly armed against all death's endeavour;
    Safe though all safety's lost; safe when men fall;
    And if these poor limbs die, safest of all.

over the frontier. Were Vichy trying to help O'Leary? Had we a friend in their counter-espionage service? These questions were still unresolved and years passed before the answers were known.[1]

In a few days, O'Leary reported that the escape of Squadron Leader Higginson, with two other R.A.F. officers and two Flight Sergeants from Fort de la Revère had been successfully accomplished on August 6th, and Langley was soon occupied with planning the next voyage of *Tarana* to bring them to Gibraltar. On September 20th, a telegram from Darling announced another triumph. The second *Tarana* operation had been carried out and Higginson had arrived safely, with Flight Lieutenants Barnet and Hawkins, Flight Sergeants Nabarro and Hickey and other aircrew from Fort de la Revère. Among the passengers was a German girl named Paula Spriewald who had acted as O'Leary's secretary in Marseille.

Squadron Leader F. W. Higginson[2] had been captured and spent several months in Fort de la Revère under the nom-de-plume of 'Captain Bennett'. Like that of Whitney Straight, his escape to England did much to improve the prestige of Room 900. He was credited with thirteen German aircraft when shot down by a pilot of the Richthofen Squadron near Abbeville, on June 17th, 1941. The discovery of his identity at Fort de la Revère would have brought pleasure to Goering, and a loss to the service. The Air Ministry urged us to effect his escape, and frequent messages concerning him were sent to O'Leary on Nitelet's set.

Higginson was one of those modest, efficient people who made the Royal Air Force what it was. He came to my flat and gave me a first-hand account of his escape from the Fort and the *Tarana* operation. But his story was of special interest, for after being shot down, he had been brought to Marseille by Cole. In December 1967, he wrote me an account of the last part of his journey with Cole over the demarcation line in July 1941. This was two or three months before the disastrous quarrel in Dr. Rodoconachi's flat, and Higginson had every reason to regard his guide with admiration.

"Cole had ginger hair, with a freckled face, and spoke French with an atrocious accent. He was dressed in plus-fours. He carried a briefcase in which he had a revolver and a mass of information on troop train departures from Lille to the Russian front. He carried a false identity card and French soldier's discharge papers which showed he had been discharged 'as of unsound mind'.

"We had crossed the river which preceded the demarcation line, and it was a very hot July day when we were stopped by a German officer and a sergeant. They began to question us. Cole did the answering. He told the officer I was simple-minded."

"I had a briefcase with a change of underwear and socks and a large slab of dark French chocolate."

"The sergeant pointed at me:

" 'He is an English soldier: he is not speaking.'

"The officer then asked for my identity card. It had been made for me by Abbé Carpentier, the priest in Abbeville with a Pas de Calais stamp.

"He seemed satisfied, but threatened to take us to the Kommandantur for questioning.

"Cole then became aggressive. He said he had seen the officer come from a café. His aunt lived at this café, and he would report both of them for drinking on duty!

"But the sergeant still pointed at me.

" 'I'm sure he is English. He is not speaking.'

"The officer then told me to turn out my briefcase on the road.

"By this time, because of the heat and my excitement, the chocolate had spread all over the contents of the briefcase and looked an absolutely frightful mess.

"Cole, with tremendous presence of mind said: 'Look, I told you he was out of his mind. Look what he has done in his briefcase!'

"The officer turned away in disgust and told me to clear off, which I did and hid in a copse.

"About a quarter of an hour later, I was joined by Cole and crossed the demarcation line that night."

Was Cole a double agent at this time, even before the confrontation at Dr. Rodocanachi's? We shall never be sure, though the evidence suggests that he first agreed to work for the Abwehr after his arrest by them on December 6th.[1] What was he doing during the quarter of an hour that Higginson was separated from him? There were many other reports to M.I.9 at this period of his coolness and skill in saving airmen from German controls under the alias of

[1]See Chapter 25. This was only two days before he betrayed the Abbé Carpentier.

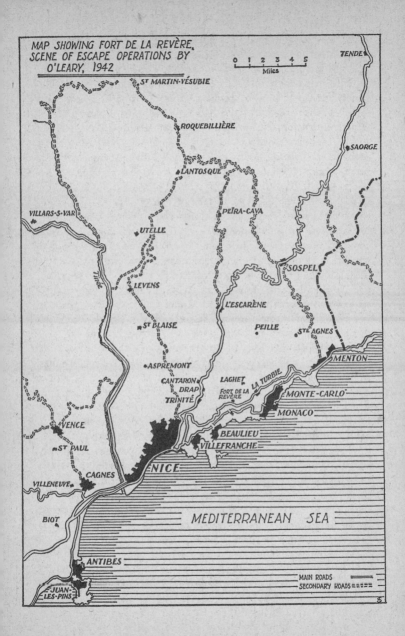

MAP SHOWING FORT DE LA REVÈRE,
SCENE OF ESCAPE OPERATIONS BY
O'LEARY, 1942

0 1 2 3 4 5
Miles

TENDE

ST MARTIN-VÉSUBIE

ROQUEBILLIÈRE

SAORGE

LANTOSQUE

VILLARS-S-VAR

PEÏRA-CAVA

UTELLE

Tinée

SOSPEL

LEVENS

L'ESCARÈNE

ST BLAISE

PEILLE

STE AGNES

ASPREMONT

MENTON

CANTARON
DRAP
TRINITÉ

LAGHET
FORT DE LA
REVÈRE

LA TURBIE

MONTE-CARLO

MONACO

VENCE

ST PAUL

BEAULIEU

VILLEFRANCHE

CAGNES

NICE

VILLENEUVE

BIOT

MEDITERRANEAN   SEA

ANTIBES

JUAN-
LES-PINS

MAIN ROADS
SECONDARY ROADS

'Paul', and many French people, especially in the Lille area, wor-
shipped him as a hero of the British Secret Service.

Higginson was later arrested and sent to Fort de la Revère where
O'Leary made contact with him. As 'Captain Bennett' he was the
senior officer, and he was provided with false papers. O'Leary had
found a reliable contact who had volunteered to act as physical
training instructor to the prisoners. This was Vladimir Bouryschkine
alias Val Williams, who in 1943, was employed by Room 900 to
organise sea evacuations from Brittany.[1] Father Myrda, a Polish
priest working for O'Leary, and Bouryschkine smuggled in a
hacksaw blade and other implements with instructions to Higginson
to select five men, all pilots, to take part in the first escape. It was
hoped that a whole series of rescues could be organised. The Higginson plan was for the airmen to slide down a coal chute from the
cookhouse of the camp, drop into the moat, then crawl through a
sewer that led outside the fort. Outside were to be two of O'Leary's
men, Jean Nitelet, his radio operator, and Tony Friend, an Australian
and an official from Monaco, armed with suitable police papers,
who would escort the escapers to Monte Carlo. O'Leary was not
optimistic. The fort was on top of a hill and strict security measures
had been introduced since the escape of Whitney Straight.

At eight forty-five p.m. on August 6th, 1942, the men began to
lever back the iron bars over the coal chute. They made an opening
and struggled through, dropping to the moat with the help of a
home-made rope. They crossed the moat and entered the sewer,
which was dangerous, for the fumes were terrible. After crawling
the length of the sewer they found its mouth covered by an iron
grille. The hacksaw blade broke and they were obliged to push with
their feet against the bars. After a great heave, the stonework which
held the grille collapsed. Suddenly they were outside, staggering
and gasping for air. The alarm was soon given, and guards and
gendarmes searched for them. But in the darkness and excitement,
they failed to make the rendezvous with Nitelet and Tony Friend.
Dawn found them lying up in bushes near a tunnel at Cap d'Ail
railway station not far from Monte Carlo.

Higginson learned afterwards that Nitelet and Friend had been
arrested and handcuffed by guards looking for the escapers. Loudly
protesting that they were on police business, they showed their

[1] See Chapter 16.

papers and were allowed to go. They were able to give the alarm
to O'Leary in Monte Carlo. Despite this misadventure, the five
airmen were lucky. While the rest lay hidden all day in the bushes
by the tunnel, Flight Lieutenant Hawkins set out for Monte Carlo.
He had been told of a tea shop kept by two Scottish ladies, the Misses
Trenchard, where O'Leary was waiting. More by chance than
design, he found the tea shop and returned to Cap d'Ail with
O'Leary.

They found the others in a depressed condition. Higginson
emerged from a clump of bougainvillaea covered in slime and
smelling of sewage. With the others, he changed into new clothes
from a suitcase brought by O'Leary. Then separating into two
parties, the escapers made their way along the beach to Monte
Carlo, where they hid in a villa rented for the purpose by Friend.
For the next twelve days, they were fed by the Misses Trenchard
from the tea shop.

This escape plan, despite the mishaps, was a model for future successes. After the war, O'Leary told me how the night of August
6th, 1942, had gone. He had many anxious moments. At his hotel,
the Vichy police came round late at night looking for Jews. They
knocked on bedroom doors and ordered every male visitor to drop
his pyjama trousers.

"I was O.K.," said Pat. "Then came another blow. Nitelet came
back early in the morning to say he had missed the party. I was overjoyed when I saw Hawkins coming towards that tea shop."

From the villa at Monte Carlo, the airmen were taken to Marseille.
Higginson was moved first. Dressed as a priest in one of Father
Myrda's cassocks, he was escorted on the journey by O'Leary and
Father Myrda himself. Hidden in Louis Nouveau's flat, he felt the
same sense of frustration, or boredom, that I had known three months
before at the Quai Rive Neuve. It was something one would never
mention to those who risked their lives to get you back. But it was
there all the same. I heard it from hundreds of others. He also gave
me a picture of the events which followed his escape.

When Langley heard of its success, he radioed O'Leary to attempt
an even bigger operation. But this never transpired. Forty-eight
hours after Higginson's escape, all officers in Fort de la Revère were
packed off to a camp in Italy. The remaining airmen and soldiers

staged a mass escape by breaking into an unoccupied part of the Fort and descending into the moat. Sixty of them got out of the camp. Thirty-four reached hide-outs of the O'Leary organisation, where they waited to be taken off by *Tarana*.

Before they could be taken off a disaster occurred.

A successful parachute drop of supplies and money from Langley had taken place the night before Higginson and his party left Monte Carlo. The reception was organised by Nitelet, Prassinos and Gaston Nègre, a legendary operator on the black market. While removing parachute containers, Nitelet and Gaston Nègre were arrested by gendarmes. Prassinos narrowly escaped to Marseille. It was a grim blow to O'Leary. He had again lost his wireless operator, and for some weeks was obliged to send messages by the forbidden method of making contact with agents of other services in touch with London. It was not till the autumn that Room 900 were able to dispatch a new man.

Whitney Straight's and Higginson's accounts of their final evacuation by sea showed some of the risks and dangers involved in this type of operation. Much depended on the choice of beach and the existence nearby of a suitable 'safe house'. This was discovered at Canet-Plage, near Perpignan. To escort as many as thirty or forty people, few of them speaking a word of French, was a formidable task. They had to be collected from their hiding places in Marseille and transported by train to Perpignan, equipped with forged papers. The trains, as usual, were crowded and, though thinly disguised in their French suits, the airmen passed the control at the station. They were concealed in a villa at Canet-Plage, not far from the beach selected by the Admiralty for the embarkation, which belonged to a Madame Lebreton, owner of the Hotel du Tennis.

Higginson and a large group of airmen returned by 'Operation Bluebottle'. On this voyage, *Tarana* was due off Canet-Plage at two a.m. on September 13th, 1942. As they waited, the airmen were crammed into the tiny villa with Paula Spriewald, O'Leary's German secretary.

"We were all standing or sitting on the floor of the villa," said Higginson, "when O'Leary appeared and ordered us to move off to the beach at one-fifteen a.m. in single file."

"But what was to happen if anyone hostile appeared?" I asked.

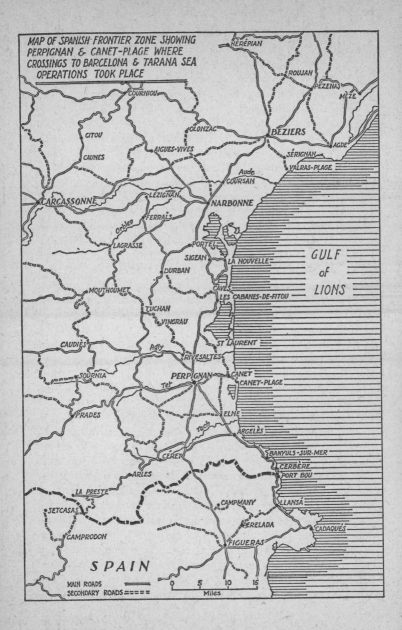

MAP OF SPANISH FRONTIER ZONE SHOWING
PERPIGNAN & CANET-PLAGE WHERE
CROSSINGS TO BARCELONA & TARANA SEA
OPERATIONS TOOK PLACE

HÉRÉPIAN

ROUJAN

PÉZENAS

MÈZE

COURNIOU

OLONZAC

BÉZIERS

CITOU

AIGUES-VIVES

SÉRIGNAN

AGDE

CAUNES

Aude

VALRAS-PLAGE

COURSAN

LÉZIGNAN

NARBONNE

CARCASSONNE

FERRALS

Orbleu

PORTEL

LAGRASSE

SIGEAN

LA NOUVELLE

GULF
of
LIONS

DURBAN

MOUTHOUMET

CAVES

LES CABANES-DE-FITOU

TUCHAN

VINGRAU

CAUDIÈS

Agly

ST LAURENT

RIVESALTES

SOURNIA

PERPIGNAN

CANET

Ter

CANET-PLAGE

PRADES

ELNE

Tech

ARGELÈS

CÉRET

BANYULS-SUR-MER

CERBÈRE

ARLES

PORT BOU

LA PRESTE

CAMPMANY

LLANSÁ

SETCASAS

PERELADA

CADAQUÉS

CAMPRODON

FIGUERAS

SPAIN

MAIN ROADS ——
SECONDARY ROADS =====

0   5   10   15
Miles

"We were to lie flat in the sand and stay there until things were sorted out."

"Did the ship arrive on time?"

"Yes, she was off the beach when O'Leary gave the Morse signal on his torch with a blue flash at two a.m. He got the answering Morse letter from the ship. Then a small boat came in and took us off in three trips."

It had been a fine night, with a calm sea at Canet-Plage. Each year in the summer, the beach is covered with holiday-makers. Few can know what tension and relief O'Leary and his agents experienced on those summer nights in 1942. Two weeks later, I saw Paula Spriewald in London. She was attractive and intelligent. Hatred of Hitler had impelled her as a German to take an appalling chance by helping enemy airmen to escape. She told me how she stood on the beach in tears, unwilling to leave for the unknown, until O'Leary firmly picked her up and put her in a small boat from *Tarana* rowed by several Scots. Her description of O'Leary was moving. Harassed by endless difficulties, the betrayal by Cole and the arrest of Nitelet, he led his group with calm authority. Nothing seemed insuperable. He spoke quietly, in perfect English, soothing the fearful and reproving the incompetent.

The next sea operation was planned for October 5th 1942 and details arranged with O'Leary once more in radio contact with London. To confirm the night of arrival of the ship, Langley sent a message on the French News Service of the B.B.C. at nine p.m.

"Les marrons sont cuites."

The tiny villa near the Hotel du Tennis was again packed with men. The weather was warm and they had a long wait, for on the first night, *Tarana* missed the rendezvous at the mouth of the river Tet. At one-fifteen a.m., O'Leary led the party, accompanied by a French-Canadian Sergeant-Major named Lucien Dumais who had escaped after the Dieppe raid and carried an iron bar to deal with intruders. They reached the area of the embarkation point at one forty-five a.m. O'Leary flashed a Morse letter in red on his torch three times before two thirty a.m., but there was no answer from the ship. A red light flashing from the north-east proved a false alarm. It came from a buoy, a mile off Canet-Plage.

At four a.m., they returned to the villa, in disappointment and exhaustion. But the message from Room 900 had made clear that *Tarana* might be at the rendezvous on either the 5th or 6th October. They waited until next evening and went to the beach again, without a sign of the ship. A humorous incident occurred when Louis Nouveau, seeing the shape of a boat offshore about a mile from the rendezvous, called the password:

"Où sont les fraises?"

He expected the answer: "Dans le jus!"

Instead, there was a flow of French obscenity from the crew of a local fishing-boat.

Leaving the men herded in the villa, O'Leary made the long train journey back to Marseille.

He signalled:

"Waited night 5 to 6 and 6 to 7 seven hundred yards from River Tet. Pas plus de bateau que de beurre au cul."

When we got this message, we sought translation of the latter sentence which proved to be:

"No more sign of a boat than butter on your arse."

This phrase, well known in the French Army, expressed O'Leary's anxiety and frustration. I learned later from Mario Prassinos, who escaped to England in 1943, that both lavatories at the villa were out or order.[1] There was also great danger of discovery by local busybodies.

At Room 900, we had a difficult decision to make, for *Tarana* had been there on both nights, and, finding no one, had begun her return voyage. It was a very serious position. If the British crew broke radio silence they would be in considerable danger. But Crockatt and the War Office, for once in agreement, saw that the O'Leary organisation might be destroyed and many distinguished pilots arrested.

Langley radioed to O'Leary:

"Vessel proceeded half mile North River Tet nights 5 to 6 and 6 to 7. Return dependant on fuel supply. Already 140 miles from Gibraltar. Instructing vessel return if possible. Next message will confirm or otherwise."

Had the ship gone to the wrong point? Or had the party waited at the wrong place? It was no use blaming the crew or the party

[1] Prassinos returned to France for S.O.E. but died of typhus in a concentration camp at Schwerin in 1945.

on the beach.[1] We could only pray that it was still possible for the
vessel to return to Canet-Plage.

A disadvantage at this critical time was that transmission and
reception periods for O'Leary's set were limited to one a day. Even
in 1942 there was considerable overcrowding on the air. This
meant a further wait for the men in the villa, even if *Tarana* were
on her way back, or another twenty-four hours. O'Leary was
compelled to stay in Marseille until the following afternoon and
communicate with Canet-Plage by risky telephone calls to the
Hotel du Tennis.

I learned afterwards that one of the organisation's chief anxieties
was their reference to 'butter on your arse', which, though expressing
their feelings, might lead to further misunderstanding when deci-
phered. They pictured Room 900 attempting to translate this
phrase into operational terms.

But the next afternoon, after contacting the ship through Darling
we were able to signal:

"Ship returning 11 *or* 12."

The men had already been hidden for over a week, and the
alternative of two nights for *Tarana's* return still left the whole
escape line in a dangerous position. When O'Leary returned from
Marseille, he found conditions at Canet-Plage had grown very
difficult. The villa was obviously being watched and the chances
of getting the men safely to the ship were slim. On the first night,
there was again no sign of *Tarana*. The men tramped back again over
the sand to the stench of the villa. Many had lost faith in the escape
organisation. They remained shuttered, silent and sullen for the
tenth day, few of them believing that the ship would really come.
Only the strong personality of O'Leary and their own danger of
re-arrest prevented them from breaking out on their own.

At last on the night of October 12th, at three a.m., a small boat
appeared 400 yards north of the correct position. Fortunately
O'Leary had posted men at several points along the beach.

"Où sont les fraises?"

"Dans le jus!"

Four boat loads went out to *Tarana* and the party was on its way
to Gibraltar.

Almost certainly there was an error in navigation. The beach

[1] Darling later reported sandbanks not on the Admiralty chart.

selected for the operation, had been changed since the escape of
Higginson and Paula Spriewald on Spetember 13th and the new
point, half a mile north of the River Tet, was difficult to identify in
darkness.

When *Tarana* arrived at Gibraltar, loud recriminations were
heaped on us, and Darling transmitted these complaints in his
characteristic style. Among the most outspoken was the tough
Canadian Sergeant-Major Lucien Dumais who was later responsible
for a brilliant series of naval evacuations from Brittany in 1943 and
1944.[1]

In London, we felt that all was not well with O'Leary. The
shadow of Cole was over the line, which in its best days had collecting points in Normandy, Rouen and the Pas de Calais. As many as
two hundred and fifty people worked for him as passeurs, couriers,
forgers and suppliers of clothes and food. How long could it last?

[1] See Chapter 17.

CHAPTER 10

The Price

BEFORE his arrest at Toulouse in March 1943, Pat O'Leary
achieved one more spectacular success after the *Tarana* sea
operations which brought out valuable Allied Servicemen.
This was the rescue of Ian Garrow, pioneer leader of the Marseille
group, from Fort Meauzac on December 6th, 1942.

Crockatt and M.I.9 had been pressing us to organise Garrow's
escape for several months. Early in November, we received a message that he might be transferred from Fort Meauzac where he was
serving a ten-year sentence for helping fellow-survivors of Dunkirk
and St. Valery to escape to Spain. This could only mean that the
Gestapo and not the Vichy police controlled his fate. Detention in
a concentration camp in Germany was the least he could expect.

Langley and I attended a meeting at M.I.9 headquarters in Beaconsfield to discuss what orders should be sent to O'Leary. O'Leary had
warned us that Garrow's transfer to the Germans was imminent.
His contacts with Fort Meauzac reported that Garrow might be
sent to the notorious concentration camp at Dachau. O'Leary asked
us a difficult question. Should he take risks to save him?

The storm was gathering for O'Leary and his organisation,
threatened with further betrayals by Cole if the latter were released
to the Germans by Vichy. Louis Nouveau of the Quai Rive Neuve
had become well-known to the Gestapo. After eighteen months
of hiding fugitives, he closed his spacious flat with the bay window
and on O'Leary's orders took charge in Paris under an assumed
name. Madame Nouveau went into hiding and early in 1943
escaped safely to Spain. She reached London after her husband's
arrest in February. Despite her cruel anxiety for him, she still
seemed the practical, cultivated Frenchwoman who had hidden me
in Marseille. For the rest of the war she worked for the Free French
in London.

At the meeting to discuss O'Leary's message, Crockatt seemed worried and ill at ease. I knew that he was in touch with Garrow's parents in Scotland, that he had great admiration for him. But there were serious hazards to the whole line and to O'Leary himself who had been awarded the D.S.O. after the last voyage of *Tarana*.

"We assume that Fort Meauzac is well guarded," said Langley. "If I know O'Leary—he will follow the model of Fort de la Revère and make it an inside job. He will bribe the guards but we have to reckon with failure. So far he has been brilliantly successful, but Louis Nouveau is not the only one in Gestapo files. If this operation leads to more arrests, the whole thing will be finished."

Crockatt was silent, and then he said: "I agree we have to face this, but I am thinking of Garrow. After all, it was he who with little money, scant encouragement and speaking no French began this escape line. I think we have a duty to take these risks."

"All right, sir," said Langley, "but as O'Leary is on the spot, all we can do is to leave him to make his own plans."

The decision was taken and there was nothing to do but keep our fingers crossed.

Room 900 was in regular radio contact with O'Leary throughout the Fort Meauzac scheme. He had an excellent operator, who reached France in October 1942. This was Tom Groome,[1] a twenty-year-old Australian. Groome spoke excellent French, his mother was born in France, and as he was intelligent and resourceful, he made excellent progress in training. He was tall and dark-haired and his round face and high colour gave him a boyish appearance. His manner was reserved, but he had an air of shy determination. In the next few months, he conducted himself with the greatest gallantry.

Groome reached the O'Leary organisation by sea in a Polish ship.[2] He quickly came up on the air and, one of his first messages, reported the departure of the Nouveaus from Marseille. O'Leary, still apparently safe, had moved his headquarters to Toulouse and was sending regular parties over the frontier to Barcelona.

Groome's short career in enemy territory was important for the part he played in the escape of Garrow, perhaps the best individual rescue operation planned and executed by O'Leary. Garrow was extremely lucky, for the German occupation of the so-called Free

[1] O.B.E.
[2] He landed at Canet-Plage.

Zone of France took place on November 30th, a few days before
his escape. When he reached London in January 1943, he described
to me how he was warned by a guard that he would be sent to
Germany in a few weeks, and managed to get a message to O'Leary.
It was then that O'Leary had radioed Room 900 who replied that he
must be the judge of what risks to take.

Meauzac was a very tough prison camp, at least as difficult as
Colditz. There were three rings of barbed wire surrounding it and
it was very heavily guarded. From the first, it was clear that escape
was only possible by the front gate. The treatment was harsh. There
were only two classes of prisoner kept there by the Vichy government on the orders of the Gestapo: those sentenced to death and
those sentenced to long terms of imprisonment. They would all be
taken over by the Gestapo at the Occupation.

O'Leary sent his best guide, Francis Blanchain, the dark young
man in the photograph of the bay window at the Nouveaus' flat,
and rescuer of Whitney Straight, to make a reconnaissance. But
while he was making enquiries about the camp, he was caught by
gendarmes at Limoges and detained. He made a spectacular escape,
but he was hopelessly compromised, and obliged to cross the
frontier to Spain, arriving in London in the early part of 1943.[1]

O'Leary now decided to take charge, aided by a dark Australian
girl named Nancy Fiocca,[2] married to a Frenchman and they made
contact with a prison guard referred to as 'Pierre' who lived at a
small house near the prison camp and earned 3,000 francs a month.
His views were strongly anti-Petain and anti-German. O'Leary was
well supplied with money brought by Groome, and he had to work
fast. He began by offering to double the man's salary for three years.
After some negotiation, it was agreed that he should receive 100,000
francs down and the balance when Garrow escaped. This made the
sum of 216,000 francs in all. Though taking a fearful risk for himself
and his family, Pierre was delighted with the money and promised
his co-operation.

The first problem was how to get a key prisoner under special
guard from a prison like Fort Meauzac. The second was to hide him
in a countryside teeming with soldiers, gendarmes and Gestapo. It
seemed that the best chance for Garrow was to wear the uniform of

[1] He married Paula Spriewald.
[2] She later worked for S.O.E. and received the George Medal.

a prison guard, and leave by the front gate when other guards went off duty. If O'Leary could obtain a uniform to fit Garrow, Pierre would smuggle it to him.

O'Leary returned to Toulouse to the house of a brave Jewish tailor named Paul Ulmann who had made disguises for him in the past. This time his request was difficult. The French guards at Meauzac wore Army uniform and he needed a complete outfit for an N.C.O. in forty-eight hours. Ulmann nonetheless produced it.

But when O'Leary arrived at Meauzac by train with the precious uniform in a parcel, he suffered a terrible disappointment. The Vichy Government had agreed with the Germans to demobilise what was left of the French Army before the Occupation. Meauzac and other prisons were to be guarded by civil gendarmes, selected from all parts of France.

After the first shock, O'Leary realised this might be an advantage to Garrow. It would mean that the gendarmes would not know each other. If a gendarme's uniform could be obtained, there was a better chance, but time was pressing. Back in Toulouse, he found Ulmann desperate. A gendarme's uniform could not be made in forty-eight hours without the right material. Nonetheless Ulmann succeeded. His former employer, who had a large outfitter's shop in Toulouse, supplied him with the correct cloth.

Ulmann and his wife worked all night. They had not merely to produce cavalry trousers, cape, cap and braid but other minute details such as the insignia worn only by Petain's gendarmes. It was a heroic performance and when the uniform was finished, it was stuffed into a suitcase, with a knife, a pistol, and false papers already prepared for Garrow.

O'Leary made another train journey, accompanied this time by Groome and two French agents who had parts to play in the escape plan. Groome had his wireless set to maintain contact with London. Travelling together was dangerous but there was no alternative, for Garrow must be recovered within a few days. At Pierre's house near the prison they made plans to hide him in an isolated farmhouse, owned by a supporter of General de Gaulle, twenty miles from Meauzac. Groome was to operate his set from the loft of this farmhouse and wait till Garrow was brought there.

Late next evening, O'Leary and the two Frenchmen, all armed with revolvers, took up their positions outside Fort Meauzac. In addition to three lanes of barbed wire, there were machine gun towers at either end. The Frenchmen were to cover these towers while O'Leary himself lay among the foothills of the mountains which rose above the main entrance, watching the guards. Searchlights shone directly on this gate and Garrow might easily be recognised.

The story, when I heard it in London, had a familiar ring. In my first attempt to get out of Colditz dressed in a home-made German corporal's uniform, the arclights of the camp had instantly revealed me as a stranger. That evening, Pierre, who was on duty, brought Garrow the uniform. Garrow went to a lavatory to change into it and locked the door. Then something unforeseen happened, someone turned the handle, shouted and waited outside.

"I stood there frozen," said Garrow later, "but there was no more knocking. Whoever it was remained standing outside the door for fully five minutes."

"Then I heard a grunt and steps down the passage. I was already in my gendarme's uniform, with my revolver in its holster and wearing my cap. As soon as all was quiet I slipped outside the door."

He hid all night in the uniform until six forty-five next morning. It had been planned that he should pretend to be coming off night duty with other gendarmes as they walked towards the first lane of wire on the way to the main gate. Pierre was waiting for him and motioned him to follow the gendarme in front, while he came behind. All went well until two gendarmes ahead of them stopped to talk. Garrow was nervous. His French was poor and after more than a year in prison, he was weak. Fortunately the two gendarmes moved on towards the main gate. When Garrow reached the gate, he saluted the guards, although one of them studied him curiously. Outside, Pierre overtook him, wheeling his bicycle, and they walked up the road from the fort.

Describing the scene afterwards, O'Leary said that crouching fifty yards from the main entrance, revolver in hand, was one of the most tense experiences of his life. Garrow's walk was painfully 'British', and he could not understand how anyone could be deceived. He was getting ready to shoot it out with the guards and hope that Garrow would escape in the confusion.

Garrow's own account of what happened after he was outside, also showed the risky nature of this operation.

"I ran straight to a car hidden in woods not far away and struggled out of my uniform into civilian clothes. The driver was the Gaullist farmer, whose name was Philippe Brègi. He pressed the starter, and nothing happened!"

"He pressed it again, but the car showed no sign of starting. The noise sounded like thunder in those silent woods, and my escape was bound to be discovered within a few minutes."

But Brègi got out, cranked up the car, and it roared away. They drove at a tremendous speed over the twenty miles to his farm, where they found Groome. After a few drinks, they went into the loft and watched Groome tap out the message to London:

"First stage successful."

At Room 900 we hoped that the rest of Garrow's escape would be uneventful. We could not know that early next morning Brègi was awakened by the barking of dogs. Outside were two gendarmes, who questioned him.

"A British prisoner escaped last night. You heard nothing?"

"Nothing," said Brègi.[1]

The gendarmes continued with their questions for a few minutes, then moved off, apparently satisfied. Brègi returned to the farm. He urged O'Leary, Garrow and Groome to leave immediately. Hiding the set, they moved carefully across country, making for another 'safe house' at Bergerac. It was hard going over the fields, through tall grass—especially for Garrow—and it was dangerous. The Germans had ordered a major search, with armed patrols and road-blocks. They threatened to execute hostages. It was clear that they were well aware of Garrow's importance.

In the evening, the party came to a small red brick house of a friend at Bergerac, where they stayed the night. But the Bergerac area too was dangerous. At dawn next morning, they took a train for Toulouse and reached the flat of Madamoiselle Françoise Dissart, O'Leary's principal organiser in the town and his successor after his arrest in March 1943.[2]

Within three weeks of his escape from Fort Meauzac, Garrow crossed the frontier to Barcelona and soon reached London by air. O'Leary accompanied him to a shepherd's hut on the Spanish side of the mountain, and the last Garrow saw of him was a figure dis-

[1] *The Way Back*, page 139.
[2] She received the George Medal.

appearing against the skyline, before the guide took him to Barcelona and freedom. O'Leary's final words had been:

"Can this go on much longer?"

In my flat at Elizabeth Street, Garrow and I sat talking far into the night. He was a big man in Highland uniform with handsome features and a soft Scots voice.

But when he discussed Cole his voice hardened. "If Cole has been released from Vichy hands by the Gestapo, he will be back again in Paris. God knows what terrible things he will do."

"We have all been fooled. We should have settled accounts with him a long time ago, but it is too late."

"What action can be taken?" I asked.

"The only thing to do," said Garrow, "is to start an entirely new organisation, perhaps in a different part of France, with agents who are not known.

"This will have to be done, because if anything happens to O'Leary the numbers of airmen and other evaders will lead to even greater dangers for those who are hiding them and cannot pass them on to Spain."

It was a clear night as we walked down Ebury Street, searching for a taxi in the blackout. In the darkness, I said goodnight to Garrow and walked back, haunted by O'Leary's last words:

"Can this go on much longer?"

Soon another disaster threatened. Tom Groome failed to come up on the air. Almost his last message had been to report that Garrow had left for Spain. A fortnight later Langley showed me a decoded message requesting a parachute drop of arms and money to the Toulouse area.

"Do you notice anything unusual about this message?" he said.

I looked carefully at the message. It was marked "Security check not given."

"They think he is in German hands," said Langley.

"Well, what do we do?"

"We shall have to pretend we don't know and keep him in play as long as possible to try and save his life."

I tried to imagine myself in Groome's place, sitting before a radio set in the Gestapo office in Toulouse. I had some personal experience of their methods, but I felt sure of Tom Groome.

After Garrow's escape, Groome, who had brought a spare set to

France, established himself at Montauban, thirty-five miles from Toulouse, with a family named Cheramy. Since the German occupation of southern France, wireless detector vans had swarmed into the big towns and already several operators of other services had been caught. This obliged Groome to move from flat to flat keeping the Cheramy house as a headquarters. His procedure was to send a young French girl, a telephonist, named Reddé as a messenger to take decoded messages to room 202 in the Hotel de Paris at Toulouse, and return with O'Leary's reply for transmission to London.

It was at the Hotel de Paris that Woollatt and I had been hidden in April 1942 before we were taken to the frontier by Francis Blanchain. This was an extraordinary place. Most of the rooms were empty and inhabited only by fugitives from the German and Vichy police. It was reserved for secret agents and escapers on the run. Beneath a glass roof there was a large, gloomy reception hall with moth-eaten chairs and a rockery. The stairs, which I well remember, climbed to a gallery overlooking the hall and off it were a maze of rather grim bedrooms. It seemed to be a place of infinite mystery, and it was famous throughout the French Resistance movement. Hundreds were sheltered here before the arrival of the Gestapo.

Sitting at her desk at the entrance was the motionless figure of Madame Mongelard, the patronne, dressed all in black with a white peasant scarf over her head. I remember, after a week of hiding in the hotel, creeping like a child from a first floor bedroom and looking over the gallery at her silent, watchful figure below. Every night gendarmes came to check up on the 'Visitors' whose false particulars she delivered to them. The Gestapo caught her at the time of O'Leary's arrest, and she suffered at Ravensbrück, but survived, a courageous, tough old woman.

O'Leary would come silently each afternoon past the figure of Madame Mongelard at her desk and wait in room 202 for Mademoiselle Reddé to bring a message from Groome. But early in January, the girl failed to appear and there was no word from Groome. It was his practice to meet her at two-thirty every afternoon but for twenty-four hours there was no news of her, so he returned to the hotel next day, having spent the night at Françoise Dissart's flat. Almost at once, there was a knock on the door, and there was Mademoiselle Reddé. He could hardly recognise her

Her clothes were in disorder, and she was barely able to speak before she collapsed. She gasped:

"Tom Groome has been arrested, they caught us both. I escaped and I think Tom jumped out of the window of the Gestapo headquarters."

O'Leary told her to leave the hotel immediately and go to Françoise Dissart.

For one terrible moment after she had gone, he wondered if this distraught girl had been sent by the Gestapo, that they were already in the Hotel de Paris and he was surrounded. How could a simple, good-natured girl like this have escaped from them?

It was a grim moment for him. He felt for his revolver, and, looking cautiously over the gallery, went down into the hall, past Madame Mongelard at her desk, and whispered to her as he left:

"Look out—Gestapo."

O'Leary followed the girl to Françoise Dissart's flat, where he found her sobbing hysterically, with the old lady trying to comfort her. She had a fantastic story. She was sitting next to Groome in the Cheramys' house at Montauban while he was transmitting five-letter groups on his set. So absorbed were they in their work— Groome with his earphones and revolver next to the set—that they did not hear someone silently enter the room. Suddenly there was a revolver in Groome's back, and a voice said:

"Finish that message. If you stop you will be shot."[1]

Groome finished the message but left out the key letter to let Room 900 know that he was in German hands.

With the two Cheramys they were handcuffed, marched out to a car and driven to the Gestapo headquarters in Toulouse. They were pushed up to a room on the second floor, where a tall thin German sat watching them. After the war, Groome told me that the man's first words were:

"Our detector vans have been listening to you for two months."

After a few minutes of interrogation, Groome suddenly refused to answer. He jumped onto the desk where the Gestapo officer was sitting, scattering his papers, and, using the desk as a springboard, flung himself against the window. The glass shattered and he dropped a distance of thirty feet into the street.

Covered in broken glass, his ankle badly sprained, he managed

[1] *The Way Back*, page 153.

to run down the street among groups of people in the middle of the afternoon.

He said later that he felt no pain at all, but driven by some tremendous force, he rushed into the doorway of a house and hid there. Tragically, he was given away to the pursuing Gestapo by a craven bystander and dragged back to their headquarters.

Mademoiselle Reddé's escape was equally dramatic. When the Gestapo rushed out after Groome, she found herself completely alone. Peeping out of the door, she looked down the corridor and saw a number of girls who worked as secretaries going down the stairs. She simply followed them and walked out of the main entrance in her crèpe-soled shoes without being challenged. Outside, she hurried into a nearby hotel, rushed up the stairs into the first bedroom she could find, where she hid in a wardrobe for half an hour. As nothing more happened, she crept out again and went to O'Leary in room 202 at the Hotel de Paris.

O'Leary was still astonished by the girl's story. He went to a local bar where he was accustomed to pick up gossip. If her story were true, someone would have heard it. Soon he heard:

"The Gestapo caught a Colonel in the intelligence service, but the girl got away."

O'Leary was recovering from the arrest of Groome, when a man called Roger le Neveu alias Roger le Légionnaire made contact with Louis Nouveau in Paris.[1] Like other German agents, he volunteered to help the line, and like Cole, began to convoy airmen from Paris. It appears that Nouveau was at first suspicious of him, but was later persuaded by the success of his missions. Roger thus became acquainted with various 'postboxes' and safe houses of O'Leary's organisation at Toulouse and Paris. The second journey undertaken by Roger disturbed Nouveau. He claimed that he and some Australian airmen had been arrested, but that he had managed to get away. This story should have reminded Nouveau of Cole but his confidence was restored by another trip which delivered airmen in Toulouse.

The inevitable net was closing round Louis Nouveau, after nearly two years of defying the enemy. A letter from O'Leary, brought by the chef of the Marseille express, arrived, asking him to report to Toulouse at once. At the beginning of February 1943, he took the

[1] See Chapters 18 and 25.

train from the Gare d'Austerlitz in Paris for the south, accompanied by Roger and five airmen.

When they reached the station, they were unable to get admission tickets to the platform, which were necessary at that time of the war. At first, it looked as though they might have to take the airmen back and hide them again.

Suddenly Roger said: "Leave it to me, I can get tickets."[1]

He hurried back five minutes before the train left with the tickets, and no one questioned how he had managed to do it. They changed to a local train at St. Pierre des Corps and found an empty carriage. A moment later, the door opened and Louis turned his back so that the newcomer should not see two vacant seats. There was a painful stab in his back, and a German voice said:

"Put your hands up!"

The end was not long in coming.

On March 2nd, 1943, Roger made direct contact with O'Leary in Toulouse. With Ullman, the tailor who had made Garrow's gendarme uniform for his escape from Fort Meauzac, O'Leary agreed to a rendezvous. Roger had offered to tell them the full story of Louis Nouveau's arrest if they could meet him at a café in the town. O'Leary afterwards remembered two men in the street outside. But he went inside. Roger was waiting for him as he studied his identity card, he saw the same two men come in and sit down. Then he said to Roger:

"Now tell me quickly, do you know who has been giving us away in Paris.?"

"Yes," said Roger, grinning. "I know him very well."[2]

Something cold and hard was pressed into O'Leary's neck and a voice said:

"Don't move!"

The news of O'Leary's arrest reached London through Victor at Geneva.

The telegram for Room 900 dated March 20th, stated that Fabien de Cortes, who was arrested with O'Leary, had arrived there. He had escaped from the train taking O'Leary to Paris by jumping from a window. He had hidden in Paris and returned to Françoise Dissart in Toulouse and had then gone to Geneva. The telegram

[1] *The Way Back*, page 159.
[2] *The Way Back*, page 171.

continued: "Fabien requests orders to be sent all organisation to shoot at sight Roger le Neveu or Roger le Legionnaire stop Roger may be associate of Cole repeat Cole stop. Message ends."

In a few days, a full report came from Geneva. Fabien de Cortes, a young Frenchman who took part in the Garrow escape plan, had been able to talk to O'Leary during the train journey to Paris. The Gestapo had beaten up O'Leary and tortured him at Toulouse. To save others, he had revealed his identity as Pat O'Leary, a French-Canadian officer sent from Britain to organise escapes, and abandoned his false identity card in the name of Joseph Cartier.

He had seen Roger talking with Germans in the Gestapo office, and he knew that the entire organisation would be arrested unless they were warned. He had already been savagely interrogated about Louis and Rénée Nouveau, and many other addresses and contacts. It was vital to get a message through to Room 900 to warn other organisations about Roger.

Whenever the train ran through tunnels, O'Leary and Fabien de Cortes were able to talk and make a rapid plan for the latter's escape. O'Leary refused to go himself, for he hoped to save his own people by taking upon himself the sole responsibility. As the train came into Paris, O'Leary rose to his feet, took down his coat from the rack above him, and in the same movement, spread the coat over the door for a few seconds. This was time enough for the carriage window to be opened and Fabien de Cortes had vanished before the Gestapo in the corridor could open the sliding door. It was an excellent escape and a tragedy that Fabien de Cortes was later re-arrested, but it was he who brought the details of Roger which we were able to circulate to all underground systems.[1]

After Victor's report, darkness descended on the fate of O'Leary until the summer of 1944, when a woman called at Brook's Club in St. James's Street, London.

"I wish to speak to Jimmy," she told the porter.

Langley was a member of Brooks's Club, but there were several 'Jimmy's' who also belonged. The porter, unused to this method of approach, was inclined to turn the woman away, but she persisted.

"I have a message from a prisoner-of-war in Germany. He is my son, and he has written to me through the Red Cross. I have his letter here. Part of it reads:

[1] Though it did not prevent his activities in Brittany in June 1943. See Chapter 18.

" 'Tell Jimmy that Pat is alive in Germany'."

After a staid consultation among the staff of the Club, a message was sent to Langley, who met the woman in the flat at No. 5 St. James's Street. Her son, she said, had been taken prisoner-of-war in 1940 and, so far as she knew, was in a camp at Bad-Tölz. There was no other clue to his connection with O'Leary.

After the war, O'Leary explained that he had been in different concentration camps, including Mauthausen, Natzweiler and Dachau. One day, he had been sent from Dachau to help unload railway waggons at Bad-Tölz station under S.S. guards. While he was heaving coal from a waggon, he noticed that the man working beside him looked like an Englishman. In a whispered conversation, the man agreed to send a message to his mother since, as a prisoner-of-war, he was allowed correspondence through the Red Cross.

It was a message from the uttermost depths, but a least there was hope. In 1945, after many tortures and privations, O'Leary was released from Dachau. He has had a distinguished career in the Belgian Army. He is now the head of their medical services under his true name—Major-General Médecin Albert-Marie Guérisse, G.C., D.S.O. A generation later, I find it impossible to think of a more fascinating organiser of underground escape than O'Leary. From being a medical practitioner at Spa in Belgium at the outbreak of war, he had become a hero of fiction. In British Admiralty records as a Lieutenant Commander, Royal Navy, he performed feats of daring unrivalled by any of his successors. From his arrival in France until his arrest, he was always on the attack.

In the front rank, too, was Louis Nouveau, who despite grave injury to a lung, when he was gassed in the First World War, endured Buchenwald with unfailing courage. Broken in health, he survived to receive the George Medal and lived at Marseille till his death in 1966, witty and uncomplaining, a magnificent and a great Frenchman.

With O'Leary, throughout his detention in Dachau, was Tom Groome. Groome had been through a nerve-wracking and terrible experience after he had omitted the key letter in his code message to show that he was in German hands. He had been told before he left England that when he was certain that we were aware that his set had been captured he was at liberty to disclose his code. This would enable us to bluff the Germans and divert attention from anything they might already have discovered. He, therefore, gave them the method of coding and decoding.

The Gestapo began the 'wireless game' by asking for a parachute operation of arms and money to be carried out near Toulouse. Such a plan had in fact been made before O'Leary's arrest and it is possible that they captured a decoded message.

The War Office and M.I.9 conducted their part of the deception, with relish. The parachute operation was cancelled on the ground that there were too many German detector vans at Toulouse! Groome was ordered to move to Monte Carlo but this did not please the Gestapo and the set remained in Toulouse.

Our next message stated that we knew that Groome had not moved to Monte Carlo because we could detect the location of his set. We proposed a sea evacuation from Genoa. After a month, the Gestapo evidently realised what was happening and Groome's set went off the air. During this exercise in double bluff, Groome's life was in the balance. But by his cool decision to give up the code, he saved his own life and enabled Room 900 to deceive the Germans. This may well have avoided other tragedies. Under interrogation, he told the Gestapo nothing of importance.

The O'Leary organisation as we had known it was gone. Although the War Office insisted that the line was finished and that no more agents, no more wireless sets, no more francs and no more reinforcements were to be sent, there was still Françoise Dissart left to carry on.

She was well known to us through M.I.9 interrogation reports. At this time a grey-haired Frenchwoman of sixty, she lived in a flat in the heart of Toulouse, near a dress shop which she owned. Her flat was close to the Gestapo headquarters, which she believed an advantage. According to M.I.9 reports, airmen and other fugitives were brought there through the back entrance and their arrival was timed for the Gestapo lunch break. The story seemed incredible but though she hid large numbers of men and sent them from Toulouse to the Spanish frontier, till the end of the war, Françoise Dissart was never captured.

When O'Leary was lying on a straw mattress in the dungeons of St. Pierre at Toulouse, he heard Mademoiselle Dissart's strange wailing voice calling outside.

"Mon Pat, où es-tu? Mon cher Pat! Pat! Pat!"

He was horrified. He knew that without regard for her safety, the old lady outside the walls was trying to make him hear.

By some miracle, she was not arrested. It may be that the guards thought her an eccentric who imagined that someone was falsely imprisoned in the horror-chambers of the prison.

Small and very French, with tremendous energy, she had remarkable character. She smoked all day long with a black holder permanently in her mouth. She seemed never to go to bed and attired in a black petticoat lived entirely on black coffee. She had a cat, well-known in the French underground, called Mifouf, who was almost as big a personality as herself. Her chief reason for helping O'Leary, to whom she was devoted, was a nephew who was a prisoner-of-war in Germany. She had also that basic hatred of Germans to be found among many French women of her generation. O'Leary was the only person who could give her orders, for she was formidable, with sharp grey eyes. The cat Mifouf, seated beside her, seemed to understand her moods.

With the German occupation of Toulouse, she had a better chance of survival. They would not imagine this unusual old lady could be part of an escape line. With the treacherous and more perceptive Vichy police it would have been different. Françoise Dissart and her cat, which lived to the age of eighteen, were almost the sole survivors of the O'Leary line. She continued to send escapers to Spain until the Liberation, escorting some from the Swiss borders herself, after Marseille had become too dangerous, with great ingenuity and indomitable spirit. By the end of the war over 600 Allied airmen and soldiers had come through this line which Garrow had started after Dunkirk and for which death and suffering in concentration camps was the price paid by more than a hundred people.

PART III

THE COMET LINE

CHAPTER II

Dédée

I N London, the loss of O'Leary was seen as a major catastrophe. It came at a time when the critics of Room 900, prompted by the arrest of Groome and Louis Nouveau, were in full cry. For many weeks, Langley and I lived under a cloud until we almost believed that we were solely responsible.

That M.I.9 had been slow to understand the menace of Cole and other agents provocateurs is true. But the real blame must lie with those who, despite the efforts of 'Monday' and Darling, for so long refused to allow sufficient recruits and wireless communications to Room 900 to create new lines. Had fresh organisations with trained agents been in the field early in 1943, to collect the growing number of airmen, they could have relieved the older lines. There would have been more chance of persuading devoted men like O'Leary to leave enemy territory before it was too late.

The early organisations had become too large and unwieldly. Too many individuals became involved about whom little or nothing was known. In the desperate struggle to hide, feed, and escort large numbers of airmen there was little time to check their loyalties. Thus the Gestapo found it relatively easy to infiltrate the escape lines compared with the more compact, and 'professional' secret intelligence circuits.

This danger accounted for much of the prejudice against Room 900 and escape lines for Allied Servicemen, which were regarded as 'amateur' organisations. However much the humanitarian role of our agents was admired they were still regarded as 'dangerous'. The amorphous nature of the escape routes made it difficult for us to counteract the menace of infiltration. Until the end of the war, we were beset by Dutch, Belgian, and French traitors posing as 'helpers' or 'airmen'. Despite all the special training given to organisers parachuted from Britain, it was impossible to prevent the deception of many ordinary families who hid airmen and their arrest by the Germans. 'Roger le Legionnaire' was transferred by the Gestapo to Brittany where in the spring and summer of 1943, he did great damage.[1]

After the arrest of O'Leary, the nature of our operations began to change. By the end of 1943, we were sending in agents to create smaller groups for specific tasks such as sea evacuation and even pick-ups by aircraft from France. We did not attempt to reinforce lines which were 'blown'. An exception to this was the Belgian organisation founded by Dédée and her father. Despite much advice to the contrary, and many more arrests, I continued to organise its support until the liberation. It achieved memorable success under the name of the 'Comet' escape line.

Secret intelligence can be reduced to mere routine by official correspondence, but the story of Dédée was amazing from the start.

It opened with a crumpled passport photograph of a laughing young woman. It was a compelling, feminine face, with her hair brushed back over the forehead. She had fine eyes and a determined mouth. Even in this faded, inadequate photograph, there was no doubt of her attractive personality.

The story began with her arrival with two young Belgians and a British soldier, a survivor of St. Valery, in August 1941, at the British Consulate in Bilbao. They had come from Brussels and crossed the Pyrenees on foot with a Basque guide.

The Consul had been astonished at the sight of this slight figure. He could hardly believe that such an innocent-looking girl had really crossed the mountains. It was an arduous journey from the foothills of St. Jean-de-Luz, made only by smugglers.

She gave her name as Andrée de Jongh, aged twenty-five, living with her parents at 73, Avenue Emile Verhaeren in the Schaerbeek district of Brussels. Her father, Frédéric de Jongh, she told the Consul, was a schoolmaster. She had been helping British soldiers and airmen in Brussels since 1940, but at first did not tell her family. In 1941 she was forced to leave Belgium and her father took her place there. They had together planned a chain of 'safe houses' in Brussels, Paris and the frontier zone. Their object was to establish an escape line to Spain.

In his report, the Consul described his conversation with her.

[1] See Chapter 18.

She told him that with sufficient money she could find guides for crossing the frontier. She and her father would in future concentrate on sending trained soldiers rather than Belgian or French volunteers.

"How much does it cost you to bring a man from Brussels?"

"Six thousand Belgian francs to St. Jean de Luz, plus fourteen hundred pesetas for the mountain guides."

When the Consul observed that this seemed expensive, Dédée replied that the guides were nervous of taking Allied soldiers through occupied territory, especially the Coastal Zone. But he was deeply impressed by her and felt that she was genuine. He told her he would refer her plan to 'Monday' at the Embassy in Madrid. Dédée said she would be back in three or four weeks' time with more men.

In writing his report to 'Monday' the Consul concluded with a hint of caution. It was always possible she might have been sent by the Germans, but he did not himself believe this. The appearance of this intriguing girl at Bilbao produced a flow of telegrams, reports and minutes lasting several weeks. Her file included the M.I.9 interrogations of those who had made the crossing with her. They spoke of her incomparable courage and firmness.

She reappeared at Bilbao on October 17th, 1941, where she met 'Monday', a big genial member of the British Embassy staff.

He was no ordinary Foreign Office type. He was outspoken, earthy, and unencumbered by protocol. There was a warm humanity in him which had made a deep impression on me when I had met him. Like Darling, he was an enthusiast for escape work, and it was clear that due to their faith in Dédée, M.I.9 had supported her scheme for a line from Brussels to San Sebastian and Bilbao from the beginning.

'Monday' explained to Dédée that the British Government were vitally concerned with recovering the crews of aircraft shot down in Holland, Belgium and France. On behalf of M.I.9 he agreed to lend the money she asked for the housing and feeding of the men on the way from Brussels and the fees for the guides at the frontier. Dédée demanded that she should be paid on each visit to Spain and that M.I.9 be refunded at the end of the war. This would guarantee her independence. 'Monday' gave her the code-name 'Postman'.

The arrival of valuable aircrew dispelled any doubts about her. Only our chief at the War Office continued to make dark hints.

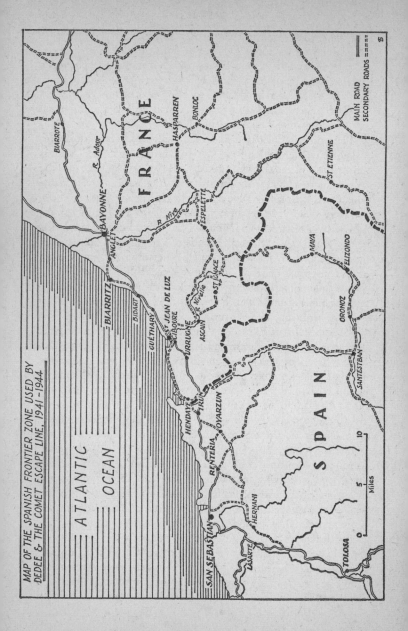

MAP OF THE SPANISH FRONTIER ZONE USED BY
DEDEE & THE COMET ESCAPE LINE, 1941-1944

ATLANTIC OCEAN

FRANCE

SPAIN

BIARROTE
R. Adour
BAYONNE
ANGLET
BIARRITZ
BIDART
GUÉTHARY
ST. JEAN DE LUZ
CIBOURE
URRUGNE
ASCAIN
R. Nivelle
R. Nive
ST IGNACE
ESPELETTE
HASPARREN
BONLOC
ST ETIENNE
MAYA
ELIZONDO
ORONOZ
SANTESTEBAN
HENDAYE
IRUN
OYARZUN
RENTERIA
SAN SEBASTIAN
LASARTE
HERNANI
TOLOSA

MAIN ROAD
SECONDARY ROADS

Miles
0   5   10

But even he was forced to change his mind. Each time she reached San Sebastian or Bilbao, admiration for her exploits grew. In her talks with 'Monday', she insisted that the line should remain in Belgian hands and although M.I.9 (and the Belgian Government in exile) should provide funds, they should not control it.

When I arrived at Room 900, Dédée and her line had been in operation for ten months. I could see that, brilliant and daring as she was, she could not continue without serious risk to her father and herself. There was no direct communication with her except the meetings with 'Monday' on Spanish territory. She had so far refused to allow a wireless operator to be sent to Brussels so that Room 900 could maintain contact with her father.

She relied on couriers to carry messages up and down the line between Brussels and St. Jean de Luz. It was an informal, even high-spirited escape line and she wanted it that way. She did not like to be regarded as a spy. Her youthful, but nonetheless effective methods were difficult for a previous generation to understand.

No one of the old intelligence establishment in the War Office had experience of an escape line covering hundreds of miles of occupied territory and they did not understand the problems.

A successful system made it essential that guides escorting the airmen by train should be inconspicuous. Dédée chose young men and women who would pass unnoticed at railway station controls and be able to explain the presence of passengers of Anglo-Saxon appearance who spoke no French. The girls in her organisation were quietly dressed and modest in appearance, but self-possessed. Their looks belied their toughness and resource. The evaders, survivors of air combat, followed them without question.

Dédée was my special responsibility at Room 900 and every week 'Monday' sent a full report to me from Madrid about the three sections of her line at Brussels, Paris and the frontier zone at Bayonne and St. Jean de Luz. Whenever she or one of her principal guides arrived over the mountains, the Consul at San Sebastian or Bilbao would signal 'Monday'. Then, in bold disregard of diplomatic protocol, 'Monday' would drive hundreds of miles to the frontier to meet her. Between July and October 1942, this slim girl, and her Basque guide, Florentino Giocoechea, personally escorted fifty-four men over the Pyrenees. Her fame grew and with it the morale of the R.A.F.

Dédée became a symbol of courage and defiance during her extraordinary career. Her lively charm and energy won over the most faint-hearted. At the Great Central Hotel, when airmen on their return spoke of her exploits, their eyes filled with tears. I could understand that in these fighting men she inspired not only respect, but also deep affection. They knew that she had saved their lives, and they were afraid for her. So were all those who knew what terrible risks she ran. But Dédée, always determined and independent, kept her own rules. She showed little interest in our admiration. She was possessed by some inner strength. And to the last, she made her own decisions.

Throughout the war, the line was organised by Belgian leaders at every stage of the journey from Brussels. Belgian pride in its independence was jealously guarded. It was not until 1943 that Room 900 provided radio links and trained agents were sent from London to reinforce it, some of whom were French.

Before the war, Dédée had thought of being an artist, had designed posters and later trained to be a nurse. When war came to Belgium in 1940, she worked in a hospital among wounded British soldiers. Their helplessness moved her to action. Early in 1941, she began to gather friends around her to hide young Belgians and British soldiers who wished to escape to England to fight. Her headquarters were the house at No. 73 Avenue Emile Verhaeren in Brussels where she lived with her father, and here she made plans to establish a route through to Spain.

She was helped by her mother, her aunt and her elder sister, Suzanne Wittek, but her most ardent supporter was her father, Frédéric de Jongh. He could remember the day in 1915 when Edith Cavell was shot for hiding British soldiers. He was a man of great purpose and principle and his country's surrender in 1940 had shocked him deeply. Although a liberal in politics and a hater of violence, he was determined to atone for his sense of shame. At fifty-eight, a bowed and scholarly man, rather short-sighted but with a resolute chin and mouth, he became a fanatic in his daughter's cause.

When Dédée paid her first visit to the British Consulate in Bilbao in 1941, her father received an unwelcome visit from the Gestapo and the Secret Police of the Luftwaffe at No. 73. The Germans sat in the demure living-room overlooking the street. They wore the regulation long dark mackintoshes and kept their hats on their heads while they fired questions at him:

"Where is your daughter Andrée?"

Her father shrugged his shoulders.

"She left here months ago. Young girls—you understand," he sighed. "Nowadays one can't keep track of what young people do."

It seemed that the Gestapo had a full description of her, though it is possible they were then looking for Andrée Dumon (Nadine), one of the guides to Paris and a girl of similar height and appearance to Dédée.

They asked Frédéric de Jongh his occupation.

"I am the headmaster of the primary school for boys in the Place Gaucheret."[1]

"Do you go there every day?"

The questioning dragged on, as the German voices grated in his ears. Frédéric de Jongh must have wondered where his admiration for youth and adventure would lead him. All his life he had been a man of peace.

In his headmaster's desk at the Place Gaucheret there were stacks of false identity and ration cards.

But the Gestapo got nothing from him. They smiled sardonically and left the house.

"We shall be back."

Their grey Opel car sped down the street.

Dédée warned 'Monday' on one of her visits to Spain, and new plans were made. The headquarters were moved from No. 73 and they remained in Brussels at the school in the Place Gaucheret until February 1942. In that month, the Secret Police of the Luftwaffe, incensed by reports of the number of airmen returning to Britain, began a further search for Dédée. They arrested her elder sister.

German Commanders-in-Chief in France and Belgium had published orders which made hiding or otherwise assisting Allied prisoners-of-war punishable by death. From this time, the Gestapo and Abwehr launched their determined campaign against the escape lines. It was to be a grim combat which cost many lives. The intervention of the Luftwaffe was significant. It is known that Goering realised the existence of secret escape organisations for recovery

[1] Now the Ecole Frédéric de Jongh.

of R.A.F. pilots and crews. He must have known its value to the Allied Air Forces. He gave orders that it was to be crushed.

Dédée's father was at Valenciennes in February 1942 reorganising the system of guides to Paris. On his return to Brussels, he too narrowly escaped arrest. The price on his head was a million Belgian francs. On April 30th, he left Brussels for ever and fled to Paris to continue operating from there.

Six days later, three of his principal lieutenants in Brussels were arrested. It was the end of the pioneer organisation formed by Dédée and her father in Belgium.

At first, it seemed to me that the Brussels organisation would collapse. But out of the confusion appeared a new chief, the Baron Jean Greindl. Since the early part of the year, he had been the Director of a canteen run by the Swedish Red Cross to provide food and clothes for poor children in Brussels. It was a voluntary organisation with offices in the rue Ducale.

Jean Greindl was thirty-six. He came from a noble Belgian family which had played a distinguished part in the development of the Congo, and much of his life had been spent in the management of a coffee plantation. He was already helping Frédéric de Jongh with food for airmen hidden in the city, and in April the Swedish canteen became a cover for the headquarters of the escape line. Here Jean Greindl operated under the pseudonym 'Nemo'.

One of his first successes was the recovery of the crew of a bomber shot down on May 13th, 1942 east of Tongerloo. The pilot, Pilot Officer Manser, stayed with the aircraft and crashed with it. He was posthumously awarded the Victoria Cross. The survivors, Pilot Officer Horseley, Flight Sergeants Baveystock, Mills and King were en route for Britain by the end of June, an early indication of the effectiveness of the line.

One of them described Jean Greindl to me. He was lean and strong, with humorous grey-blue eyes, and spoke in a quiet, ironic voice. He had divided Belgium into regions for the collection of survivors of crashed aircraft, with reporting centres at Gand, Namur, Liège and Hasselt, to which patriots in surrounding villages and farms were to bring the airmen. This new system brought splendid results for Dédée until the end of 1942. He also recruited a new series of guides to take the men by train to Paris.

In the early days of the escape line, Dédée and her French friend,

Elvire Morelle, had taken the men direct from Brussels to Bayonne without a halt in Paris. But by 1942, the controls had grown stricter at Quiévrain, the Belgian frontier post, but they could still cross the Somme by boat. Five names appeared regularly in M.I.9 interrogation reports until the end of the year. They were Peggy van Lier,[1] Count Georges,[2] and Count Edouard d'Oultremont,[3] Baron Albert Greindl, younger brother of 'Nemo' of the Swedish Canteen,[4] and Jean Ingels.[5] In the spring, they replaced other guides who had been forced to flee from Belgium or who were already in German hands. Among these was the other Andrée—Andrée Dumon, alias Nadine—a nineteen-year-old girl who took twenty men to Paris before her arrest in the summer. She was the 'Andrée' whom, it is believed, the Gestapo mistook for Dédée. Andrée Dumon survived Ravensbrück, but her father, who worked for Frédéric de Jongh, disappeared for ever in the programme of mass extermination. His younger daughter, Micheline Dumon, alias 'Michou'[6] became one of the line's most successful operators in 1943–44. After several hair-breadth escapes, she reached London safely in May 1944.

As I sat in box-like Room 900, I tried to visualise this new group under Jean Greindl. They were none of them, except their chief, over twenty-five. Even in the wooden English of interrogation reports, I could feel their high spirits and gaiety. They were not professional agents, but as guardians for bewildered airmen they were superb. I had reason to hope that with the strong personality of Jean Greindl in Brussels, the line would revive.

But these were the days before the storm. I was less happy about the Paris section of the line. After his hurried departure from Brussels, Frédéric de Jongh was reunited with his daughter. Dédée, too, was unable to return to Brussels and travelled continually with parties of airmen between Paris and Spain. She had not seen her father since January, when she had paid a daring visit to Brussels and escaped through the back garden of her home seconds before two officers of the Secret Field Police invaded the house.

Frédéric de Jongh refused all his daughter's entreaties to escape

[1] M.B.E.—now Mrs. J. M. Langley.
[2] M.B.E., M.M.—see 'Ormond', Chapter 20.
[3] M.B.E.
[4] See Chapter 13.
[5] Shot at Brussels October 20th, 1943.
[6] George Medal. See Chapters 20 and 21.

to England. He was determined to continue. As Dédée told me afterwards, he could not bear to leave. His wife and elder daughter were in danger in Brussels, and it would seem like desertion. He stayed in Paris till the end.

The Paris organisation had rented a huge, ugly villa at St. Maur to hide airmen before their transport to the south. In charge of it, as housekeeper and cook, was Elvire Morelle.[1] This brave French girl had made one crossing of the Pyrenees with Dédée in February 1942. With Florentino, their Basque guide, they had begun the return journey from San Sebastian to France on February 6th, in driving snow. Elvire slipped in the darkness and fell, fracturing her leg. Florentino, quick to appreciate the danger, for it was getting light, went off in search of a mule from one of the mountain farms. Elvire, in great pain, was mounted on it and taken back down slippery ways to a farmhouse near Renteria. But thanks to the skill of a Basque doctor from San Sebastian, she recovered, and returned to Paris.

Dédée and her father now searched for a suitable flat and found one on the fourth floor of a modern block at No. 10 rue Oudinot, where they made their headquarters and prepared false papers. With his French friends, Robert Aylé of the rue Babylone and Aimable Fouquerel,[2] masseur from a nearby hospital, Frédéric de Jongh organised the hiding of more and more airmen as the months went by. The pressures on the organisation grew. Through 'Monday', I sent money to them, but I began to make plans to equip the line with trained agents. I still hoped that Dédée and her father would escape to Britain before it was too late.

Two courageous French assistants of the line were René Coache and his wife Raymonde, of Asnières, a northern suburb of Paris. Raymonde Coache[3] organised food and civilian clothes for the evaders. She and her husband hid no less than thirty men in 1941 and 1942 in their small apartment at Asnières. They still live there today. The rooms are modest and the furniture unchanged from those dangerous months. Their flat on the second floor is reached by a winding stone staircase. There is no way of escape. How often must

[1] M.B.E.
[2] Both were shot at Mont Valerien, Paris, March 28th, 1944, with Frédéric de Jongh.
[3] M.B.E.

they have listened for the tread of the Gestapo at their door. Here the Coaches lived their finest hours. They were both to suffer terrible hardships for their service. Madame Coache was arrested at Lille in 1943 and emerged thin and starved from a concentration camp two years later.

Coache, a French Post Office engineer, escaped to England in the same year. Although he was nearly forty, I persuaded him to become a radio operator for what had then become the Comet Line. With the code-name 'Dover' he went in 1944 to Brussels. He was arrested by the Gestapo whilst operating his set a few weeks before the liberation of the city, but fortunately survived.[1] His training and subsequent mission for Comet were my personal responsibility. He was a brave and modest Frenchman who went back to enemy territory after I had been obliged to break the terrible news, at the flat in St. James's Street, of his wife's arrest.

The organisation in the south was controlled by an indomitable Belgian lady, Madame Elvire de Greef, known as 'Tante Go' after her deceased pet dog.[2] With her husband, Fernand, and her son and daughter, she had tried to escape to England via Bordeaux in 1940, but, forced to remain in France, she rented a villa at Anglet, not far from Bayonne.

From the earliest days, Madame de Greef worked closely with Dédée. When the airmen reached the frontier zone, she made all the arrangements for hiding them in St. Jean de Luz before their journey to Spain. She was involved in numerous black market operations to obtain the best possible food, and by these activities lulled suspicion of her real work. She knew all the local smugglers and under-cover agents in the bistros of Bayonne and St. Jean de Luz and on more than one occasion she blackmailed German officers by threatening to reveal their possession of black market goods and thus escaped arrest.

Her husband, Fernand de Greef[3], worked as interpreter at the German Kommandantur in Anglet. He had access to official stamps and supplied his wife with blank identity cards and special passes for the Forbidden Zone along the Atlantic coast. Her son Freddy acted as her courier, and her pretty eighteen-year-old daughter,

[1] See Chapter 23.
[2] The dog was named 'Go Go'.
[3] M.B.E.

Janine, escorted the men from the station at St. Jean de Luz to safe houses in the town. Despite their constant underground activity, the de Greef family miraculously avoided capture and were still in action at the liberation of France. It is estimated that between June 1941 and August 1944, when they were met by the redoubtable 'Monday', who motored to Biarritz, no less than 337 airmen and soldiers of all the Allies passed through their hands before reaching Spain. With Dédée and Micheline Dumon ('Michou'), Madame de Greef received the George Medal after the war.

The image of Madame de Greef and the deep impression which she made on the evaders became a source of wonderment to me, chairborne in London. I could only marvel at her resource and daring. A photograph of her came into my possession at this time. I forget how it reached me. Not every airman had been trained in security, and one might have brought it as a souvenir. She was slight, with a round face and high cheekbones. (Her eyes were prominent, grey tinged with green, and she had short, dark hair.) Even from this photograph I could understand the impression of energy and dedication which she gave. In this she was like the other Belgian and Frenchwomen who worked under the leadership of Dédée, but far more ruthless.

It was some years before I met her in Brussels, when she gave me an account of her exploits in her brisk and unemotional way. She is an extraordinary woman. She was a match for the Gestapo over three years of continuous underground activity. She bribed, cajoled and threatened the Germans and deceived them to the end. Her contribution to victory was tremendous. She is now a widow living in Brussels, but still keeps her air of mystery and resource. She was one of the most skilful and dangerous enemies the Germans ever had. Like Dédée and Michou, who survived these endless dangers, she is strikingly untouched by time. All three of them have kept their vitality and good looks, despite their perilous and often heartbreaking experiences. They are wonderful examples of the triumph of will-power and feminine subtlety.

Nor is there anything neurotic about the famous Basque guide, Florentino Góicoechea.[1] Every man who reached the Great Central Hotel spoke of him with awe. From the autumn of 1941, he took Dédée and other members of the organisation across the Pyrenees

[1] He received the George Medal.

until the early part of 1944. He is still to be seen in his native village of Ciboure, adjoining St. Jean de Luz, a great, powerful man of the mountains. His features are majestic and wild. He speaks no word of French or Spanish, only Basque. Twenty-five years ago, he could carry a man on his shoulders across the torrent of the river Bidassoa, which forms the frontier at Irun. He was indifferent to fatigue or danger. Without him, Dédée and the Comet escape line which followed her could never have rescued so many airmen.

During the summer of 1942, I received reports that an Englishman was working with Madame de Greef and taking turns with Dédée to escort parties over the frontier. It was some time before there was any reliable information about him. He told the airmen very little about himself. His name was Albert Edward Johnson, generally known in the organisation as 'B'. Before the war, he had been secretary and chauffeur to Count Baillet-Latour in Brussels. In 1940, he settled at Anglet with the de Greef family under the name of Albert Jonion.

Johnson was a quiet, pale Londoner with large, sensitive brown eyes and the greatest endurance and loyalty. Admiration for him among the aircrew who came back was unbounded. Between June 1941 and March 1943, he was responsible for the return of 122 men to Spain. It is not to anyone's credit that he only received the M.B.E. for this work. Like many agents who started in the field, unattached to a military intelligence establishment, he was classified as a 'civilian' and eligible only for the Order of the British Empire. Those trained in Britain were given commissions in the Intelligence Corps or General Service Corps, which made them eligible for military decorations. But a civilian carrying out secret work in enemy territory in wartime ran a greater risk of torture and execution than someone claiming military rank.

The case of Johnson was especially unfair. He was one of our best and most dedicated agents. But he never complained. He died in 1954, and it is sad that he received so little recognition for his daring. My thoughts turn to him when I think of some recent awards of the M.B.E.

CHAPTER 12

The Maréchal Affair

THROUGHOUT the remaining months of 1942, Dédée, Johnson and Jean-François Nothomb ('Franco')[1] a young Belgian who had joined her line, crossed the Pyrenees in all weathers with parties of airmen. Between July and December, Dédée made nine such journeys, Johnson eight, and Nothomb one.

I interrogated many of the airmen on their arrival, about the system of guides.[2] They described how Dédée herself escorted the parties from Paris with Nothomb or Madame de Greef's daughter Janine. When they reached St. Jean de Luz Madame de Greef organised their reception and hid them with families in the neighbourhood.

Their route to the frontier avoided the main road to Hendaye by a rough track to a farmhouse at Urrugne. Here they were received by Francia Usandizaga, a Basque farmer's wife, with bowls of hot milk and soup before they continued their journey. Very often they stayed the night there if the weather was bad in the mountains. The farmhouse has changed but little since Dédée and Florentino brought parties there almost every week during the last months of 1942. But Francia has gone. She paid for her devotion at Ravensbrück.

At nightfall, Florentino led the party, followed by Dédée, into the hills. They were an extraordinary pair, this huge rugged man and the slight, tenacious Dédée. The airmen described Florentino's fabulous knowledge of the mountains. He was able to find his way in all weathers, even under the influence of cognac. He could always scent danger. When there was fog, which hid every landmark, he could still find the path. He would stop for a moment and tap the

[1] D.S.O., now priest of the Order of the Petits-Frères de Jésus.
[2] They were first questioned by Darling at Gibraltar who reported any operational information to Room 900.

ground with his espadrilles. Then, finding the way, he would move off at a great pace, with the party stumbling and slipping behind him. It was useless to ask him to go more slowly. Often, on the blackest of nights, he could find a single tree trunk or a rock. He would search rapidly, and bring out a spare pair of espadrilles or a bottle of cognac which he had hidden months before. He spoke no language but Basque. His French vocabulary was limited to 'douce-ment, doucement' and 'tais-toi'.

Before they left Francia's farmhouse, Dédée would give orders to the men. They were to march in single file and in complete silence until they were in the mountains. At all times they must follow and obey Florentino on the journey. Before departure, Florentino sat packing a large rucksack, frequently taking a long swig at a bottle of cognac. He then inspected the feet of each man and the fit of his espadrilles and gave him a stout stick to support him on the march. Watching them was Dédée, dressed in blue fisherman's trousers, with a small bundle harnessed to her back.

They followed Florentino from the farmhouse until, about eight miles inland from St. Jean de Luz, they saw the beams of the lighthouse at Fuenterrabia circling over the hills and valleys. Within an hour came the twinkling lights of Spain and below them the frontier town of Irun, at the mouth of the river Bidassoa. The next part of the journey was dangerous, especially in changeable weather, for they had to descend towards the river. If snow or rain began to fall, the path grew slippery, and despite their stout sticks the airmen often fell heavily. As the path sank into the shadows of the river gorge, the lights of neutral territory began to disappear.

Everything depended on a safe crossing of the Bidassoa. If it were in flood and unpassable on foot, the party had to make a long detour to cross a bridge. This was risky, as the bridge was lit by floodlights. A mile down the valley, they saw the faint grey gleam of the road-way which runs on the Spanish bank of the river. From time to time a car passed along the frontier road, its headlights shining briefly on the torrent. Parallel with this road there was a railway, on a step of sheer rock.

A few minutes later, they could hear a deep sound which swiftly became more distinct. It was the roar of the torrent bounding to-wards the sea at Irun.

Reaching the bank, they saw the white foam dancing in the

darkness and, crouching among the trees, watched the Bidassoa twisting among the rocks below. Florentino held up his hand for silence and peered towards the brightly lit frontier post on the far side. On a clear night, the frontier guards could be seen patrolling the Spanish road. They would not hesitate to fire if they saw anything moving.

Florentino would then give a signal to Dédée, who quietly ordered everyone to remove their trousers and tie them in a bundle round their necks. Florentino climbed down first, to test the depth. If the river was fordable, he would take the first airman by the hand and lead him across with the water up to his waist. It was essential for the party to cling together. One false slip would mean drowning.[1] Dédée would come last, often helping the airmen over herself. Her strength and vitality amazed them.

Shivering from the icy water, they put on their trousers and waited. The sternest test was yet to come. They must climb a rocky embankment, cross the railway line and then the frontier road, followed by a steep slope on the far side. Florentino would lie flat, hidden by a thorn bush, watching the road. He could see lights from the windows of the frontier post and a guard patrolling only a hundred yards away. When the guard turned his back, Florentino gave a grunt, clambered over the railway, jumped to the road and scrambled up the opposite slope. Pulling himself upwards with the help of roots and bushes, his great strength enabled him to get clear and out of sight in a few seconds. The tired airmen followed him. Sometimes one would fall back into the road with a clatter. Dédée would always wait to see that every man was safely across and sometimes would seize one and push him up the bank. How could the men fail before this extraordinary girl? By sheer force of example, she drove them on into Spain.

There were nights when they were lucky to escape. In July 1942, Dédée and Florentino were ambushed in the foothills on the French side by two German soldiers. The party of airmen scattered, until Dédée collected them and took them back to the farmhouse at Urrugne. They crossed safely two days later. Only rarely was a man lost in the darkness and found himself arrested by the Spaniards and sent to the concentration camp at Miranda del Ebro. Across the frontier, Florentino began to march powerfully uphill towards the

[1] Jean Greindl's successor in Brussels, Count Antoine d'Ursel, was drowned in the Bidassoa in December 1943.

peaks known as the Trois Couronnes. The panting fugitives struggled after him. One man told me that he was only able to continue by watching Dédée's slim legs in front of him in the dawn light.

There were several hours of marching to come. If a man lagged behind, Dédée would return and speak to him, giving him encouragement. She would sharply reprove anyone for drinking wine or cognac until they were nearer safety. On the Spanish side of the mountain, they were soon among fresh fields and the tinkling of sheep bells. Moving down into a valley, Florentino and Dédée kept watch for the green uniforms and shiny hats of the Spanish guards. They approached a lone farmhouse and while the party hid in some bushes, Florentino flung a pebble at the window. When the door was opened by the farmer's wife, the men hurried into the warmth of the kitchen. There they dried their clothes and ate a splendid potato omelette.

While her charges slept in the farmhouse there was no rest for Dédée. She changed from her blue trousers into a blouse and skirt, and walking five kilometres across the fields, came to the town of Renteria, where she took a tram to San Sebastian. At the flat of her contact, Bernardo, she rested until dark. Then, returning with him in his car to the farmhouse, she collected the men. They drove towards San Sebastian until Bernardo stopped by a car parked at the roadside. 'Monday' himself emerged and shook hands. He held a short conference with Dédée and Bernardo, then bustled the men into his car and drove to the British Consulate in San Sebastian.

There was little time for Dédée to wait. She must rejoin Florentino in the mountains before dawn broke, to return to the French side. Carrying messages and money for Jean Greindl and her father, she waved goodbye and drove back with Bernardo to the farmhouse.

This was the story that I heard almost every week at the end of 1942. It would have moved the most cynical and complacent. M.I.9 must take every possible step to support Dédée and, if possible, prevent her from falling into German hands. This was something that no one dared to think about. But Dédée herself had few illusions. She would never willingly have left her work. She asked of us only sufficient money to support the line and its helpers. With Madame de Greef and her father, she remained in complete control. Her successes did much to alter the lukewarm attitude of the British authorities to escape lines. Each telegram from Madrid with the names of airmen she had brought through gave us fresh en-couragement and it would not have been human if the two-man staff of Room 900 had not sought to take a little credit.

It was occasionally my task to take an airman back to the station from which he had flown. The effect on his friends of suddenly seeing a man they had thought dead or taken prisoner weeks before was tremendous. It began to have a striking influence on the morale of all aircrew. In 1942 the appearances of those presumed lost might seem miraculous. A year later, when several hundred had been rescued, it was widely known throughout the Allied Air Forces that if a man landed in occupied territory by parachute, he had at least a fifty-fifty chance of getting home. The history of the escape lines confirms this. That it became possible was due to those great exponents of escape organisation, Dédée and O'Leary.

Dédée and her father were still reluctant to have a radio operator in Brussels or Paris, a view supported by our boss at the War Office. They were afraid that wireless contact with London might weaken their independence and that Room 900 would give them orders. Dédée expressed her distrust of radio operators to 'Monday'. Many secret organisations had already been broken up by the capture of wireless sets. It was better for escape organisations to be without them. Their task was to help men escape over the Pyrenees, not to send messages to London. Since Dédée was not concerned with air or sea operations, it seemed the safest course even if communications were slow. But once Jean Greindl was established in Brussels, there was always the risk that, if arrests were made, the links between Brussels, Paris and St. Jean de Luz would once more be broken.

In the autumn of 1942, I wrote to 'Monday' asking him to discuss with Dédée the sending of an operator by parachute to Belgium. She agreed to talk to her father in Paris and put the plan to Jean Greindl. On her next crossing to Spain she told 'Monday' that Jean Greindl would welcome a wireless operator. He needed money and information, all of which had to be conveyed to him by courier from Paris. It was a clumsy and unreliable system.

My great difficulty was to find a suitable Belgian for training as an operator. Room 900 was still a poor relation, and Langley had struggled for months to obtain an operator for O'Leary. To employ and train a Belgian national for a secret mission, it was necessary to have the agreement of the Belgian Government in exile whose

Intelligence service, or Sûreté, had their headquarters at No. 38 Belgrave Square, in London. The supply of volunteres in the United Kingdom was strictly limited in 1942. Later in the war, considerable numbers of young men escaped through Spain and volunteered for such tasks. The Belgian Government were extremely proud of Dédée and her triumphs. They were among the first, not excluding the Air Ministry, who sensed the contribution that she was making to the war. They gave me their support and in the next two years I recruited many fine agents on behalf of Room 900.

After weeks of searching, Commandant Jean Delloye, the Assistant Air Attaché, who, like myself, was devoted to helping the line, proposed a young Belgian to work for Jean Greindl. His name was Sergeant Henri Decat, then serving in the Belgian Army and a native of Louvain. He began his training under the pseudonym of Lieutenant Drew. Reports of his progress in radio and codes were sound, if uninspiring. I was present during his parachute training at Ringway aerodrome, near Manchester. He was physically tough and loyal, but inclined to boast. This may have led to his mysterious death in Belgium in April 1943.[1]

In further talks at 38 Belgrave Square, I convinced Delloye that we must build a reserve of organisers for the Brussels line. At any moment it might be necessary to replace Dédée or her father. I was introduced to Count Jacques Legrelle, a shy but charming and intelligent Belgian. He was thirty years of age at this time and a lieutenant in the Belgian forces. He was too well-known to send to Belgium and I planned that he should work in the Paris sector of the line.

Legrelle started his parachute training at Ringway in October 1942, but on one of his first jumps broke a vertebra in his back and remained in plaster until the end of the year. He recovered, and a year later, despite this injury, went overland from Gibraltar to join the organisation in Paris.[2] But many tragic events were to occur before he was fit to leave or Sergeant Decat was parachuted to Belgium.

Since the Cole affair, we had warned both agents and escapers

---

[1] 'Monday' reported the finding of his body near Rouge Clôitre in Belgium. He had been murdered.

[2] This sending of agents over the frontier by land into occupied France was known to Room 900 as 'waltzing'.

that double agents or Germans posing as airmen might be used again. But as we had already discovered in unoccupied France and through denunciations by Cole in Paris at the end of 1941, escape lines run by untrained patriots were easy game for German agents. It was difficult to keep a check on the loyalty of large numbers of helpers and whether men claiming to be R.A.F. or Americans were genuine. While both sensed the danger, neither Room 900 nor Jean Greindl's group in Brussels were adequately prepared for the attack by the Abwehr in November 1942. Using two of their operatives disguised as American airmen they set a trap for the Brussels organisation. Jean Greindl himself had foreseen this, but the defences were weak. In the same period, an escape line from Holland run by S.O.E. for their own agents was used by the Germans to destroy S.O.E. circuits in France.

After O'Leary's report on Cole in April 1942, 'Monday' had given Dédée instructions that all evaders were to be interrogated when they were first in contact with the line. The O'Leary organisation often asked for confirmation of a man's identity by radio and this became the regular practice. But Dédée and Jean Greindl had no such means of insuring that an airman was genuine. The questions supplied to them for these checks were, however, too general. Where had the man been shot down? From what station had he taken off and in what aircraft? Where was his home?[1]

These were insufficient to unmask a trained enemy agent. Later, in 1943, we prepared long and detailed questionnaires which included information about types of aircraft and the whereabouts of pubs and night clubs in London, and items of R.A.F. slang and and current flying procedures unlikely to be known to an enemy.

Most of our French and Belgian helpers knew little English, and until organising agents briefed on Air Force detail and trained in security were sent into the field, they were liable to fall into the sort of trap set for them in November 1942. Later, the improved methods of interrogation had their effect. After 1942, the Germans seldom employed bogus airmen, but relied on Dutch, Belgian, or French traitors who offered their services as 'guides'.

The tragedy in Brussels began on November 19th, 1942 when a sealed green envelope was pushed through the letter-box at the

[1] The questions were given to Dédée by 'Monday' and regularly changed. They included food prices and the airman's last meal before taking off on the raid.

house of Monsieur Georges Maréchal of the Avenue Voltaire in Brussels. Maréchal and his wife, an attractive Englishwoman, had been hiding agents and Allied Servicemen for a long time. They were great admirers of Edith Cavell and trusted agents of Dédée and Jean Greindl. Their eighteen-year-old daughter Elsie,[1] was employed to meet airmen arriving in Brussels from the provinces. After the war, Madame Maréchal was able to tell me her own story of the day which led her to terrible suffering in a concentration camp. Thinking the letter might be for Jean Greindl, she handed it to her daughter. Curious, the girl broke the seal and read the tiny slip of paper inside.

"Deux enfants pour jeudi."

Elsie gasped.

"But I don't understand—why has the message come here?"

Madame Maréchal was worried. She was already suspected by the Gestapo, and messages for her were always delivered to another address. When men arrived from the provinces, a guide named Albert Marchal[2] took them to the steps of St. Joseph's Church in the Square Frère Orban in Brussels and waited for Elsie to collect them. No such arrangement had been made for November 19th. Before there was time to take the decision to inform Jean Greindl, the door-bell rang. Outside was twenty-seven-year-old Albert Marchal, with two men dressed as Belgian workmen.

"They are here already!" exclaimed Elsie. "However did they get here?"

Marchal was bewildered. He had been expecting Elsie at the rendezvous at St. Joseph's Church and, finding no one there, had brought the men direct to the Avenue Voltaire.[3] They had been delivered to him by a 'contact' in Namur for escort to Brussels. He was also anxious. He knew no English, but there was something unusual about the two men. He confided his suspicion to Madame Maréchal, and left the house, to be arrested next day.

One of the 'airmen' who spoke English with an American accent was short and neatly dressed, the other tall, with a long, pale face.

"We are Americans in the R.A.F.," they explained. Then they fell silent. They appeared to Madame Maréchal to have hangovers.

[1] Madame Claude Courtois.
[2] Shot at Brussels October 20th, 1943.
[3] This was contrary to his instructions.

"We had a terrible party last night." The taller man got up, white in the face. "Can you show me the cabinet?"

The cabinet! This seemed to Elsie a strange expression for an American to use. Perhaps this was the only word of French he knew.

The 'Americans' could eat little.

"You don't look like Americans," said Elsie. She spoke perfect English, like her mother, and one of her tasks was to question evaders. There was a strange silence. Elsie set paper in front of them and asked them to write their names and numbers, where they were shot down and in what aircraft. They wrote slowly and they seemed nervous and irritable. Then they asked if they could walk in the fresh air, and reluctantly, when they promised to return in an hour, Madame Maréchal let them go. A request to walk in the 'fresh air' in enemy occupied Brussels was very suspicious. Madame Maréchal sent Elsie to Jean Greindl at the Swedish Canteen. Her anxieties were growing. The men wore khaki shirts and not R.A.F. blue and their behaviour was unlike that of any Englishmen she had hidden in the past. But, she reflected, she had not met any Americans.

When the girl arrived at his office, Jean Greindl studied the note delivered that morning at the Avenue Voltaire. It was written in pencil.

"Deux enfants pour jeudi."

The names of the men and the 'd' of deux' had more than a suggestion of German script. He listened to Elsie and then said quietly:

"Elsie, you must go back. Stop these men from leaving at all costs. Interrogate them carefully. Then come back. If you suspect them, you and your mother must leave the house immediately."

Meanwhile the men had returned to the house at the Avenue Voltaire. They sat sullenly with Madame Maréchal. She was surprised that Americans should talk so little.

"What part of America do you come from?"

The tall, pale man answered:

"New Jersey."

The bell rang again, and she rose to open the front door. The 'American' pushed past her and dashed towards it, while the other swung her round from behind.

He held a revolver.

"Madame, the game is up!"

The open front door revealed a grim figure in a long black rain-coat wearing glasses.

"Where has your daughter gone?"

"Where is your chief?"

"Where is his headquarters?"

Madame Maréchal fought for time, but the trap was set. Elsie walked straight into it. When she arrived home, the front door opened of its own accord. She was taken with her mother to the Gestapo headquarters.

The small 'American' laughed.

"You'd better talk, Elsie. Your mother didn't want to and something has happened to her."

Georges Maréchal, her father, was arrested when he arrived home that evening. By then, there were eight Gestapo or Luftwaffe secret police agents drinking tea (a rare delicacy) in his dining-room.

Jean Greindl watched darkness fall in the Rue Ducale. He was with Peggy van Lier and twenty-five-year-old Victor Michiels, a new recruit. There was no news of Elsie Maréchal.

"Victor, go to the Avenue Voltaire and spy things out. On no account try to go into the house unless you are absolutely certain there is no danger."

Victor, a bold young man, took the route followed by Elsie.

It had grown dark, and there was nothing to be seen or heard outside the house in the Avenue Voltaire. He watched for half an hour. There was no movement. Then he went to the door and rang the bell.

A torch flashed.

"Halt!"

Three German Field Police came from the shadows with Lügers pointing at him. Victor backed with his hands up, then decided to chance it. It was very dark. He ran a few yards. Two shots struck him as he ran. The third shot brought him down, and he lay dead in the gutter.

At dawn next day Dédée's French guide, Elvire Morelle, arrived in Brussels by train from Paris and went, by arrangement, straight to the Avenue Voltaire. There had been no means of warning her. She reached the door and rang the bell and was immediately arrested. She was taken to the Gestapo office in the rue de la Traver-sière in handcuffs and interrogated in a room with a portrait of

Goering, in a white uniform, holding the jewelled baton of a Reichsmarshall.

In this same room, the night before, the Secret Police of the Luftwaffe, reinforced by the Gestapo, had interrogated the Maréchal family. Under the portrait of Goering, the bastards beat eighteen-year-old Elsie until she was covered in bruises and unable to lie on her back for weeks. All night long the inmates of the prison of St. Gilles in Brussels could hear her heart-breaking sobs. I thought of her when, as an official of the Tribunal at Nuremburg, I met Goering in his cell three years afterwards.

The Maréchals and Elvire Morelle gave nothing away, and for the moment, Jean Greindl and the Swedish Canteen were safe.

CHAPTER 13

A Winter of Disaster

THE grim chapter which began in Brussels on November 20th, 1942, was not ended by the arrest of Dédée on January 15th, 1943 before she set out on her nineteenth crossing to Spain.[1] In a few weeks, the Gestapo struck savagely not only in Brussels, but all the way to the south. It was a concerted attack on all the lines. In February and March Louis Nouveau, Jean Greindl, and, finally, O'Leary fell into their hands.

In Brussels alone, one hundred people were arrested as a result of the Maréchal affair, and many never saw their homes again. 'Monday' and Darling reported the inevitable fear and distrust which these blows occasioned among families who had been willing to hide and feed airmen. Accusations of treachery and bad security flowed out of occupied territory from those who escaped the terror.

The loss of great leaders like Dédée, O'Leary, Louis Nouveau and Jean Greindl were more than personal tragedies. For a time, the escape movement seemed to falter and lose confidence. That it revived and made history was entirely due to the faith and courage of those who stayed at their posts. Of these, Madame de Greef, Jean-François Nothomb, and Françoise Dissart, of Toulouse who succeeded O'Leary, set a memorable example, and richly deserved the high decorations which they received.

Theirs was an example which, predictably, was not followed in certain parts of the War Office in London. The very existence of Room 900 and its contacts with underground escape lines was threatened. Langley and I were subjected to violent criticism of the potential dangers of escape work to military information and sabotage. In vain we protested that the saving of a bomber pilot's life could be as important as blowing up a bridge. The suggestion that much of the intelligence received from occupied territory had less

[1] If return journeys are included she did 36, an amazing feat.

relevance to the war than the recovery of a fully trained aircrew was curtly dismissed.

That Room 900 was not reduced to an impotent staff organisation without secret facilities owed much to the determination and persuasiveness of Brigadier Crockatt. He realised that if escape lines were allowed to continue without any direction, the dangers to security would be even greater. Other organisations responsible for sabotage and intelligence, would take pity on shot-down airmen and be tempted to organise their return.

Crockatt sought and found a degree of support in the Air Ministry. He could point, despite terrible casualties, to the large numbers who had already returned and were again on flying duties. With their aid, he was able to overcome this negative campaign. Our supervisor at the War Office, destructive at first, and determined to put up the shutters at Room 900, was by May 1943 temporarily appeased.

The security of our escape lines was a complex problem. It could be said that with more trained agents, many of the disasters of that winter could have been avoided. But working with a multiplicity of experienced agents in the field, other organisations were even more disastrously penetrated by the Gestapo during the same period.

It was a bitter conflict while it lasted. I was aghast at the cynical belief that fighting men shot down by the enemy were of minor importance to other intelligence branches. Unfortunately it was the truth. Throughout the war, Room 900 with its junior officers had to fight every inch of the way to help rebuild the escape lines.

In my depression, I met three times a beautiful auburn-haired girl, then married her in December 1942. She restored my will to fight on and to complete my part in this story. I could not but marvel at my luck. Twelve months before, I had been a mere number in a prison camp, one of the thousands whose fate lay in Nazi hands. During our short honeymoon in January events moved fast in Belgium and France.

Jean Greindl decided to send out his principal guides, Peggy van Lier, Georges d'Oultremont and his cousin Edouard. The Maréchal affair had put them in mortal danger.

They reached Paris in safety, where they said goodbye for the last time to Frédéric de Jongh. Their thoughts were for him and for Jean Greindl, their chief, left behind in Brussels to face the music.

Darling housed them on their arrival in Gibraltar, and in the first week in January, 1943, they arrived in England.

I was still on my honeymoon but Langley, meeting them instead in London, fell in love with red-headed Peggy van Lier as she stepped out of the aircraft. He married her a year later, and they live happily in Suffolk witn their five children.

Peggy was one of the luckiest survivors of the Maréchal disaster. I met her for the first time at the flat at Ebury House, 39 Elizabeth Street, near Victoria Station, belonging to my wife's aunt, where I lived and interviewed agents during the rest of the war. It was here also that my wife played her part in our organisation by providing the best wartime hospitality. Peggy had been well-described by the returning airmen. A slight, fresh-faced girl, with splendid bronze-red hair. The daughter of a Belgian businessman of Hal, near Brusssels, she was twenty, with clear-cut features and strong blue eyes. She symbolised the spirit and enthusiasm of the young people led by Dédée. I knew that she was serious and brave, but until I talked to her in London that January, I did not realise the peril she had experienced. Instead of marriage and security in Suffolk, her story might have been that of those who emerged like wraiths from the stinking corruption of Ravensbrück and Mauthausen. She was distressed at leaving Jean Greindl in Brussels and she was not consoled by her narrow escape.

I was anxious to know everything about Jean Greindl and Dédée for I had difficult decisions to take. I had cancelled the mission of Sergeant Henri Decat, the radio operator, just in time. News of the arrests in Brussels arrived twenty-four hours before he was due to be parachuted.

Peggy sat opposite me, earnest and sad.

I asked her about Jean Greindl, and she sighed.

"He was our chief. We younger people would do anything for him."

"How did you meet him?"

"I met him in 1941. He wanted to encourage resistance to the Germans. So we used to write secret notes to each other. We were planning a line to help young Belgians escape to England. Later we met Dédée and her father and agreed to help them. From the early part of 1942, Jean Greindl was diverting bags of rice and flour from the Swedish Red Cross to the escape organisation. Soon he and I were deeply involved in the work of the Line."

"We continued to use the canteen to feed poor children, but it soon became the Brussels headquarters of the line."

"What is Jean Greindl really like?" I asked. "We have only a shadowy picture of him here."

"He is slender and immaculate, but very tough. We used to call him 'Le Kas', or the 'Boss' as he was known in the Congo. He has been accustomed to command, but he is also a kind man—and," Peggy faltered, "a brave one too. His wife Bernadette and two children are in Belgium. I'm sure he will be afraid to leave them."

"But is he known to the Gestapo? Did they question you about him?"

Peggy calmly sipped her glass of sherry, then told me her own story of November 20th. She had waited with Jean Greindl at the canteen after he had sent Victor Michiels to find out what had happened to the Maréchals. When he did not return, they went to their homes. Fearing the worst, Peggy lay awake all night, but Michiels was already dead. She remembered with horror that Elvire Morelle would arrive from Paris in the early morning and go straight to the Maréchals' house in the Avenue Voltaire. But there was nothing she could do to save her.[1]

She left Hal for Brussels at nine, feeling something terrible would happen and packed a huge handbag with her toothbrush, underclothes and money.

As she spoke, she seemed to be reliving the experience.

"When I got to the canteen that morning, there was still no news. No one would risk a telephone call to Victor Michiels' family."

She volunteered to call at their house though warned that it might be a trap. The Michiels family lived in a large white house near the canteen in rue Ducale. Peggy boldly rang the bell and the door opened immediately. There stood a cadaverous man with deep-set eyes, a typical Gestapo agent.

"What do you want?"

"I've come to see Josée Michiels."

This was Victor Michiels' sister.

She was pushed into the sitting-room, where a frightened family was guarded by two Germans. To her horror, she found the key of the garden gate of the canteen in the pocket of her dress. She managed to slip it beneath the cushion of her chair.

[1] She could not leave home on account of the curfew imposed by the Germans.

"That afternoon, I was taken by car to be interrogated at an office near the Cinquantenaire.

"The Gestapo officer said to me in the car: 'You may as well know that we had to shoot young Michiels last night.'

"'Oh, but that's not possible!' I said.

"My hand went to my mouth," said Peggy. "I had claimed I had never met Victor Michiels.

"But the German seemed upset by the young man's death. He did not appear to notice my mistake. He told me to say nothing about it or things would go badly for me."

At the Gestapo office, a tall, fair woman came into the waiting-room. She showed no sign of recognition, but Peggy felt a pang of horror. It was Elvire Morelle.

Few conversations since I started my work for Room 900 brought me so close to the dangers of underground escape work. The straightforward story of this young girl caught up at the age of twenty in the toils of the Gestapo made a lasting impression. But Peggy clearly thought the risks were worthwhile. I wished that our detractors had been there to understand her meaning.

She continued calmly.

"I was interrogated by a fat, evil, rat-faced S.S. officer. I spoke in German, which impressed him. Did I really not know Victor Michiels? How did I know his sister? Why did I want to see her? Where did I learn German?"

"Did he mention Jean Greindl or the canteen?" I asked.

"No. They seemed to believe me. Suddenly, they released me. I was so surprised, I shook the German by the hand. When I had walked a hundred yards from the office, I burst into tears."

"Were you trailed?"

"Apparently not. I got in touch with Jean Greindl and was packed off to Paris next day with Georges and Edouard d'Oultrement."

I asked her about the future for Jean Greindl. She declared that he would start the line again, but after a hundred arrests of guides, shelterers and their relatives as innocent hostages, it would take time to recruit volunteers. The line had lost nearly as many of their own people as they had brought back airmen.

"What about sending a radio operator? When will it be safe to parachute him, do you think?"

"Jean Greindl is bound to be suspicious of anyone who contacts him. The links with Dédée are for the moment broken, and Dédée herself must surely be in danger."

"Can you give me any password or sign I could give the man who is going to be dropped? Something that would make it clear to Jean Greindl that you have arrived here? That it must have come from you?"

Peggy thought for a moment.

"Before I left Belgium, I gave each of our group a little medal made for our local church, Notre Dame de Hal. I have still got some of them. If they were to show these, he would know they came from me."

When Peggy had gone, I thought over what she had said. If Jean Greindl was in danger, he must be persuaded to come out. Sending Decat was a risk, but at least we could communicate directly with Brussels. It might be possible to influence Greindl to choose a successor and escape before it was too late.

During the first week in January 1943, I saw Georges and Edouard d'Oultremont, who gave me much the same account of the situation in Brussels and Paris. Georges had been a prominent guide for the Jean Greindl organisation. He was a cheerful, laughing character. He had replaced Andrée Dumon, alias Nadine, who since August had been in the prison of St. Gilles at Brussels. His gaiety and high spirits were extraordinary. Edouard, his cousin, a tall, handsome military person, also escorted airmen from Brussels to Paris. Soon after his arrival, he joined the Allied Forces in Britain, where he served throughout the war. Georges was later to play a memorable part in the story of our operations in France.[1]

When I had spoken to these survivors of the Brussels catastrophe, I decided that Decat, also known as 'Lieutenant Drew', should go to Belgium without delay. At last the moment, another young Belgian known as 'Lieutenant Boeuf', who had been trained as a courier, was chosen to accompany him. I imagined that in restoring the line to Paris, Jean Greindl would be glad of closer communication with Britain and I know that he welcomed these plans and felt he could start again.[2]

The parachute operation for the two men had been approved,

[1] See Chapter 20.
[2] Conversation with his widow Baronne Jean Greindl after the war.

the dropping zone near Waterloo agreed, and they were to be dispatched in the third week of January 1943; but on January 15th, the Germans delivered their second blow.

I shall not forget the telegram from Madrid.

"Saturday from Monday. Deeply regret Florentino reports Dédée arrested with three pilots at Urrugne. Imprisoned Villa Chagrin at Bayonne. Attempts being organised for her escape."

Dédée had been a vital flame. We had known that she was in danger. But it was hard to believe that one who had performed so many miracles should have been taken. The moment, dreaded for so long on both sides of the Channel, had come. The worst thing of all was to be chairborne in London and unable to do anything but wait for news. It was at this time that I resolved that, should the opportunity occur, I would myself go back to France. But that was to be many months afterwards and in very different conditions.

Slowly I was able to piece together the story of Dédée's capture. With her father, now nearly sixty, she had moved to another flat in Paris at the Rue Vaneau, south of the Seine. Here quiet, short-sighted Frédéric de Jongh would sit stamping forged identity cards and organised the reception of airmen from Brussels, while he waited for his daughter's return from her crossing to Spain. On the evening of January 13th, 1943, with her father, and the three airmen, Dédée left Paris for Bayonne. She had at last persuaded him that he was doomed and he must leave for England. Since the Maréchal affair, all was quiet in Brussels and the Paris organisation was under control.

"He left Paris with a heavy heart," she told me, years afterwards. "He hated the thought of leaving me."

"In my turn, I was afraid for him, I felt I could better face the dangers of my mission if I knew he was safe."

But at Bayonne, Madame de Greef told them that the plan to take Frédéric de Jongh to Spain was impossible. For days there had been torrential rain, and the Bidassoa was in flood. It would mean the extra five hours' march to cross a suspension bridge. At Monsieur de Jongh's age, such a journey in bad weather was too hazardous. Madame de Greef persuaded him to stay at her villa at Anglet and wait until the rains had gone. Dédée would take the men over alone and return for him. So she set off on her last journey, having brought over one hundred and eighteen men since her first arrival at San Sebastian in 1941.

Her father was bitterly disappointed, but they never saw each other again. The road from St. Jean de Luz to the farm at Urrugne was a river of mud and in all her adventures, Dédée had never seen a storm of such violence in the mountains. They reached the farmhouse, where Dédée and Florentino hurriedly conferred. Florentino decided not to attempt a crossing on that black, tempestuous night, and returned to his home at Ciboure, hoping that the party could leave the following evening.

Next morning the storm had subsided, though a cold grey mist covered the mountains. About midday, the sound of a car was heard and as it drew closer to the farmhouse, one of the pilots rose and drew his sheath-knife.

"The Gestapo!" he cried, and everyone laughed.

Then Dédée saw through the window the field-grey uniforms of German police. She motioned the men upstairs, but it was too late. The door burst open, and ten Germans invaded the kitchen, covering the group with rifles and machine pistols.

Dédée, Francia Uzandizaga and the three pilots were led into the courtyard, where they stood shivering while the farmhouse was searched from cellar to lofts.

"Where is the fifth? Is he hiding here?"

No answer. But Dédée knew they meant Florentino.

"You will talk, my friends. You will talk."

As the rain began to fall again, the group started on the two-hour march to Ciboure and over the bridge to St. Jean de Luz. They were in single file, with their hands above their heads and five gendarmes with rifles on either side. Dédée thought of diving over the bridge into the estuary below, but it was low tide. At dusk they were in the town prison.

Why was Dédée arrested?

It was impossible to get any clear information at the time. At first, I supposed that the Gestapo had uncovered the whole organisation in the south under Madame de Greef and linked this with their arrests in Brussels. This was not correct. Madame de Greef and her husband survived the whole of the war and were still in operation at the end. The Gestapo seem never to have realised Dédée's true significance, though they were hunting high and low for her father in Paris.

On the evening of January 13th, Madame de Greef was certain

that something was wrong. She had spies everywhere, at the local telephone exchange and in the bars of St. Jean de Luz. Before the party arrived from Paris, she learned that some of the families in the town who hid airmen for her were being watched by Gestapo agents. The latter wore the same kind of tie so that they could recognise each other. But the man who actually betrayed Dédée was a humble Spaniard, who had been employed at the farm, and he sold her for money. During the night before their arrest, Dédée, Florentino and the three airmen sat before a fire in the farmhouse kitchen to dry their clothes. Darkness had fallen, when a dog barked outside. Francia was agitated. She told the others not to move and sent her small boy to see what it was. He returned and spoke to his mother in Basque language.

Francia, still frightened, said to Dédée:

"There is someone at the door who knows you and who knows that I am helping you to get men to Spain."

The door opened, and the Spanish farm-hand entered. Dédée was not pleased to see him. She had once employed him as a guide, until she suspected him of stealing from her rucksack and dismissed him. Why should he now return to the farm? When Florentino had left for his home at Ciboure, she remained worried at this incident. But there was nothing to do but wait for the storm to subside.

She was sharply reminded of the Spaniard when the gendarmes invaded the farm. They had demanded to know the whereabouts of the fifth person, evidently Florentino. Who else could have known that there had been five visitors at the farm?

Today, the Spaniard remains the chief suspect. But he has disappeared. At the time of the liberation of France, he escaped to Spain. It has emerged, too, that one of the agents of Madame de Greef, whose responsibility was to warn her of danger through her faithful agent, Jean Dassié, supervisor of the telephone exchange at Bayonne, suddenly took fright that evening and fled to Paris.

Fortunately, a Red Cross visitor known as Madame 'X' recognised Dédée in prison, and sent to Dassié the agreed message of disaster:

—"La petite cousine est malade"—which he passed to the organisation.

From the Villa Chagrin prison at Bayonne, to which she had been moved, Dédée smuggled out the pitiful message:

"Les enfants ont parlé et dit tout ce qu'ils savent."

She meant the airmen with whom she had been arrested. They had been told by the Gestapo that if they did not co-operate, they would be treated as spies. One of these men gave way. He disclosed to the Gestapo the name of the family who had hidden him at Bayonne. It was that of one-armed Jean Dassié, a veteran of the First World War, who had exposed himself to every danger by sending messages through the Bayonne switchboard.

From the last week in January, Madame de Greef, Albert Johnson and Jean-François Nothomb who became Dédée's successor, under the pseudonym of 'Franco', made fruitless attempts to rescue her. They made their plans in the Bar Gachy in Bayonne, opposite the prison, where the proprietor was a friend of Madame de Greef. They first tried to get Dédée out in a large soup-container, but the Germans suddenly removed her by car to the Gestapo office in Bordeaux, returning her the next day.

Next, they bribed a plumber who visited the prison to force open the ventilator of her cell. They hoped that she could escape through this into the courtyard and reach a home-made rope ladder thrown over the outer wall of the Villa Chagrin. But Nothomb, climbing to the top at night with the aid of grappling-hooks, saw there was a twelve-foot inner wall.

The prison was poorly guarded, mainly by Frenchmen, and there were only three Germans. For their next scheme, Nothomb and Johnson planned to dress in the stolen uniforms of German officers, enter the prison and engage the remaining German guard in conversation while his two comrades were entertained in the Bar Gachy. They hoped this would give Dédée time to struggle through the ventilator, drop into the courtyard and dash through the gates. But on February 3rd, the day arranged for the escape, when the plumber came to force the ventilator he discovered her cell empty. Dédée had been moved to another prison, the Maison Blanche at Biarritz. Madame de Greef was still ready to take any risk before the Gestapo discovered Dédée's true identity. She had given her name as 'de Tonga' and this appeared on her cell door.

Like the Villa Chagrin, the Maison Blanche was not well guarded, but before another escape plan could be made, Jean Dassié of the Bayonne exchange was arrested at home with his family. After further interrogation, the airman who had revealed the name

Dassié to the Germans was taken by them through the streets of Bayonne and pointed out the house where he had been concealed after arriving from Paris on the morning of January 14th. This led the Gestapo to believe that the headquarters of the escape line in France must be in the south. They made the airman take them along the route he had followed that fateful evening to Urrugne.

Dèdèe soon realised that the Gestapo were hot on her father's trail. They believed him to be the chief of the line. She therefore told them the truth, that she was its chief and that she had started it—She abandoned her story that the line was directed from Bordeaux and that she was a guide or courier, named 'de Tonga' living in the region. With this alibi in mind, she had dyed her hair black, but her own was fair and it was beginning to show through. When the plumber entered her cell, he reported she was 'grey-haired'. She was taken with Jean Dassié and confronted with the airmen. For the one-armed Frenchman who had hidden them, it was hopeless, but neither he nor his wife and sixteen-year-old daughter would admit anything. They were beaten, tortured, and later deported to Germany but they never talked. At the end of the war, they returned to France where, after a few days, Jean Dassié died of his sufferings and his wife sometime later.

Madame de Greef, with characteristic energy, bicycled round Bayonne, warning her helpers. She succeeded in saving Robert and Yvonne Lapeyre, two loyal agents of the line, just before the arrival of the Gestapo. With the assistance of Albert Johnson, they escaped safely to London, where I met them and heard the details of Dédée's arrest. By February 6th, Johnson and Nothomb resumed the line to Spain and the flow of airmen.

The Gestapo soon ceased their enquiries in the Bayonne region, but they remained sceptical of Dédée's story that she was the real chief. It was now too late to save her. The last sight of her was at Bayonne station when, handcuffed, she was seen walking with the Dassié family to the train for Paris. Over the window of their compartment the Germans had fixed an iron grille.

This was the end of Dédée's marvellous career but not of her legend. She survived the horrors of concentration camps and though she has suffered in health, has continued to follow her profession as a nurse. She is recognised as one of the great heroines of the Second World War. She has been fêted and decorated by all the

Allies. But she remains unaffected and faintly amused by all these honours.

What made her so brilliant an underground leader?

Like her father, she did not see war itself as glorious, but, unlike him, she lived to realise that the sacrifices were not in vain. Her motives were uncomplicated. She saw in the Allied airmen she was saving the instruments of victory over the Nazis.

Her second great contribution lay in the example which she set to other young people. She and her friends were full of youthful scepticism, many were only teenagers. But they had a cause and a faith and she continued to inspire them even when she was gone. And it was her story that led others to carry on her work, for the line was broken and mended many times before the war was over.

A fortnight after Dédée's arrest, I decided to continue with the plan to parachute Decat and 'Lieutenant Boeuf' to Jean Greindl in Brussels. The operation was risky, for no one knew how much the Germans had discovered about Dédée.[1] At Room 900, Langley and I discussed this anxious problem. We feared that we were sending our first Belgian radio operator and his companion into a trap.

"From the latest message from Jean Greindl, all is quiet in Brussels," I said.

"Ominously quiet?"

"Perhaps, but we have taken all precautions. The men have an address where they can hide. They will have no direct contact with Greindl until they know he is safe."

"How will he know which night to expect them?"

"He has given us, through 'Monday', the B.B.C. message to send on the French news service."

"When is the next opportunity?"

"Tomorrow. It is nearly the end of the moon period. I feel they should go. If we have radio contact, we may be able to persuade Greindl to leave Belgium. Besides, he needs money and moral support."

So, on a rainy January night, I saw the two young Belgians at the flat in St. James's Street and gave them their final briefing. They

[1] She was interrogated nineteen times by the Secret Police of the Luftwaffe, by the Gestapo twice. These organisations were enemies. The Luftwaffe sent her to Germany to spite the Gestapo—this may have saved her since she became 'lost' in the concentration camp system (Dédée to the author, January 11th, 1969).

were to be at Jean Greindl's orders, and to maintain communications with London and Paris. I gave them their false identity cards and they recited their cover stories. Each of them took half of 500,000 Belgian francs for the organisation in their money belts.

Finally, I gave them the precious medals from Notre Dame de Hal, as reminders to Jean Greindl of Peggy van Lier.

The rain was still falling as we left the flat in a khaki-painted Humber driven by a girl in uniform. I was more nervous than the two young Belgians. They were excited by their adventure but, for my part, I felt the responsibility for their lives. War is dangerous, especially behind the enemy lines. What is inexcusable is not to feel for the safety of others. We drove fast through the blacked-out countryside to a 'resthouse' for agents on the outskirts of Godmanchester. Here we waited tensely for the weather report. A night and a day passed, and on the second evening the weather over the dropping-zone near Waterloo was reported fine.

As they were to be dropped 'blind'—without a reception committee—my chief anxiety was that they would not reach the safe address, or that it would be compromised. Decat carried his wireless set, a shortwave transceiver, weighing about thirty pounds, in a small suitcase. I wondered how his cover story would stand up if he were stopped in the early morning.

At ten, on the night of their departure, I drove with the two agents (or 'Joes' as they were known to the R.A.F.) to the 'special duties' aerodrome at Tempsford, ten miles east of Bedford. I sat with them and the crew of the Halifax from 161 Squadron R.A.F. which was to take them on their mission, drinking coffee until midnight. After helping them equip with parachute, revolver, money and identity cards, I saw them into the Halifax. Then, standing back from the roar of the engines, I saluted as they took off into the night.

But the train of disasters had not finished and I shall never forget that winter. A fortnight before the arrest of O'Leary, I had to break the news to Peggy van Lier and the d'Oultremonts of the arrest of Jean Greindl. Only a few days after landing in Belgium, Sergeant Decat, in Brussels, came up on the air with the message:

"Nemo (Jean Greindl) arrested sixth of February."

Then all was silence. We never heard from Decat's set again and until the news of his death in April 1943 there was no record of him.

If only Jean Greindl had listened to his friends' entreaties. Dédée had seen him in Paris at her father's flat in the rue Vaneau a few days before her own arrest in January, and she has told me of their conversation.

"You realise that there are nine chances out of ten that you will never come out of this alive?"

'Nemo' had said nothing. He had simply smiled. But Dédée knew that he had accepted his fate.

In Brussels he saw his wife, who had just had her second child, a son. He saw her in secret, fearing deperately that he might be followed. She too has recalled to me their poignant meeting as she pleaded with him:

"You are going to stop and escape to England before it's too late?"

"No, I'm going on till I find my successor. Dédée has persuaded me."

"It is sheer madness."

Jean Greindl shrugged his shoulders, and in a moment he was gone. Next day, he heard of Dédée's arrest.

The end came for him on Saturday, February 6th at the Swedish Canteen. Why he risked going back after the Maréchal disaster, we shall never know. But a month before, in Paris, Dédée had warned him: "Don't go near the Canteen."

The radio silence from Decat prevented me from getting further details until the end of February, when Jean Greindl's brother, Albert, one of the guides to Paris, escaped from Brussels to England. On February 14th, he crossed the Pyrenees, guided by Florentino, with a party of American pilots. I met him at Euston when he arrived and, by special dispensation of the R.V.P.S., took him to the Goring Hotel near Victoria. It was already eleven o'clock at night, but it was vital that I should have the latest news, and we discussed Jean Greindl's fate.

Albert Greindl was a dark young man, polite and apparently unruffled by his narrow escape. He had managed to salvage many incriminating documents from his brother's flat just before the Gestapo arrived. Though he was pale, shaken and tired, he was anxious to tell me what had happened.

"Of one thing I am certain, the line will be carried on. But—" his quiet voice faltered—"I ask you to do everything to save my brother's life."

There was nothing I could promise to do.

"How was he arrested?" I asked.

"He went back that morning to the canteen. He knew it would be all up with him if he stayed much longer, but he felt for his wife and family and he refused to leave until his successor was chosen. We pleaded with him, but he would not go. He used to call himself 'the last of the Mohicans'—the name seems tragic now."

Albert Greindl continued:

"I have found out a little, because one of the friends who was arrested with him has been released. He told me that they could hear the clatter of plates as the children began their meal in the canteen below my brother's office. Suddenly, the door opened. Four men with automatics stood over them.

'German Secret Police. No one move.'

"A small, dark, greasy man in a heavy raincoat, with his hat pulled down over his eyes, waved his automatic.

'At last, "Nemo", we've got you'."

The Gestapo drove Jean Greindl to their office at the rue Charles Legrelle. There he had a terrible shock. His wife was there too. They took each other's hands for a moment, and she held her rosary before him.[1]

It was midnight when I left the Goring Hotel and walked down Ebury Street to my flat. Was there nothing we could do to save Jean Greindl? His brother had said that the line would continue, but for the next few weeks there was complete silence in Brussels. Jean-François Nothomb, Dédée's successor, came through to Spain on March 20th with a party of airmen from Paris, but he could only confirm the worst.

A week before, Albert Edward Johnson had made his last journey over the frontier to Britain. After a magnificent contribution to Madame de Greef's group at St. Jean de Luz, he had been arrested by the Germans, in company with her, a week before. But a brilliant exercise in blackmail by Madame de Greef, who threatened German officers with exposure for possessing black market food, saved him.

But Johnson's time had come. He had crossed the Spanish frontier fourteen times, and 122 Allied servicemen owed their liberty to him.

---

[1] Information from Baronne Jean Greindl. She was released after a short period.

CHAPTER 14

Gibraltar Meeting

BARON Jean-François Nothomb, son of a Belgian senator and novelist, doggedly continued the Comet escape line. He was twenty-three and already had achieved marvellous success. He had worked with Dédée since October 1942, and a year later had completed fourteen journeys across the Pyrenees with Florentino and parties of airmen. When Johnson was forced to escape in March, he was joined by an assistant, Max Roger.[1] Between July and October 1943, they were bringing over as many as twelve men a month. Nothomb and Max Roger brought through two parties in July, four in August, and six in September. Nothomb himself made crossings on July 24th, August 13th, September 2nd and 28th, and October 6th.

On all these occasions, he had talks with 'Monday', who was deeply impressed by his faith and endurance. But by October, 'Monday' thought that he was exhausted and that he should be persuaded to come to England. He telegraphed me from Madrid suggesting a daring plan. He would smuggle Nothomb in the boot of his car across the Spanish frontier at La Linea, for a meeting in Gibraltar. With the fate of Dédée always in my mind, I was determined to prevent another tragedy. I hoped that I could persuade Nothomb to return with me to England though the line was independent and I could not give him orders. I replied to 'Monday' I would be in Gibraltar at the end of October.

I knew that Nothomb would have painful messages about Dédée's father. In April, Frederic de Jongh, hoping for news of his daughter, had stayed on at the rue Vaneau in Paris under the name of M. Moreau. He was still taking men across Paris from station to station for the journey south. He had abandoned all thought of escape to England. Judging from 'Monday's' letters, his grief at the

[1] Executed 1945.

166

arrest of Dédée and his elder daughter, Suzanne Wittek, had aroused in him reckless activity. Nothomb, Madame de Greef, and Darling implored him to leave for England. They warned him that his arrest might mean the death of his daughter, that his frequent appearances at the Gare d'Austerlitz and the Gare du Nord were imprudent. He sought by all means to save his daughter's life, though little was known except that she had been moved to Fresnes prison, in Paris. Through Nothomb, he sent pathetic messages to me, asking M.I.9 to intercede for her through a neutral power, and for this purpose he made a hazardous journey to Switzerland, where he saw Victor, at the end of March.

The possibility of intercession by a neutral power for Dédée and Jean Greindl was often discussed, but invariably condemned. Had there been many German agents to exchange, something like the modern negotiations with the Soviet authorities might have been undertaken. But in 1943, the Gestapo had captured large numbers of secret agents working for the Allies, and mediation would have been futile. M.I.9 regarded such démarches as highly dangerous to those in enemy hands since it would recognise their guilt as spies and saboteurs. The family of Jean Greindl in Belgium had asked Marshal Mannerheim of Finland to intercede with Goering. I have seen the correspondence which, in the circumstances of his death, could not have saved him, and had he lived, the chance that Goering would have pardoned him was slight. For Dédée, whose real significance remained in doubt, such representations might have led to her execution.[1]

Throughout the spring, the indomitable figure of Frédéric de Jongh alias Monsieur Moreau was seen in Paris. The Gestapo, though he did not know it, had already found him. Once again, despite warnings from 'Monday', the organisation had been penetrated. In April 1943, he acquired a new guide for the route from Brussels to Paris, who called himself Jean Masson, a Belgian from Tourcoing, on the French frontier.[2] Subsequent reports described him as about twenty-five, small, with untidy blond hair. Only his prominent round blue eyes made him unusual. Frédéric de Jongh felt he would do well as a guide. The controls at the Belgian frontier

---

[1] She changed identities with another girl in a concentration camp. Had a special search for her been made, this might have been discovered.

[2] See Chapter 25.

at Quievrain and Blanc-Misseron had been greatly strengthened. Jean Masson claimed to have many contacts in the region, and he produced a quantity of blank frontier passes with the stamp of the Feldgendarmerie for Lille. It was from Lille that Madame Raymonde Coache of Asnières, after her husband René's escape to Britain, was guiding airmen to Paris by train. At the rue Vaneau, Frédéric de Jongh discussed the new man with his friend, Robert Aylé, who lived nearby at No. 37 rue de Babylone. They decided to try him.

On May 15th, they sent Jean Masson to Brussels to collect airmen, bring them to the Gare du Nord in Paris and then pass them to Nothomb. Raymonde Coache had been meeting parties from Brussels at the station since the middle of April 1943, and transferring them to the Gare d'Austerlitz for the journey south. This I knew from M.I.9 interrogation reports.

A few days after he was sent to Brussels, Jean Masson arrived with no less than seven airmen. He was met at the Gare du Nord by Frédéric de Jongh and Robert Aylé. They were full of praise for this success and asked him to continue working for them. But they enrolled a most dangerous traitor. At the beginning of June, Jean Masson called at the rue Vaneau.

"Be ready for June 7th," he said. "I have a large party from Brussels. You will need all your helpers to take them over on arrival in Paris."[1]

Jean Masson's tone, it is said, was peremptory and nervous. Unsuspecting, Frédéric de Jongh arranged to send Raymonde Coache and another girl to Lille to meet him with his party. With Monsieur and Madame Aylé, he would be waiting for them at the Gare du Nord at half-past four on the afternoon of June 7th. The new guide arrived punctually from Brussels at Lille. He took the airmen to a waiting-room, where he met the two French girls. Raymonde Coache took one of the airmen to a small café opposite the station to wait for the train to Paris. There was a hand on her shoulder, and the airman raised his arms above his head to face a drawn revolver. The other girl, Madeleine Bouteloupt,[2] had got into the train with her charge, a small Cockney airgunner. She thought that Coache had missed the train. The door was flung back, and two men in civilian clothes stood in front of her.

[1] Conversation with Madame Robert Aylé in 1954.
[2] Died in 1945 as a result of her detention at Ravensbrück.

"Papers!"

She handed one of them her identity card.

"Madeleine Bouteloupt," the man said slowly, and put the identity card in his pocket. "Come with me. German Secret Police."

She was led to a compartment at the far end of the train where a blonde German policewoman searched her, then struck her across the face.

In Paris, Frédéric de Jongh left his flat for the last time as the clock struck four. Monsieur and Madame Aylé were waiting for him on the platform. They were pleased with the new successes of the line. Jean Masson arrived with the remaining five Englishmen and one American airman and advanced towards them. He was smiling broadly, and they all shook hands. Seconds later, they were surrounded by at least twelve policemen. All, including Jean Masson, were handcuffed and pushed towards the headquarters of the Railway Police. They were then taken to the infamous Gestapo office at the rue des Saussaies.

Madame Aylé described the scene to me in her apartment at the rue de Babylone after the war. As they waited to be interrogated, a door opened and Jean Masson stood there smiling. He was no longer handcuffed, and he spat on the floor in front of them.

"Well, you fools," he sneered.

Madame Aylé felt his face to be the most unpleasant she had ever seen. It was repellent in its triumph. Jean Masson laughed and bowed contemptuously. Then Robert Aylé rose and struck him with his fist and the traitor shrank from him. The door opened again, and they were forced up dark steps to an office, where three grim figures at a desk awaited them. Jean Masson, whose real name was Desoubrie, was tried and executed for treason at Lille after the war. His work for the Germans cost Frédéric de Jongh, Robert Aylé and many others their lives.[1]

Nothomb told 'Monday' that, eight days later, he returned from Spain and opened the door of the flat in the rue Vaneau with his own key. On the table in the sitting-room were blank identity cards and a pen. The window was still open. At first, he thought that Frédéric de Jongh had just left, so he changed his clothes and searched everywhere for a favourite tie, but could not find it. Then he went into the kitchen and saw a saucepan on the stove. Lifting the lid,

[1] See Chapter 25.

he saw vegetables covered with mildew, and in the cupboard found rotting fruit. He suddenly realised the truth, stuffed the false papers and all the money he could find into a suitcase, and fled from the flat.

He was able to make contact with his lieutenant, Max Roger, and next morning they went to No. 37 rue de Babylone, home of the Aylés. They turned at the top of the staircase to see the seals of the Gestapo on the front door. They decided to take an even greater risk. They went back to de Jongh's flat in the rue Vaneau. But as they went up in the lift, they heard German voices on the fourth floor, where the schoolmaster and his daughter had lived. By a miracle the lift stopped only at the fifth floor, to save electricity in war time. With Max Roger, Nothomb stood motionless, not daring to move, expecting the Germans to climb the stairs and take the lift. Then with a sigh of relief, he heard their footsteps descending, and both men made their escape.

Such was his determination to help his old friend and save what could be saved, that Nothomb actually returned to the flat the same evening. He removed the seals from the door and searched secret hiding places for money and papers. He managed to remove a number of identity cards and papers undiscovered by the Germans. I had this particular action in mind when I recommended him to Crockatt for the D.S.O. for which, as a lieutenant in the Belgian Army, he was eligible, and which he received after the war.

Before I visited Gibraltar in October, the news of the death of Jean Greindl had brought great sorrow to London. Shortly after her father's arrest on June 7th, Dédée was moved from Fresnes and sent to Brussels to appear as a witness at the Luftwaffe court-martial of Elvire Morelle, her principal French guide, arrested at the Maréchal home in the Avenue Voltaire. In a waiting-room at the Palace Hotel in Brussels where the trial took place, she saw Jean Greindl for the last time. He was thin and pale, and months of imprisonment and torture had aged him. She was full of admiration for his cheerfulness and courage in the short conversation which they were able to snatch.

The characters of these two great Resistance workers were in contrast, but they understood each other well. Dédée was indifferent to fear; she scoffed at indecision, and she was always eager to do battle. Jean Greindl, a married man with a family, was more tranquil.

He was more sensitive of the dangers, but he faced the consequences with resignation.

Dédée was astounded at her own good fortune. Although she had told her interrogators the truth to save her father neither the Gestapo or the Secret Police of the Luftwaffe were prepared to believe that so young a girl could be the real architect of this underground conspiracy. She was therefore confident that she could withstand interrogation, and her fears were for others.

Jean Greindl and his friends of the Swedish Canteen had already been condemned to death in April, and despite the entreaties to Goering there was little hope for them. He was occasionally allowed to see his wife for a few minutes, when he was brought blindfold to the Gestapo office. He was able to tell her that he was imprisoned in the artillery barracks at Etterbeek, a suburb of Brussels.

Throughout the summer, there were rumours of a reprieve, but in August a letter from Marshal Mannerheim suggested little hope. Goering was intent upon revenge for the escape of so many Allied airmen, and smarting under the defeats inflicted on his Air Force. But it was not Goering and the Luftwaffe secret police who brought death to Jean Greindl. On September 28th, Nothomb, on his arrival in Spain, told 'Monday' a story of tragic irony.

On September 7th a large force of Allied bombers and fighters attacked the Brussels area. A single bomb fell on the artillery barracks at Etterbeek. It went straight through the roof of the stables, where Jean Greindl was imprisoned, and burst on the floor of his cell. For a few days, there was no news, and then a curt message that he was dead. On September 10th, his father and brother-in-law[1] were granted permission to recover his body. It was evident that he had died instantly, and the body was filled with splinters, as if the bomb had burst at his feet.

On September 12th, permission was granted for the body to be removed for burial, which took place at his family home at Zellick.

In London, I had to break the news to Albert Greindl. That his brother, who had done so much to save Allied airmen, should have been killed by them seemed a cruel act of fate. He consoled himself with the thought that he had been spared further imprisonment and execution. It has been said that Jean Greindl was deliberately imprisoned in the barracks as an obvious military target. He

[1] Baron Jean-Charles Snoy et d'Oppuers.

was the only one of the group from the Swedish Canteen who was held there, probably because the Germans attached enormous importance to his arrest.

For his companions, the end came on October 20th at six a.m. when, accompanied by the Austrian chaplain, Monseigneur Gramman, they were taken to their execution. Their names were: Eric de Menten de Hornes, Jean Ingels, Albert Marechal, Henri Rasquin, Ghislain Neybergh, Gaston Bidoul and Robert Roberts Jones. They were shot at the Tir National, the rifle range of Brussels, where Edith Cavell had paid the same price on October 12th, 1915.

A week after their execution, I arrived in Gibraltar with a senior officer from M.I.9 at Beaconsfield, Colonel Cecil Rait.[1] My purpose was to discuss the future of the Comet line with Nothomb and Darling, and my plans for the collecting of evaders during the invasion period. This, with the code-name 'Marathon', covered France, Belgium and Holland.[2] There was also the more immediate and exciting project of the new series of sea evacuations which Langley had prepared. This was to be organised by a team of French-Canadians working with patriots in Brittany under the code-name 'Shelburne'. It was originally named by me after the eighteenth-century Whig Prime Minister, but turned out to be the name of a town in Canada and seemed appropriate.[3]

The necessary arrangements had been made for me to meet 'Monday' and Darling, and for Nothomb to be smuggled into the fortress of Gibraltar. Since he was referred to as 'Franco'—his pseudonym in the Comet line—in telegrams between Room 900 and Madrid, confusion arose when messages containing this name passed through uninformed hands. For one absurd moment, a political section imagined that a meeting was about to take place with General Franco, the Head of State.

The operation was a dangerous one for 'Monday', expert cutter of diplomatic red tape that he was. He had first to bring the dark young Belgian, obviously of military age, in his car from Bilbao to Madrid, and then all the way to Gibraltar. The Spanish police might easily stop him and question him about his passenger. The

[1] M.C.
[2] See Chapter 20.
[3] See Chapter 19.

crossing of the frontier at La Linea also involved considerable risk. It would be necessary for Nothomb to get into the boot of the car, unobserved, when they were a few miles from the Rock. Then would come a hot, uncomfortable ride in total darkness until they reached the Spanish frontier post. Bent double in the boot of the Bentley, Nothomb would have to wait until 'Monday' had shown his diplomatic papers and parleyed with the Spaniards before being driven to Darling's office. If the operation failed, it would evoke a diplomatic row, but 'Monday' had already had success with this operation. It was in this way that O'Leary had entered Gibraltar for his conference with Langley in April 1942.

Rait and I were to fly in civilian clothes in a K.L.M. aircraft with a stop at Lisbon.[1] There was a regular drill for military people flying to Portugal and onwards. They were required to pose as civilians, carrying their uniforms in suitcases. There was not much risk of trouble in Lisbon, where the Portuguese were accommodating to anyone with a British passport. The main danger lay in the flight in an unarmed aircraft. A K.L.M. machine, with the actor Leslie Howard aboard, was shot down on its return from Lisbon on June 1st, 1943.[2]

There seemed to be a good deal of unnecessary nervousness in the War Office about my journey. My passport described me as a 'barrister', with a photograph of a youthful person in a check suit wearing an obvious regimental tie. I had long ago abandoned the pseudonym of 'Captain Newton' and other fanciful names, but I discussed with Room 900 what should be my story were I kidnapped by the Gestapo in neutral Lisbon. I eventually decided to say that I had come to defend a British businessman on a charge of fraud in Portugal, though the Gestapo would have had very little difficulty in establishing my real identity.

We flew from Bideford in Devon, with a party of men dressed all alike in Army trenchcoats. Before we took off, an improbable incident occurred. As we sat in a Nissen hut which served as a waiting-room, a Special Branch detective, stepped forward.

"Major Neave!" he shouted.

I rose and followed him, amused by the disclosure of my true identity, and entered an office. A security officer shook my hand. "A

---

[1] K.L.M. planes were on charter to B.O.A.C. at this time.
[2] After this, flights to and from Lisbon were made at night.

man called Windham-Wright[1] has been phoning you frantically from Room 900. He told me to tell you that Brigadier Crockatt is very angry about the Lesbians' false teeth and wants you to ring before take-off. You seem to have funny sort of agents in M.I.9."

It was already one o'clock in the morning and the aircraft was about to leave, but there was just time to get through to Room 900. I heard Windham-Wright's anxious voice.

"Crockatt rang just as you left," said Windham-Wright apprehensively. "He's had a bill for £70. They have both ordered complete new sets of teeth on your authority. Crockatt says he won't pay, and he's furious with you."

The aircraft engines were revving up outside, and the security man was chuckling.

"You tell Crockatt that these women risked their lives to save airmen and he should pay. I'll take all the responsibility. After all, they might have been sent to a concentration camp where the Nazis would have stolen all their teeth."

I put down the receiver and ran to the aircraft laughing, but I was not allowed to forget the dentist's bill for a long time. In the autumn of 1943, two elderly French ladies who had hidden evaders in their Paris flat escaped to England. On arrival in London, they both complained of toothache. They were also dissatisfied with the lodgings which I found for them in Kensington. I listened to them patiently. They threatened to write to Members of Parliament and their acquaintances in the British aristocracy. In view of their obvious bravery—and also to keep them quiet—I had agreed that M.I.9 should pay for their new dentures. It seemed a just reward for courage and the bill was paid.

The aircraft, with its blacked-out windows, rose into the night. The heat inside was stifling and it was difficult to sleep, but at dawn we landed at Lisbon. I felt sure that something would happen to me at the airport. Although it was nearly eighteen months since my escape, I was still apprehensive about controls. A Portuguese customs officer examined my passport with a sceptical expression. Then he opened my suitcase, and under the thin disguise of civilian shirts studied my Sam Browne belt and other articles of uniform. He handed back the passport.

[1] Major P. J. S. Windham-Wright, M.C. and Bar, joined Room 900 in the summer of 1943.

"Good luck, Major Neave, and a pleasant journey."

My Lisbon story was a cheerful anti-climax, and a few hours later the plane, carefully hugging the neutral Spanish coast, landed at Gibraltar.

Darling, our man on the Rock, was waiting for us. For months he had brought imagination and humour in his newsletters signed 'Sunday' to the confused mixture of gossip and fact which was poured out to him by new arrivals in Gibraltar. As soon as they set foot on British soil, agents, helpers, servicemen and other less defined characters told him their stories. Often, it was his task to sift blood-curdling rumours of treason and inefficiency intermingled with intrigue, financial scandal and inter-organisation disputes.

Darling had his own system of disguising the correct names of people he was writing about by using witty and complex nicknames. I spent many hours trying to solve the puzzle of his letters. Had the Germans captured any of them they would never have made any sense. His humour was unique. 'Monday' also rose above protocol, with his own incisive style. In this triangular correspondence between Room 900, Madrid, and Gibraltar, I joined them both in poking fun at our superiors and the Germans. While disputes and complaints about the operation of escape lines were unavoidable, we nonetheless managed to avoid some of the unnecessary strife which occurs in all secret intelligence organisations. As Commissioner of Criminal Organisations at Nuremburg in 1945, I was to be astounded at the evidence of the bitter rivalries between the Gestapo, the S.D., the Abwehr, and other enemy counter-espionage services which we were fighting.[1]

'Monday' had already arrived at Gibraltar and Nothomb, badly in need of rest, was hidden in one of Darling's five flats. My first meeting with him was relatively public. We had decided that in view of his personal gallantry, he should be received by the Governor of Gibraltar, Lieut-General Sir Noel Mason-MacFarlane, who would give him messages of encouragement to pass on to the Comet organisation. On the morning after my arrival, Nothomb was driven into the courtyard of Government House. We assembled in a large, spacious room overlooking the Bay—'Monday', Darling, Nothomb, Colonel Codrington of the War Office (known in our

[1] See Chapter 25. S.D., the Sicherheitsdienst or Security Service, and other secret police branches are described.

correspondence as 'Fish Paste') and myself. It was a sombre occasion, for I sensed that Nothomb, like Dédée and her father, was determined to go back to occupied territory after our meeting. Mason-MacFarlane was a tall, white-haired man with a long, intelligent face. He was dressed in a bush shirt and khaki shorts, for it was a very hot day. I could see that Nothomb was slightly surprised to be received in this uniform. He was in a green tweed so familiar to illegal passengers from France.

I studied this young Belgian aristocrat who had nearly rivalled Dédée in the number of men he had brought to freedom, and whose conduct at the time of Frédéric de Jongh's arrest showed him to have nerves of steel. He was dark, rather Latin looking, and though pale and strained, very sure of himself. I knew that, like the others, he had an unshakeable faith in his mission and he would see it through to the bitter end. Mason-MacFarlane clearly sensed the occasion, and he spoke to his brave visitor from outer darkness in excellent French:

"On behalf of His Majesty the King and the Belgian Government I am asked to convey our gratitude for your magnificent work. Please give this message to all members of the Comet line and with it the sincere thanks of the Allies. Tell them that the day of Liberation will soon come."

I looked out of the window for a moment at the dazzling waters of the Bay of Gibraltar. We would remain safe on British soil, but Nothomb must soon return over the mountains to the unknown perils of his mission. Surely he must not go back. I must convince him that he was certain to be arrested if he stayed too long. In the afternoon, I talked to him in the stifling flat where he was hidden. He was dreadfully exhausted. Boils which had broken out on his neck were giving him pain, but he was inflexible in his decision to leave Gibraltar the following day.

I asked him about his reception by the Governor.

Nothomb replied in his polite, firm voice:

"It was delightful, mon Commandant, and so informal I did not expect the Governor in shorts."

"He meant all he said to you."

"It is wonderful," said Nothomb, "to be here in this great fortress, if only for a day. It has given me great hope. I feel for the first time that the forces of evil will not prevail."

We spoke for a while of the Comet line.

"I am sending someone to help you in Paris. He will have to come overland as he injured his back during parachute training. We call him 'Mr. Lewis'."

This was Legrelle and Nothomb frowned.

"It still remains a Belgian line? You are not trying to control it?"

"No. You must give the orders. We provide money and communications. We have always respected that since the days of Dédée."

But he was not convinced. He would wait till he met 'Mr. Lewis' on his next visit to Spain. It was painful to both of us to talk of Dédée and her father, and his account of the arrest and death of Jean Greindl was heart-rending. I could see that he was sick and tired. But how could I prevent him going back? I did my best, but I had no authority to order him to stay in Gibraltar.

"Franco, you are ill. Come to England and rest for a few weeks. We can return you to France later." I hoped that Max Roger would replace him, reinforced by Legrelle. He looked straight at me with his fine, dark eyes and I felt almost ashamed at this suggestion. I saw in them that same look I had seen months ago in the face of the girl who had guided me through the streets of Annemasse in April 1942.

Nothomb was scornful of the danger.

"No," he said quietly. "This is my work. This is war. There are scores of pilots to bring out, and I am responsible. I promised Dédée and her father that I would carry on. When I have found a successor, then I will talk about taking a rest."

If courage be the mistress of virtues, faith also gave him determination to continue.

Next morning, I watched him climb into the boot of 'Monday's' car. I followed in another car, with Darling, through the controls at La Linea and drove into Spain. A few miles out, we stopped and sat for a while at a café. It was difficult to be cheerful as we drank a bottle of wine. At sunset, I shook hands with him and watched 'Monday' speed along the dusty road towards Madrid. I felt certain I should never see Nothomb again. But he had three more journeys to make across the frontier before disaster overtook him. These were on November 6th and 27th, and December 23rd. In all, he made seventeen journeys and was personally concerned in the return of two hundred and fifteen men.

I returned to London very worried and unhappy, for I knew that Nothomb had not chosen his successor. I realised that he was suspicious of any British attempt to control Comet and I had no intention of doing so. Since the arrest of Jean Greindl and the mysterious death of his radio operator, Decat, in April 1943, we had been without direct communication with Brussels. The situation in Paris was also disturbing and obscure. I decided to send Legrelle to Spain, and if Nothomb agreed, for him to go to Paris. I was certain that Legrelle, now recovered from his accident, would prove a discreet and capable organiser in Paris though he could no longer parachute. Since it was impossible to drop him in France, I radioed Darling to make arrangements for him to be smuggled from Gibraltar to 'Monday' to meet Nothomb when he next arrived in Spain.

At the end of October, I went with Legrelle by train to Pembroke Dock, where an R.A.F. squadron of Sunderland Flying Boats was stationed. We arrived there in the late afternoon, and looked out over the waters of Milford Haven. The Air Force were much intrigued by us. They found it difficult to understand why an Army Major should be living on their station, accompanied by a quiet blond man in civilian clothes introduced to them in the officers' mess as 'Mr. Lewis'. If only I had been able to explain to them what 'Mr. Lewis' was going to do for them.

The following day, Legrelle took off for Gibraltar, where Darling reported his safe arrival. We had succeeded in smuggling agents in the boot of 'Monday's' car on more than one occasion, but the La Linea operation could not be tried too often. This time we tried another scheme. After a few days at Gibraltar, Legrelle was brought from his hiding place in Darling's flat, and put aboard a naval craft at night. This was one of the special ships, like *Tarana*, used for clandestine operations along the Spanish coast. Innocent in appearance it was armed to the teeth. After a short voyage, a rendezvous was made at sea with a Spanish fishing vessel, to which Legrelle was transferred. After thirty-six hours of discomfort, he was landed at Valencia, on the southern coast of Spain, disguised as a fisherman. He was taken to the British Consulate, and from there driven to Madrid, where 'Monday' hid him for two or three days.

On his next journey to the frontier zone, 'Monday' took Legrelle by car to San Sebastian, where they met Nothomb. 'Monday' reported their meeting to me at the time, and Legrelle has since described it.[1] 'Monday' introduced Legrelle as Mr Lewis, and Nothomb replied:

"I don't want an Englishman in the line, and I don't want any English influence."

The atmosphere of suspicion was increased by the fact that I had given Legrelle a code with which to communicate with Room 900. Comet had no wireless in Paris and relied on couriers to San Sebastian. It was essential, if anything happened to Nothomb, for Legrelle to be able to send messages in code. Owing to the injury to his back, he could not cross the frontier except in emergency. It was a delicate position. On the one hand, I had agreed with the Belgian Sûreté and Nothomb that, as in the days of Dédée, the line should remain in complete Belgian control. On the other hand, it was my responsibility (and the Belgian Sûreté agreed with me) that we must at all costs maintain the line. The Belgians had made many cruel sacrifices, but it was essential to find replacements for the leaders in the event of their arrest.

I was very disturbed at the suggestion that we were trying to deceive the members of Comet by sending Legrelle, armed with his own code, and I replied to 'Monday's' letter, urging him at all costs to reassure Nothomb when he next visited Spain. At the end of the year, 'Monday' replied that the trouble had been avoided. Legrelle and Nothomb had become good friends. Nothomb had at first suspected that he was to be 'supervised' by Legrelle, who was the older man. It was also decided that the considerable quantity of money which I had given Legrelle should not be the subject of a separate account. Nothomb has since confirmed that they worked together in mutual confidence. The mists of misunderstanding over this incident have been dispersed by Madame de Greef, since the war:

"We received many suggestions and much advice from M.I.9 which were very useful, but never direct orders. Until the end, the line was our own affair and no one else's."

While M.I.9, through Room 900, were in control of the operations of other escape organisations in France, they stuck to their bargain with Dédée when she first came through to the British Consulate at Bilbao in August 1941.

Legrelle arrived safely in Paris and established his headquarters

[1] Rémy, *Réseau Comète*, volume III.

at a flat in the rue de Longchamp, and the line continued. But the Gestapo were closing in on them both. On January 18th, 1944, on his return from Spain, Nothomb went straight to this flat. He has since said that as he walked to the door he had a sharp presentiment of danger, but he rang the bell. The door was opened immediately, by a Gestapo agent.

"How are you, Franco? We are pleased to meet you at last."

The evening before, the same thing had happened to Legrelle, after only four months in Paris.

From information which we received down the line, it was clear that Jean Masson was at work again and we had lost these two valuable agents. When Nothomb was taken to the Gestapo head-quarters at the rue des Saussaies he found Jean Masson was there. Although they had never met, Nothomb realised who it was.

"I am Jean Masson,"[1] said this young man with the prominent blue eyes. "It is I who has betrayed all of you."

He seemed to speak with a kind of insane pride. When Nothomb was released, very ill, from the concentration camp, he was present at the trial of Jean Masson, in his real name of Desoubrie at Lille. The tables were turned but Nothomb, who entered the priesthood shortly afterwards, forgave him. Jean Masson, who was illegitimate, had never known a proper home and had no doubt, like other traitors, been tempted by the financial rewards of the Gestapo.[2]

A strange surprise awaited Nothomb at his interrogation when an elegant Gestapo official came up to him.

"Well, Franco, why did you take the seals off the door at the rue Vaneau?"

"I have not been there for months."

"Don't lie. You had better think this over."

Nothomb stared at the German, and then his face broke into a smile.

"What are you laughing at, Franco? Things look bad for you."

"Nothing."

The Gestapo official was wearing the long-lost favourite tie for which Nothomb had searched at the rue Vaneau after Monsieur de Jongh's arrest in June 1943.

---

[1] He later used the name 'Pierre Boulain'. See Chapter 21.
[2] See Chapter 25.

PART IV

WOMEN AGENTS

CHAPTER 15

Mary Lindell

ONE of the most colourful agents in the history of Room 900 was Mary Lindell, Comtesse de Milleville. She was a woman who combined a passion for adventure with extremely blunt speech. That she did not have more success was due to a number of misfortunes. But she was responsible for the return of several men, including two survivors of the famous raid on Bordeaux harbour, known as the 'Cockleshell heroes'.[1]

I first heard of her on July 27th, 1942, when a telegram from Barcelona arrived at the War Office. I stared at it that morning in astonishment. A woman dressed in French Red Cross uniform, with a British passport in the name of Ghita Mary Lindell, had arrived at Barcelona from France having crossed the frontier by train as a 'stranded governess'. She had told our man in Barcelona that the American Vice-Consul in Lyon had obtained her visas for travel to Spain and Portugal, and an exit permit from the Vichy Government, to whom she had declared that all her papers and money were stolen. She was an 'important member of the French Red Cross' and had arrived in Barcelona 'in uniform with numerous First World decorations.'

"Crikey!" said Langley. "This is fantastic. Read on."

The telegram continued. In 1940 Mary Lindell had driven Captain James Windsor-Lewis, Welsh Guards,[2] from Paris over the demarcation line to Limoges. She had been arrested in Paris in 1941, court-martialled for helping escapers and imprisoned in Fresnes for nine months. She was now offering to return to France and start a new organisation with a radio operator, and would shortly arrive in London from Lisbon.

Our first reactions were wary. We sent for Windsor-Lewis'

[1] G. E. Lucas Phillips, *Cockleshell Heroes*, Heinemann, 1956.
[2] The late Brigadier James Windsor-Lewis, D.S.O., M.C.

interrogation report. He had been captured at Boulogne in May 1940 with a serious wound in the leg, and taken to hospital in Liège. This was during that period of confusion in occupied France that I remember so well. It brought back to me my own stay in hospital in Lille and unsuccessful plans for escape. In those days, the escaper had to rely on his own initiative and hope that he would fall among friends. Windsor-Lewis certainly did both. A nurse in the hospital helped him to get civilian clothes. Though his wound was not healed, he walked out of the hospital, undetected, and hid with a family in Liège known to his nurse, who put him on a train to Brussels. He was very English-looking, handsome and military. He spoke no word of French, and he had no contact with any escape organisation in Brussels or anywhere to stay the night. He found a café and managed to order a meal, but the owner, seeing his weak condition, was anxious to help him. Two Belgian policemen were called.

I was struck at this stage of the story how as early as July 1940 the Belgian police, instead of handing him over to the Germans, sent him to a hospital in the Schaerbeek district of Brussels. This was the same district where Frédéric de Jongh had lived with his family. It must have been at this time that the schoolmaster and his daughters were wondering how they could aid the Allies. Several months later Dédée, by her arrival at Bilbao, established their line to Spain.

In Britain, we should not forget that ordinary Belgian and French people, even in the first dark hours of occupation, were ready to take these risks.

Windsor-Lewis, in Belgian worker's clothes, looked as if he had just come from the Guards depot at Pirbright. But he was a determined, resourceful and attractive man, and he found another sympathetic nurse in the hospital at Schaerbeek. She treated his wound and put him on a train from Brussels to the Belgian frontier. After some difficulty with frontier guards on the train, he took the road to Paris, thumbing a lift from a German Army lorry. At the United States Embassy in Paris, he said he was an American who had lost his passport and belongings in the bombardment of Ostend. Embassy officials, not surprisingly, refused to believe him, but as they were about to turn him away, an Englishman, Colonel Cecil Shaw, appeared. Astonishing as it may seem, Shaw, married to an American wife, was still living at the Ritz Hotel, under German occupation, and engaged in various underground activities.

Shaw introduced Windsor-Lewis to Mary Lindell, who lived, as she still does, at the rue Erlanger under the name of the Comtesse de Milleville. In June, Mary had started to ferry sick children across the demarcation line on behalf of the French Red Cross in her car. She now proposed to drive Windsor-Lewis to Limoges in unoccupied France, a journey of several hundred kilometres. He remained hidden in her flat for thirteen days while she obtained the necessary pass from the Germans to convey the latest 'sick child' to safety.

When I recall her subsequent adventures during the war, I was not surprised to hear that she had called at the office of Count von Bismarck in the rue St. Honoré for the necessary pass and a permit for eighty litres of petrol. She told the great-grandson of the Prussian Chancellor:

"I have to fetch a poor little child from the other side of the border and bring it to Paris."

"It is in order for the Red Cross to go," said von Bismarck affably, and turning to a secretary, "Kindly make out the necessary papers for the Comtesse."

The papers included permission for Mary to be accompanied by a mechanic.

Windsor-Lewis told M.I.9 how Mary had driven him off at five o'clock in the morning in the direction of Etampes. All went well until they met, by the side of the road, a young German pilot in flying kit, who stopped them and asked where they were going.

Mary wanted to go to Orleans, but the German wanted to go to Chartres. So Chartres it had to be. She drove in that direction, the pilot beside her and the 'mechanic' sitting in the back. The pilot apologised for his poor French and asked if she spoke English.

"Yes, a little," said Mary cautiously.

The German laughed.

"That's good, I haven't had an opportunity to learn French yet, we have been too busy bombing England. This morning I nearly did not come back."

"What happened?" asked Mary.

The pilot declared that his mission had been to bomb Bristol but there was a heavy mist and no bombs were dropped. As he was making for home, his aircraft was nearly shot down by Spitfires. It was losing height and, as he was unable to reach the aerodrome, he and his crew had baled out.

Even in the extraordinary story of Mary Lindell, there were few
such crazy incidents as this.

Suddenly, the German turned and looked behind him.

"Who is that?"

"My mechanic."

"He doesn't look very intelligent."

"No, you're right. He's a little simple-minded," she replied.

She drove to the Kommandantur at Chateaudun, where she was
introduced to the Kommandant who thanked her for her kindness
to the pilot and offered her a thick wad of petrol coupons.

"With our compliments," said the Kommandant, bowing. "They
can be used at either French or German pumps."

She hoped that this was the end of her suspense, but the exuberant
young airman wished to be taken to the aerodrome near Chateaudun
where he was stationed and of which he was inordinately
proud.

"Look at these wonderful aircraft!" he cried.

He asked her to drive round the perimeter of the aerodrome, with
Windsor-Lewis seated uncomfortably in the back, and admire
the rows of German bomber and fighter aircraft.

After a quarter of an hour's study of enemy aircraft and a drink
in the officer's mess, the pilot directed her back to the main gate,
where he said goodbye. As he did so, Mary saw that Windsor-
Lewis' shirt sleeve had rolled up, revealing the badge of the Welsh
Guards tattooed on his forearm.

But the amiable German did not notice.

"For God's sake, sew your damn shirt buttons on in future,"
said Mary as they left the aerodrome.

She drove to Cloyes, a small town near Chateaudun and stayed at
the Hotel St. Jacques. There they spent the night, though the hotel
and its dining-room was a German officers' mess. As the proprietor
led them to their bedrooms, he made a strange remark.

"I'd like to point out, Madame, that your rooms are at the end
of the wing, and should you get nervous in the night, you can always
climb out of your window and go through the garden to the river
bank where a boat is moored."

The hotel, to which I have often been, has a charming garden and
orchard leading to the river Loir which, rising near Illiers, beloved
of Marcel Proust, joins the Loire at Angers.

"We've come here to sleep, not to swim," replied Mary.

Early next morning, they drove a hundred and fifty miles without difficulty to Ruffec, not far from the demarcation line. At Ruffec, a market town near Angoulême, Mary marched into the Kommandantur with Count von Bismarck's pass and demanded permission to cross the line the following morning.

"Very well, Countess," said the town major deferentially, clicking his heels. "I will inform the N.C.O. in charge of the guard to expect you."[1]

At the demarcation line the guards did not even ask Windsor-Lewis, her 'mechanic', for his identity card. They drove to Confolens and Limoges, where Mary brought him a ticket for the train to Marseille. At the station, they said goodbye. They were to meet again in London eighteen months later. The rest of the Windsor-Lewis story was typical of the early history of escape from France.

He spent two weeks at Cap Ferrat with Lord and Lady Furness, still living on the Riviera. Mary had given him an Irish identity card in Paris and after making three attempts to cross into Spain, he applied to the Eire Embassy in Vichy and obtained an Irish passport. He was now able to travel to Portugal as a 'neutral' and take a flying boat to Poole and the train to London. All this happened in the gay days of 1940. By the time Mary escaped to England in July 1942 life had become much more dangerous in unoccupied France, soon to be under the control of the Gestapo. Windsor-Lewis, like many other escapers, fought with great distinction to the end of the war.

When I had studied these reports, there were still a number of questions in my mind.

I could well believe that Mary Lindell bore a charmed life. Her escape, with an exit permit from Vichy, would be a simple matter for her, though it sounded like the adventures of a lady of title in the wars against Napoleon rather than 1942. The American Vice-Consul in Lyon who had given her papers as a 'British governess' was a contact of O'Leary. But we still had to be cautious. What was the truth about her arrest by the Gestapo and imprisonment in Fresnes? Why should she want to go back to France? Two days later, I was with Langley at the flat in St. James's Street, when

[1] Barry Wynne, *No Drums No Trumpets*.

there was a ring at the front door. I went down the dark flight of stairs and opened it.

She was standing in the sunshine, dressed in the royal blue uniform of the French Red Cross, with a row of French and British decorations. She was at this time about forty-five, but looked considerably younger. She had dark brown eyes and chestnut hair, and her face was finely proportioned. Her figure was slight, and her uniform well-cut. She seemed very feminine, but in her expression there was an intensity, a stubbornness which somehow did not fit her smart appearance.

As soon as she spoke, I understood why. She was very definitely English and used to getting her own way.

"I have received several messages at my hotel asking me to meet Captain Langley," she said, commandingly, "Does he happen to be in?"

Her tone was peremptory and English in every inflexion. I might have been the butler answering the door. She looked me up and down. Then she laughed.

I was shaken, but said:

"Let me introduce myself. I am Airey Neave of M.I.9. We are expecting you."

She shook my hand heartily and with me climbed the stairs. I could think of nothing to say to her except that it was a nice old house, which seemed a rather lame opening. She walked with determination into Langley's sitting-room, and we sat down. Despite her gruff manner, she was still beautiful, and I could see why she had been able to fool Count von Bismarck and other susceptible Germans.

The conversation started badly. Langley asked her not to see Windsor-Lewis, for we had a strict rule that people arriving from occupied Europe whom we had not interviewed should not discuss their adventures with escapers.

Mary frowned.

"I have already seen him, of course," she said.

I could not help thinking that this was to be expected after all the dangers they had seen together.

We began to question her. She had been born in Sutton, Surrey and when the First World War came, volunteered as a nurse. Tiring of being a V.A.D., she crossed to France and joined the French

Red Cross, where she served in field hospitals with great distinction for the whole of the war. Since 1919, she had lived in Paris with her husband and three children.

I noticed that she wore two English decorations in front of her French Croix de Guerre, loudly proclaiming her nationality. She gave an immediate impression of fearlessness, independence and not a little arrogance. Although she had lived for so long in France, she had abandoned nothing of her English background. Her contempt and disdain for the Germans was enormous. I asked about her arrest by the Gestapo. If she really wanted to return to France—and she might still be a potential agent—it would be some months before it was safe to send her back. How much did the Gestapo really know about her?

She told us that at Christmas 1940, her flat was searched by the Gestapo, who fortunately missed her British passport and a .38 pistol lying on the top shelf of her daughter's wardrobe. The following day, they came again and took her for questioning. They appeared to know about Colonel Shaw of the Ritz who had put her in touch with Windsor-Lewis.

She denied all knowledge of him. They then asked her a number of very awkward questions.

She told them she was very sorry but she knew nothing about him.

"But you had the gentleman in your flat," said the Gestapo.

"It is the first time I've heard of it," she said, "Was he handsome?"

"Yes," said the Gestapo. "Very handsome."

"What a pity I missed him. He sounds just my sort."

She wondered if she had been betrayed by someone in the American Embassy, for no one else could have known all the names. After a long series of interrogations, she was court-martialled. Apparently the American Embassy made arrangements for a lawyer to represent her. She gave us a description of her sensational trial with a mixture of humour and anger. She still talks of it today with disdain.

The President of the court-martial had begun the proceedings by saying:

"You will be given a fair trial . . ."

"How can I have a fair trial if my defending counsel has not arrived yet?"

"The court will adjourn for a quarter of an hour," said the President.

"Later," said Mary, "my counsel came rushing in. He had been held up on the Paris metro!"

She was charged with assisting the escape of British officers and insulting the German Army. She was found guilty on all counts and sentenced to eleven years' hard labour. When the President rose to announce sentence, Mary again intervened.

"I said to him, may I please have it explained to me when and how I insulted the German Army?"

"The President looked at his notes and told me, 'Your words were: "These swine are going to arrest me.".'

"Are you not aware of the meaning of the word swine in English? It does not mean 'pig'. It means a wild boar, an animal of courage and ferocity. Therefore in my context I was praising the German Army, not deriding it."

The President was baffled. Her counsel took the opportunity of offering the President her 1916 citation for the Croix de Guerre. The President handed it to a German officer who sat with him, who promptly stood up and saluted her. The President then ordered the interpreter to read the citation to the court, whereupon, to Mary's greater embarrassment, the entire court stood up and saluted. After this Chaplinesque performance they retired, and on their return reduced her sentence to nine months' solitary confinement.

As we listened to her story, Mary began to laugh loudly.

"I found this completely ridiculous," she said, "so I remarked to the court, 'Just sufficient time for me to have a baby with Adolf.'"

There was a horrified silence. Her counsel nearly fainted and the interpreter went white.

"What has the prisoner said?" demanded the President.

Fortunately the interpreter hesitated. At that moment her lawyer could be forgiven for arriving late, for with great courage he rose and said, 'The accused said that in the circumstances she considers the sentence fair'."[1]

When she told us that her favourite author was Kipling and her heroine, familiarly enough, was Edith Cavell, I could quite believe that all this had really happened.

[1] Barry Wynne, *No Drums No Trumpets.*

"And you still want to go back to France after all this?" asked Langley.

"That is what I am here for."

"Have you contacts in France who are still safe?"

"Yes, a large number."

When she had gone into the bright sunshine in St. James's Street, I turned to Langley.

"Well, what do you think of that?"

Langley gasped: "I've nothing to say at the moment, except that I want a very large whisky and soda."

Mary Lindell was the first woman specially trained by Room 900, and she returned to France by Lysander in the third week of October 1942. After our sensational meeting at St. James's Street in July, I was placed in charge of her training. We had, with some misgivings, agreed that she should return to France.

I asked her what had happened after her court-martial in Paris, anxious to discover whether the Gestapo had traced her to England.

She completed her sentence at Fresnes prison in November 1941, disappeared from Paris and got in touch with the American Vice-Consul in Lyon, an old friend of escape organisations. He arranged for Spanish and Portuguese visas for her to travel as a governess on her British passport. But she was still on the run. As a result of other arrests in Paris, the Gestapo again began a search for the Comtesse de Milleville and instructed the Vichy police to do the same. This sounded serious enough, but did not entirely rule out the chances of a successful mission.

Mary was well aware of the dangers of returning to France and that it would be impossible for her to operate from Paris. Her best chance was to establish an escape chain to Spain from an area as far from the scene of the interrogation by the Gestapo as possible. She had many contacts at Ruffec near Angoulême, where she had obtained permission from the Germans to cross the demarcation line with Windsor-Lewis two years before, and there was no reason to think she was suspect there. It was known to us that a number of R.A.F. and American pilots had been shot down in this part of France and it was therefore agreed that Ruffec should be the headquarters of an organisation to develop a new route to Spain. Since she was well known to the American Vice-Consul in Lyon, she should use him as a means of contact with Cartwright and Victor in Switzerland.

During the next few weeks, I made a careful assessment of her qualities. I had no fear of her ability to argue her way out of any difficulty. Today in the rue Erlanger, at the flat from which she set out on her famous journey with Windsor-Lewis, her contempt for authority is undimmed, her spirit, despite much suffering in concentration camps, undaunted.

I did not doubt her capacity, as one accustomed to obedience, to shepherd evaders past railway officials or sentries. My fears were of a different kind. I felt that her return might endanger her own life and those of others. Yet she was not the only agent of our organisation, known to the Gestapo, who volunteered to return to Occupied territory. Georges d'Oultremont, who had escaped the débâcle in Brussels at the end of 1942, returned to Paris in 1943, to reinforce the Comet line.[1] There was also René Coache of Asnières, their radio operator in Brussels, who had escaped the Gestapo, and others who made more than one mission of this kind before the end of the war.

It was not easy to resist Mary's enthusiasm and fearlessness, though she did not endear herself to the Establishment in London by her outspoken behaviour. She went through a 'crash' course in coding with great aplomb and application, and took a course in night landing operations with Lysander aircraft. This involved the training of agents in the laying out of flare paths and signals to the pilot. It needed considerable discipline on the part of 'reception committees', many of whom had only the most primitive equipment. Agents had to be taught how to place the flares correctly and pass on these procedures to others in the field. Since Lysanders were fitted to hold only two passengers, they also had to be trained to warn the pilot of approaching enemy fighters.

Her incompatibility with Tom Groome, who had by now joined O'Leary, compelled me to search for another wireless operator. Mary wanted to take a Belgian whom she had befriended in Lyon before his escape to England, but it would take six months to train him as an operator. In view of the number of airmen reported in hiding, her mission became urgent, and time would be required to secure his release from the Belgian Army. Room 900 had no other

[1] See Chapter 20.

recruits in training as radio operators and the only possible plan was to send the Belgian by parachute at a later stage. She would have to rely on couriers to Spain and Geneva to maintain contact with Room 900.

I felt the greatest sympathy with her annoyance at having to leave without a radio operator. She did not spare M.I.9 with her pungent comments. But she knew the need to act quickly. There were other reasons for her urgent departure for France. 'Monday' had already noted the first signs of Gestapo counter-measures in Brussels and Paris, which were soon to bring catastrophe to Dédée and Jean Greindl and the German occupation of the unoccupied or Free Zone was only a month away. I therefore hoped that with Ruffec as her headquarters, she would be secure until we had radio contact with her.

Langley and I discussed with her a false identity, but she insisted that she should continue to work under cover of her Red Cross uniform. She had her French identity card from the First World War as a nurse in the name of Ghita Mary Lindell and a French Red Cross card forged by M.I.9 in the name of Ghita de Milleville. She wanted both these cards to use 'according to circumstances'. We did not know that the Germans had arrested others in Paris who had worked with her in 1940, had set up a search for her and condemned her to death in her absence in the name of de Milleville. Had we done so, her mission might well have been cancelled and the return of the two surviving 'Cockleshell heroes' would probably not have been possible.

CHAPTER 16

The Commandos

ON October 20th, 1942, I gave Mary Lindell a final briefing at St. James's Street and at dusk drove with her to the R.A.F. Station at Tangmere, where Lysanders of 138 Squadron operated to France on moonlit nights. Like many such journeys it was an unhappy experience for me. Though I did not doubt that Mary had the boldness and capacity to lead a réseau, the thought of sending a woman on such a dangerous task was unpleasant. That women made admirable organisers, especially in escape work, was never in doubt. It was the possibility that they would be subjected to the most degrading methods of torture, if captured, which distressed many intelligence officers of my generation. It was an attitude which many women agents scorned as Victorian, and perhaps it was. Those, who, like Mary, fell into German hands, showed conspicuous courage, and of S.O.E.'s many women agents, three were awarded the George Cross, two posthumously.

I was also at a turning-point in my emotional life, for I had become engaged to the girl with auburn hair who had first rescued me from my post-Colditz depression. I could not tell my fiancée that plans were being discussed for me to accompany Mary to France in the Lysander. S.O.E. had agreed that Mary should fly to one of their reception committees near Limoges, but Langley and I disliked the idea of sending her to the landing zone without escort. Who was to accompany her? The 'conducting officers' used by S.O.E. were primarily concerned with the training of agents. They remained with them until they were safely aboard the aircraft but never flew on the actual mission. Since Room 900 had only two officers at this time, we acted as our own 'conducting officers' when our few agents left England.

By 1942, the rule was also firmly established in the War Office and S.O.E. that staff officers directing secret operations from London should not risk capture by the enemy. This particularly applied to heads of sections with knowledge of the names of agents, their missions, and the overall plan of underground activity. Room 900, with only two such officers, was responsible for escape work in the whole of north-west Europe. The capture of either of them, since they shared all the secrets, could not be contemplated. We were relieved from our anxieties next day, by the decision of S.O.E. to send one of their own agents to France in the same Lysander. My duties were to be confined to seeing Mary safely off at Tangmere. I have no hesitation in recalling my deep sense of relief, but the question recurred when we started sea evacuation from Brittany in 1943.[1]

Though angry about the Belgian wireless operator, Mary showed no trace of anxiety on the journey. Cool and relaxed in her blue uniform, she seemed to look forward to her mission. When we reached Tangmere, the Squadron Commander took us to the briefing room. The reception committee organised by S.O.E. was at a point sixty miles south-east of Limoges and fifteen from the small town of Ussel. She was to break contact with them on arrival and make for Ruffec. The Frenchman who travelled with her was to join the S.O.E. group responsible for the reception. Since we had strict security rules to prevent agents of different services knowing too much about each other, I asked her not to discuss her mission with him. Characteristically, she thought this ridiculous, until she found that the S.O.E. agent had been given the same instructions.

Before take-off, there was a moving moment when she was introduced to the pilot of her aircraft. He was a Canadian, a slight young figure, and a battle of Britain hero, and with several decorations. He took both her hands in his and said:

"I just wanted to say thank you for going over there. I can't tell you what we feel about it, but all the boys have tremendous admiration for what you are doing."

These simple words gave expression to the whole purpose of our work. A few minutes later, I was equipping her with her parachute harness, Mae West and an inflatable dinghy. Then we walked to the

[1] See Chapter 19.

all-black Lysander standing silhouetted against the moonlit aerodrome. There was something mournful and sinister about its
appearance. Within minutes, the engine roared and the aircraft
rose like a great bird into the sky.

Mary Lindell was on her way back to France and a few hours
later, 138 Squadron and S.O.E. reported her safe arrival. I knew that
her intention was to make for Limoges, using her French Red Cross
card as Ghita de Milleville. Her reason for this choice of identity was
that she was 'so well known in hotels in most parts of France', which
I did not find reassuring. For the next few weeks there was little
news of her, though a message reached us from Geneva that she
had contacted the American Vice-Consul in Lyon, with whom it
had been arranged through Geneva that she was to receive additional
funds. Shortly afterwards, she was badly injured in a road accident.
Accompanied by a French guide she left Lyon to return to Ruffec,
deciding to cross the demarcation line at Blois, on the river Loire.
A place existed on the river where it was possible to walk across a
sunken lock only a few inches beneath the water. But when she
reached it, two German soldiers could be seen across the river, their
bayonets glinting in the winter sun. As this crossing place was only
guarded on occasions, there was no alternative but to wait for them
to be withdrawn.

For a second reconnaissance, Mary obtained a tandem bicycle
and pedalled with her French guide towards the river. They had
only travelled a short distance when a car struck them from behind.
The Frenchman was hurled into the air and Mary on to the car's
radiator. They were both severely injured, Mary being knocked unconscious. With the greatest difficulty, patriotic villagers carried
her and the Frenchman to a remote farmhouse. Mary was placed
on the farmer's bed and, since she appeared to be dead, he began to
dig a grave for her in his garden. Fortunately, a friendly chemist
arrived, pronounced her alive and refused to sign a certificate.
In the greatest secrecy, she was removed to a hospital in Loches,
where it was found that she had five fractured ribs, a serious head
wound and injuries to her leg and arm. For many days she hovered
between life and death, attended by a valiant Dr. Martinez. But
the local Gestapo, having heard that 'an English agent' had been
seriously injured, came to interrogate Dr. Martinez, and later
arrested him. Three of their men searched the hospital from top to

bottom, but the staff had hidden their patient in the cellar behind a pile of wood.

Shortly after Christmas, with the aid of her son, Maurice de Milleville, Mary returned, though still very ill, to Lyon. The accident displayed her courage and toughness, but it came at a most unfortunate time. On December 1st, 1942, the British submarine *Tuna* sailed down the Irish Channel towards the French coast on operation 'Frankton'. The order, signed by Vice-Admiral Lord Louis Mountbatten, Chief of Combined Operations, on October 30th, 1942, was for a small group of Royal Marine Commandos to paddle up the river Gironde in canoes and place limpet mines on shipping at Bordeaux. The submarine was to take them within nine miles of the mouth of the river.

"Thus was put in train one of the minor operations of the second great war which in boldness of conception, care in planning and courage in execution, was not excelled by any other of its kind, and one that a German officer described as 'the outstanding Commando raid of the war'."[1]

Aboard the submarine were twelve Royal Marine Commandos, whose task was to man six canoes. They were divided into two Groups, A and B. The leading canoe (*Catfish*) in A Division was manned by Major H. G. Hasler[2] and Marine Sparks, and their target area was the west bank of Bordeaux harbour.

Before the raid began, M.I.9 discussed with Combined Operations the possibility of putting the crews in touch with an underground escape organisation to find their way to neutral territory. They had otherwise no choice except to be taken prisoner for they could not return to the submarine, which left the area after the canoes were launched. Until this time no aircrew or Commando even on a special mission had ever been given the location in occupied territory, let alone a contact address, or an escape line. It was considered far too dangerous to give such details to any operational troops, who inevitably risked capture and interrogation. The reason was a sad one. Late in 1941, a returned airman had given addresses of French families to a friend in his squadron, but the friend was shot down and killed. The addresses were found on his body by the Germans, who traced the families and shot them.

[1] C. E. Lucas Phillips: *Cockleshell Heroes*.
[2] Lieut.-Colonel H. G. 'Blondie' Hasler, D.S.O., the Atlantic yachtsman.

Despite the terrible consequences of this breach of security, it seemed to Langley and myself that there were exceptions to the rule in the case of airmen or soldiers specially trained for a secret mission. It was decided that Major Hasler and his Commandos should be told that on completion of their mission, they should make for the town of Ruffec, where they would find an organisation equipped to get them back. While it was the responsibility of Room 900 to protect the security of their agents, this decision seemed to me to have the worst of both worlds. I did not see how those of the party who escaped could be certain of making contact with Mary or her friends in the Ruffec area. Nor had she been warned that the Commando raid in the river Gironde was taking place.

On December 8th, the canoes were launched into the night and, keeping good formation, paddled into the Gironde about three a.m. They were at this time some forty or fifty sea miles from Bordeaux harbour. After a series of disasters, they were reduced to two canoes, including Hasler's, the others having disappeared in the darkness. On the first day, they lay up without being spotted by the Germans, and on the second night continued up the river for a further twenty-five miles. They lay up on land for the second day without being detected. On the third night, they made further progress and by six-thirty a.m. were in the waters of the river Garonne, on which lay Bordeaux itself, only twelve miles away.

Hasler had intended to make his attack on the enemy ships the coming night (December 10th), but they had not gone far enough up the river to enable this to be done with any chance of withdrawal afterwards. Moving round a bend of the Garonne at about ten o'clock, they saw with a thrill of anticipation what they had come so far to hunt—two large ships moored at the quayside on the eastern bank. They waited among the reeds during the day of the 11th, as Hasler made his plans to attack that night. He decided that he would himself in *Catfish* work up the western bank of the main docks some three miles away, and he gave orders to Corporal Laver that *Crayfish*, the second remaining canoe, was to make along the eastern bank towards Bordeaux east docks.

At nine-fifteen that night, the canoes slid quietly out through the reeds. Hasler could soon see that seven ships lay ready for them, and with Sparks he brought *Catfish* right up to the quay. Then he continued up the line of ships, and with Sparks placed limpet mines on the side of a large cargo ship. They moved along each ship in turn. As he turned back downstream, he had placed eight mines on five separate ships. Suddenly, a sentry on one of the ships shone a torch down onto the water. They remained motionless, but since nothing happened, they moved quietly downstream, planted two limpets at the stern of a cargo ship, and quietly shook hands. They had not gone far when they met *Crayfish*, manned by Corporal Laver and Marine Mills. They had mined two ships, five limpets on the first ship and three on the second. Together, the two canoes swept back into the Gironde. For five successive nights they had been at large in enemy waters, covering a total of ninety-one sea miles or 105 land miles by canoe. At dawn, they decided to separate and this was the last that Hasler ever saw of Laver and Mills.

On the morning of December 12th, the limpet mines went off one after another and caused enormous damage, to the extreme anger of Hitler. In London, there was no news of the fate of the Commandos. All we could do was hope that the survivors would make for Ruffec, seventy miles from Bordeaux. When they had parted from *Crayfish*, Hasler and Sparks scuttled their canoe and started a night's march in a north-easterly direction. They met a number of farmers who helped to disguise themselves as French peasants. With the aid of special maps and compasses with which they had been supplied by M.I.9 they continued marching until, at dawn on December 18th, weak and hungry, they reached Ruffec. They had walked nearly a hundred miles.

By an extraordinary chance they made immediate contact with the Mary Lindell's organisation. At the Hotel des Toques Blanches in Ruffec, a small establishment well known to her, they ordered a meal of soup, vegetables (which did not require food coupons) and two glasses of rough red wine. The patronne caught their eye and brought them second helpings. Since she seemed kindly and sympathetic, Hasler took out a pencil and wrote "We are two escaping English soldiers. Do you know anyone who can help us?" Then he asked for the bill. The woman came over, named a sum, and Hasler handed her a five-franc note with his message folded in it. There was no expression on her face as she brought back the change and laid it on the table. With it was her reply, on a piece of paper.

"Stay at your table until I have closed the restaurant."

At closing time, she locked the door and beckoned Hasler and

Sparks to follow her into the kitchen, where her husband, the chef, was still clearing up the dishes.

"Who were you told to contact in Ruffec?" he asked.

"We were given no names," Hasler answered. "We were told that friends of England would be on the look-out for us and would help us."

"Why did you come in here?"

"Because we were hungry and this looked a good place."

. They stayed the night in great comfort. Their clothes were washed and they woke fully refreshed on December 19th. During the morning, two Frenchmen arrived and interrogated them and at two p.m. took them in a baker's van to a point close to the demarcation line south-east of Ruffec. They walked with their guides to a farmhouse, entered a lighted kitchen, and the door was locked behind them. This was the property of Mary's agent and guide, Armand Debreuil, and known as 'Farm B'. In spite of their inadequate briefing, Hasler and Sparks had miraculously made contact with Mary.

On Christmas Eve, 1942, Maurice de Milleville said goodbye to his mother in hospital at Loches and returned to Lyon, where he found a letter from Debreuil stating that 'two important parcels of food' awaited him. Realising that the message was urgent, he returned to the hospital where Mary gave him instructions to tell Debreuil that the men would be picked up on January 6th and taken to Lyon. This was the reason for her hurried departure from hospital shortly after Christmas. At Lyon she was able to organise the reception of the two Commandos and at that time, her plan was to get them across the French frontier into Switzerland. She had so far failed to establish a route across the Pyrenees and told Hasler that it had 'folded up' for want of a guide. Both men would have to wait in Lyon till they could be smuggled into Switzerland.

On their first meeting, she strongly objected to Hasler's large blond moustache and upbraided her son Maurice de Milleville, who had brought the men to Lyon, about it; she fetched a pair of scissors and made Hasler cut it off. The men were then moved from house to house, coming to rest at the home of a Monsieur Belvaise in the Place Bellecour, Lyon. They were given a severe lecture on security and Mary's remarks to Hasler on the subject of 'girls' are worth quoting:

"We've got only one rule for Englishmen in our care—NO GIRLS. From past experience we know that once they meet a pretty girl everything goes to hell. So we shall take care to keep them away from you."

Hasler gave a splendid description of her on his return. She had taken them by tram to a photographer's studio in Lyon for new identity cards. As they followed behind her, she shouted across the street to them in English:

"Here we are!"

Amusing as these stories might be, they were bound in the end to incur disquiet in London and later in the year, they brought M.I.9 near to apoplexy. Being young, I was delighted with her unconventional ways, but they became increasingly difficult to defend with the Establishment, and later I was sharply forbidden to send a radio operator to her.

Meanwhile, the fate of the 'Cockleshell heroes' remained unknown in London. We were completely out of contact with Mary and, since the German occupation, the American Vice-Consul who had rendered us such signal service had been withdrawn. I had told her that if she were in difficulties she must reach Cartwright or Victor in Switzerland. This she did, bringing with her a coded message from Hasler for Combined Operations. She crossed the frontier with the help of the Swiss Intelligence Service in a fishing boat on the Lake of Geneva. This was a brave effort—her leg had not long been out of plaster—and her arm was in danger of gangrene. By the time she had reached the waiting-room at the British Legation, she was ill and in pain.

Cartwright seems at first to have doubted her identity,—he was a cautious man—and Room 900 was not in direct contact with him but with Victor at Geneva. On February 23rd, 1943, I received a telegram from him at the War Office, announcing her arrival in Berne. It told me for the first time of her accident in December, and that she was badly in need of medical treatment. It also revealed that Hasler and Marine Sparks were hiding in Lyon and that a coded message from Hasler was on its way to Combined Operations Headquarters. Loud was the rejoicing in London and Portsmouth at the news of the two Commandos. Crockatt at Beaconsfield was showered with congratulations, though it had only been by the merest chance that the two men had gone to the Hotel des Toques

Blanches at Ruffec. But the existence of Mary Lindell and her communications with Berne made possible the subsequent return to England of the only men to survive the raid.

Hasler's message presented Combined Operations with a baffling problem for he had forgotten some details of the code. But brilliant work by Second Officer Marie Hamilton W.R.N.S. and Major Ronald Sillars (of M.I.9) broke it and news of the success of the operation became known. The fate of the other canoes, however, remained a mystery for some time. While decoding was in progress, Langley and I discussed what I should reply to Cartwright. Why were the men at Lyon? From Cartwright's telegram it seemed that Mary could not ensure their safe passage over the Spanish frontier but would try and get them into Switzerland. We were not in favour of this plan for Hasler and Sparks were needed in London. The Government was waiting to hear their story and a stay in Switzerland would delay their return to England. Was there any way of putting them in touch with O'Leary, now in Toulouse? We decided that, after Groome's arrest, this would be too hazardous. Mary would have to get treatment for her injuries in Switzerland and then try to get them from Lyon to Spain. It was better to wait for her recovery since it would have been a tragedy if Hasler and Sparks had been captured. I replied to Cartwright that he should ensure that Mary had fully recovered before she returned to Lyon with additional funds. We were obliged to tell Crockatt and the Admiralty that it would be some time before the Commandos reached Spain.

But we had already lost control of the situation; we never had much. The impatient Mary 'escaped' from Cartwright. She met a member of the Swiss Intelligence Service, well known to me as one of our firmest allies, at a party who made arrangements for her to return secretly to Lyon. Despite her injuries, she again crossed the frontier, this time at Annemasse. In a few days, she told Hasler that she had found a guide to take him with Sparks over the Spanish frontier. At Room 900, there was some misunderstanding as to the truth and it was thought when Hasler returned that he had been transferred to another escape line. It seems she was still feeling desperately ill, and knew that she must return to Switzerland for treatment. Before she went, she was able to put them in the hands of a guide named Martineau who took them to Perpignan at the end of March. They crossed the Pyrenees with a Belgian in the R.A.F., Flying Officer Prince Werner de Merode, and Flight Sergeant Dawson, R.A.F., and arrived safely in Madrid.[1]

If M.I.9 were unfairly critical of Mary's exploits in February and March 1943, their attitude can be explained by the feeling that, audacious though she was, her methods appeared hair-raising. Luckily she has survived to debate the subject with me many times. She did not know that Room 900 had to contend with senior intelligence officers, who, like Cartwright, did not regard her imperious methods with the same sympathy as the younger generation.

Hasler and Sparks were naturally full of praise for her, and loud in their demands that she should receive greater support from Room 900.

They were the only survivors of Operation Frankton to reach home alive. Six of the remainder are known to have been shot under the infamous 'Commando Order', the others presumed drowned. These cruel murders of the Marine Commandos were among the vilest things the Germans ever did. I have elsewhere described what I felt when I entered Field Marshal Keitel's cell in October 1945:

"It was this man, sitting before me, who had carried out those brutal orders. Keitel, the toady to Hitler, the time-serving Staff Officer, the square-headed murderer. No crocodile tears for Keitel."[2] I was thinking of this amazing Commando raid, of Mary, and the escape of Hasler and Sparks.

If Room 900 did not especially distinguish themselves on this occasion, and we were criticised, Langley and I had one consolation. I became Commissioner for Criminal Organisations at Nuremburg in 1946 and reported on the Commando Order to the International Military Tribunal by which Wilhelm Keitel, who signed the 'Commando Order', was convicted and hung, and which condemned the S.D. and Gestapo who carried it out as criminal organisations.[3]

When Mary had recovered after a further stay in Switzerland, she resumed her efforts to create a new escape line from Ruffec and we remained in uncertain contact with her through Cartwright.

---

[1] The accounts of the Bordeaux raid and of the escape of Hasler and Sparks are taken from Brigadier Lucas-Phillips's *Cockleshell Heroes*, by permission of the author.
[2] *They Have Their Exits.*
[3] See Chapter 25, *Trial of the Major War Criminals*: Volume XLII, pp. 1–153.

In May 1943, she suffered a further disaster through the arrest of her son, Maurice, though he was later released after brutal treatment by the Gestapo. It was evident that they were hot on his mother's trail. They seem to have searched for her everywhere except Ruffec. In Switzerland she had changed her identity to the 'Comtesse de Moncy' and began a system of guides for airmen to cross the frontier at Andorra. But on November 24th she was arrested at the railway station at Pau by the S.D.

She maintained that she was the Comtesse de Moncy but it was evident that the S.D. knew her as the Comtesse de Milleville alias Marie-Claire for whom they had been searching for over a year. Despite the supply of a large sum of money by Victor in Geneva for her ransom, she was eventually removed from the S.D. Headquarters in Biarritz by train to Paris. The War Office, always strongly opposed to bribery of German counter-espionage services, was outraged by Victor's action and sharply reproved Room 900. On the way to Paris, she dived from the train in an attempt to escape, but was shot in the back of the head by a guard. Another bullet pierced her cheek. Taken to hospital in Tours, she was operated on by a German surgeon who saved her life. She recovered only to be taken in February 1944 to the prison of Dijon where she remained for eight months under savage treatment by the S.D. On August 31st, a message reached Berne that she was in cell Number 108, under the name of Docteur Marie de Moncy. She was transferred to Ravensbrück concentration camp on September 3rd, 1944, from which she was released on April 24th, 1945. At Ravensbrück, she worked indefatigably in the camp hospital and succeeded in saving several women from the gas chamber, including one of the agents of S.O.E. It was in this camp that several girls in the service of S.O.E. were detained before they were taken elsewhere and shot.

Mary Lindell, now over seventy, is one of the extraordinary personalities in the chronicle of escape. She continues her charitable work in France for other victims of Nazi persecution. She was intractable and often unlucky and she did not achieve the success for which I had hoped. But her career, as an Englishwoman defying the Germans by sheer pertinacity and daring, was almost without precedent. Her journey with Windsor-Lewis and the recovery of the two Commandos from the Bordeaux raid are among the great stories of underground war.

CHAPTER 17

Trix

OCCUPIED Holland in 1942 presented a difficult problem for escape work and a route to Brussels was badly needed. Recruits in England were difficult to find. The Dutch in London seemed to have more than one secret service and many quarrels. In the autumn, Dr. Derksema, who worked independently of their official intelligence departments, introduced me to Miss Beatrix Terwindt.[1] Trix, as she was known, was the only woman volunteer besides Mary Lindell sent to enemy territory by Room 900. She had escaped from Holland to Brussels and Switzerland, arriving at London in August 1942. Before the war, she had been an air hostess for K.L.M. airlines and offered her services to Dr. Derksema, whose headquarters were then at Chester Street in London. Trix, twenty-seven years old, was slim and dark with intelligent grey eyes. In our first conversation, I found her quiet and thoughtful and eager to return to Holland. I had no doubt that she possessed both courage and resolution, qualities which she was later to demonstrate in awful circumstances.

In 1939, the pre-war Allied information network in Holland had been destroyed through successful penetration by the Abwehr. This had resulted in the famous 'Venlo incident' when two British Intelligence Officers, Captain Payne Best and Colonel Stevens, were kidnapped at the Dutch frontier in 1939. In 1942 only S.O.E. had regular communications and throughout that year they parachuted large numbers of agents and wireless sets.

When I arrived at Room 900 the file on Holland consisted of a number of addresses disclosed by the few airmen who had been shot down there and escaped to Spain. These addresses were almost impossible to check since we were without radio communications and it seemed that it would be too great a risk to rely on them. The

[1] Now Mrs. Beatrix Scholte-Terwindt.

creation of an escape route to Belgium would, therefore, depend on sending an agent who could be received and helped by an established group. This could only be done through co-operation with the S.O.E. Dutch section. Although it was contrary to M.I.9 policy to mix escaping with another subversive activity, I was given permission to seek their assistance. In October S.O.E. undertook not only to train Trix through their own resources but to parachute her to one of their reception committees later in the year.

Meanwhile I wrote to 'Monday', who, through Dédée, passed a message to Jean Greindl in Brussels and in November 1942 I received his reply. Though the number of airmen arriving from Holland was relatively small, Greindl was anxious to have a link on which he could rely for a system of guides from the Hague and Amsterdam. It is significant that he appeared to be worried about the trustworthiness of some Dutch guides who had brought evaders into Belgian territory.

I have no wish to rake over the unhappy story of the S.O.E. Dutch section. Their successful deception by the Abwehr has been recounted in great detail.[1] In June 1942 the Abwehr captured an S.O.E. agent and, using his wireless transmitter, played it back to London. The deception was not discovered. Oberst Giskes, head of the Abwehr and S.S. Sturmbannführer Schreieder of the S.D. in Holland operated an ingenious plan under the code name of 'North Pole'.[2] The coup was also known as the 'England Spiel'. By means of more captured wireless sets Giskes was able to organise 'reception committees' in Holland for the parachuting of S.O.E. agents, radio operators and stores. He received large quantities of arms destined for the Dutch underground. Over fifty Dutch subjects despatched by S.O.E. from England dropped straight into his hands and forty-seven of them are said to have been executed. Eventually, Giskes became tired of this horrible farce, and in the spring of 1944 sent a message to S.O.E. revealing the truth.

The only woman parachuted to Holland in 1943 and who survived this appalling episode was Trix. During her training, I saw her frequently in London and discussed her mission. Despite her unassuming manner, it was obvious that she was both capable and resolute. Her experience with K.L.M. had given her a knowledge

[1] Especially by E. H. Cookridge; *Inside S.O.E.*
[2] Giskes, *London calling North Pole*, Arthur Barker, 1966, is the German version.

of aeroplanes and pilots. Since she spoke good English and French, she seemed an admirable recruit as a principle guide for airmen between Holland and Belgium. The difficulty of obtaining a Dutch wireless operator when volunteers were scarce meant that she would have to go alone. But as she was cautious and responsible I hoped that after breaking contact with the S.O.E. reception committee she could assemble a number of Dutch people who would shelter airmen before their passage to Brussels.

Before her escape from Holland, she had already met a number of people who had done this work. She had a strong personality, but she would not easily be noticed on trains or at control points and she seemed like many of the girls employed by Comet. She was efficient and practical and, with a supply of Dutch money, I concluded that she would be able to help with the many domestic problems involved in sheltering airmen. Though she never had the opportunity to put these attributes to the test, she might have become a Dutch equivalent of Dédée.

During the latter part of 1942, S.O.E. gave her their regular course of training at a school outside London. Their reports on her were satisfactory and I felt fully justified in my choice. I was, however, afraid than an air hostess with many friends in a large organisation such as K.L.M. might easily be recognised, though she would be able to explain her apparent disappearance from Holland by saying she had been in hiding from the Germans. I considered whether her appearance should not in some way be altered. Plastic surgery of the face to alter distinctive features was used on rare occasions during the Second World War, but this drastic method seemed unjustified. I took her to a sumptuous apartment at Albany in Piccadilly where we interviewed an expert in theatrical make-up who had nothing more original to suggest than altering her shoulders and hipline, by padding out her coat and skirt.

In December, S.O.E. made their plans to parachute her to Holland under the code-name Felix. Though they did not know it, they were in direct communication with the Abwehr and S.D. who announced that all arrangements had been made to receive the new agent with a number of containers of arms and a radio set. I had given Trix the address of a man named Smit of the Bally shoe shop in the Hague and a password. Smit had been housing R.A.F. evaders and his name had occurred in M.I.9 Interrogation Reports in the last few weeks. I also gave her the names of two Dutchmen, suspected of working for the Germans. But shortly before Operation Felix was due to take place, news was received from 'Monday' of the Marechal affair in Brussels followed by the escape to Gibraltar and London of Peggy van Lier and the d'Oultrements.

Until early in January 1943 I did not know that Jean Greindl would be able to continue and it was essential that Trix should not contact his organisation until the extent of the catastrophe became known. It seemed wiser, therefore, to postpone her departure and S.O.E. agreed to wait until February. This meant a dismal period of waiting in London for her. The secrecy which we imposed on agents was depressing for this conscientious girl. She had now left the Training School and was obliged to remain alone in a dreary bed-sitting-room in Kensington. I could understand her feelings but she realised the tremendous risks of associating with other Dutch agents. That she knew very little about S.O.E. and its organisation may well have saved her life.

Though S.O.E. had taken full responsibility for her training and dispatch to Holland, her mission as an escape organiser remained in my hands. I find it difficult to write of what happened to her. On the evening of February 13th, 1943, I went with her, by car, to the aerodrome at Tempsford. Those journeys sitting beside an agent on the way to unknown dangers are unforgettable, but my memories of this night are especially poignant. Before she left London, I had received the news of the arrest of Jean Greindl but decided not to postpone her departure a second time. I warned her that on no account must she seek out the Comet Headquarters in Brussels until the line had been reformed under new leadership. She should spend the next few weeks preparing the ground in Holland and recruiting helpers.

At midnight I helped her with her parachute harness and gave her a quantity of Dutch money with her identity papers as a hospital nurse. Before she climbed into the Halifax, I shook hands with her and stood saluting, with a group of Dutch and British Intelligence Officers, as she took off on her ill-fated mission. Next afternoon, with surprising promptness, a message was received by S.O.E. announcing her safe arrival and 'a welcome to a gallant woman comrade'. The Abwehr were enjoying themselves.

Trix Terwindt is living today in Holland and in May 1968 she wrote me her own account of that dreadful night.[1] As result of it, she suffered two years of hell and every detail is stamped on her memory. She made a normal landing but wind caught her parachute and on falling she slightly injured her face. The reception appeared to work perfectly and she was at once surrounded by several Dutchmen. She was asked to hand over a code, hidden in her cigarette lighter, which she carried for S.O.E. So far, nothing had occurred to alert her. The Dutchmen then collected the S.O.E. containers and in one of them found a radio set which they assumed was for her use. This surprised her, for I had sent no set with her, though she had been told to expect an operator later in the year. The set was, in fact, destined for an S.O.E. group in complete German control.

She noticed that the Dutchmen seemed a 'rough bunch of men', but, for the first few minutes, their conversation was not unusual for agents in the field. They asked her if she had a personal code and she replied that her orders were to divulge it to no one. The Dutchmen complained, as agents do, that communications were bad and that London did not understand their problems. Nor did S.O.E. realise how dangerous conditions in occupied Holland had become. As they walked across the field, one of the Dutchmen remarked that the chief of the organisation would not be pleased to have a woman working in the Dutch underground. While this annoyed Trix, it did not make her suspicious.[2]

S.O.E. had given her instructions to remain under the orders of the reception committee for twenty-four hours and then break contact. The Dutch traitors working for Giskes now tricked her into giving them the address of Smit at the Hague. They claimed that they had orders from London not to release her until this address and password had been confirmed. At first she resolutely refused. But the Dutchmen insisted. They tried a further trick. This was to suggest to her that the false identity card given to her in London was badly printed and it would be dangerous to travel with it. It is impossible to say whether this was justified, but, believing the Dutchmen to be genuine S.O.E. agents, she gave them the address. It was nearly a year since her escape from Holland to England and

---

[1] She also gave evidence to the Dutch Commission of Inquiry after the war.

[2] Giskes, in *London calling North Pole*, states that he had not been warned by S.O.E. to expect a woman.

she felt that the reception committee would be better informed about German controls and identity documents.

The night was dark and it had now begun to rain. Her escorts took Trix to a wooden shed where one of them threw a blanket over her shoulders, saying that her raincoat was too light in colour. She might be noticed moving across country in darkness to their headquarters. As he did so, he pushed her lightly in the back. Then she received a shock.

"I put my right hand behind me to feel what had happened. My wrist was caught and my hands were shackled behind my back."[1] At first she laughed: "Don't make silly jokes. You think I'll be frightened because I'm a woman?" She kept her head, hoping that this 'rough bunch of boys' were communists.

She reflected that they had already told her that women were unsuitable for the Dutch Underground. Perhaps these men were testing her courage? But, inside, she was furious with them. She kept silent, trying feverishly to guess what had happened. One of the Dutchmen called in a German soldier who apparently stood guard outside. He explained that the German was 'helping the underground'. Trix did not give up hope. Before her escape to England, she had known of an Austrian soldier who had done the same.

Her anger was increased by the boastful and impertinent behaviour of the Dutchmen who behaved like 'Red Indians'. As the truth began slowly to dawn, her fear was for Smit. She was horrified at the thought that his arrest and death, if indeed he were still free, might lie at her door. A German in civilian clothes now entered the hut, an official of the Abwehr, and she knew that all speculation was over. She had been dropped straight into the hands of the enemy.

She made an effort to put a poison pill in her mouth but her captors prevented her. Then, handcuffed, she was driven to the Abwehr headquarters in Dreibergen where German sentries stood on guard. During the journey she sat with her eyes closed, thinking hard. Her S.O.E. training told her that she must alter her cover story. Despite the tremendous shock which followed the tension and excitement of her departure from England, she felt able to withstand interrogation. There had been warnings in England that some

[1] Letter to the author May 13th, 1968.

S.O.E. groups had been penetrated by the Germans. What filled her with rage and humiliation was the discovery that the whole operation, including wireless communication with S.O.E., was in their hands. Surely the British were not so incompetent? Her first thoughts turned to the indiscreet talk of other Dutch agents in London.

Very detailed enquiries were made into the 'North Pole' affair after the war. At one time Giskes was operating no less than fourteen captured S.O.E. sets to London, and early in 1943, he had gained almost complete control over their circuits in Holland. It was a coup without precedent in secret service work. Those responsible in London and Holland have suffered enough and my task is only to recall the conduct of Trix Terwindt, surely one of the bravest of many brave women agents of her generation.

She was examined at Driebergen by a German doctor, a blunt, humourless officer. She describes this as the first of many humiliations. When she shed tears, he ascribed them to sorrow at her plight and made a clumsy attempt to comfort her, trying to appare sympathetic to her cause. In reality, Trix was made of sterner stuff, she was weeping with fury and disillusionment.

Her interrogation lasted for three or four days and nights with only one interruption for sleep and a bath. The S.D. in Holland co-operated with the Abwehr on 'North Pole', and it was S.S. Sturmbannführer Schreieder himself who led the questioning. He was assisted by other officers who followed each other in a continuous process of cross-examination. During this period, she took meals with the Abwehr and S.D. staffs and their secretaries. Schreieder began by telling her that he had sent a message to S.O.E. saying that:

"Felix had landed safely in spite of wind and rain." There is ample evidence that Trix refused to tell him anything of her mission or give her personal code.[1] Schreieder promised that, if she co-operated, she would not be sent to a concentration camp. Later the friendly attitude changed and she was told that he had other means to make her talk, but he did not employ them.

Early in her interrogation, Schreieder called one of the Dutch members of the reception committee into the room. Trix recognised his name as one of the two men suspected of working for the

[1] Cookridge, *Inside S.O.E.* Schreieder was not declared a war criminal and is still living.

enemy about whom she had been warned in London. The Dutch-man stated that on landing she had admitted having a code, but Trix denied this. She told Schreieder she had been boasting in reply to the contemptuous attitudes of the reception committee towards women.

On the third day, Schreieder, still friendly, asked her if she would go and find Smit at the contact address in the Hague. This she refused saying that she would weep for shame if she had to go there.[1] Schreieder must have supposed at this time that she would co-operate with him. He appeared to Trix to be the cleverest and most 'professional' of the S.D. officers. He was evidently favourably impressed by her courage and contemptuous of the British for sending a girl. After the war, she gave evidence at the trial of S.D. members in Holland and learned that Schreieder had even considered releasing her.

Trix was moved to the prison at Haaren and her questioning was pursued. Not realising the extent of the damage done to S.O.E. by 'North Pole', she was aghast at the detailed knowledge which the S.D. possessed of the training school for agents. They were aware of many names and meeting-places. Since she knew little or nothing about S.O.E. except their training system, they obtained no useful information from her and she was able to avoid disclosing that she was, in reality, an agent of Room 900 and did not belong to S.O.E.

Until May 7th, 1944, she remained at Haaren, confined in a cell, lonely, bored and miserable. This terrible period was relieved only by the introduction of another girl into the cell in December 1943 to spy on her. But she still gave nothing away. She arrived in Ravensbrück concentration camp on May 10th and suffered appal-lingly in health and mind, despite rumours that she would be released in exchange for German Air Force prisoners-of-war. In January 1945 she was transferred to Mauthausen and about a week before the end of the war reached Switzerland through the Inter-national Red Cross.

She has never indulged in recrimination and bitterness. She has treated her nightmare experience as one of the fortunes of war. It was this quiet faith and serenity of spirit which brought admiration from her captors. Thanks to her refusal to talk, she was one of the

[1] She gave nothing away about Smit's activities. He was arrested and died in a concentration camp without the Germans discovering his escape line.

few survivors of 'North Pole' who escaped death. As she wrote to me afterwards:

"I was an amateur but in war risks have to be taken. I played a game of cat and mouse with the Gestapo with the only difference that I was caged and the cat was free."

If the history of Room 900 and the escape lines is one of human success and sacrifice, this is one of its saddest episodes, redeemed only by the splendid example of this young Dutch girl. The first attempt to set up an organisation in Holland had been a tragic failure and I never sent a woman on a similar mission from England during the rest of the war. In contrast, later Room 900 operations in that country in 1944 and 1945 were to bring striking success.

PART V
BRITTANY

CHAPTER 18

Val Williams

THE need for an escape route by sea from Brittany had long been discussed by Room 900. Two early attempts in co-operation with the Free French were not successful. On each occasion, French naval officers were sent over the Spanish frontier to Brittany to organise evacuation by ship. One was recognised and denounced by a former colleague, the other was shot by a German officer in a café brawl.

During the latter part of 1942 and the early months of 1943, Allied raids on Brest, Cherbourg and other important ports left behind a large group of airmen hidden in different parts of Brittany. There was no means of getting them to Spain. The O'Leary organisation had been unable to set up a new line to southern France before it was overwhelmed, though Louis Nouveau during his short-lived activity in northern France had made contact with the leader of a Resistance Group.

This was François Le Cornec, of Plouha, a village on the north coast of Brittany, fifteen miles from St. Brieuc and two miles from the shore. Le Cornec was a dedicated patriot and a clear-headed organiser. He obtained his release from a prisoner-of-war camp as an agricultural worker in 1941 and soon formed a Resistance organisation consisting of friends in the region and the local gendarme. Among their activities was the hiding of airmen. This little group of Breton fishermen and farmers formed the base for a series of brilliant sea operations at the end of 1943 and the first months of 1944.

In the autumn of 1942, Langley began plans for a naval rescue service from the coast near Plouha. His choice for the mission was Vladimir Bouryschkine, whom he nicknamed 'Val Williams'[1] after

[1] Mr. Williams checked this chapter for me shortly before he died in France in August 1968.

Valentine Williams, author of *The man with the Club Foot*, *The Crouching Beast* and other adventure stories of the nineteen-thirties.

Val Bouryschkine Williams, as he was known after the war, will be remembered as the 'physical training instructor' and contact man for O'Leary during preparations for the Higginson escape in July 1942 from Fort de la Revère at La Turbie near Monte Carlo. Born in Moscow, in 1913, he had grown up in the United States, where he became a basketball champion. In 1940, while working for the American Red Cross, he met the Reverend Donald Caskie in Marseille after both had escaped from German occupation in Paris.

Caskie encouraged him to remain in France and help survivors of Dunkirk to return to England. Williams evolved an ingenious 'cover story' for this work. He obtained the job of coach to the basketball team of the Principality of Monaco, and armed with this official status bicycled to Fort de la Revère to see the Commandant. He declared to this officer that under the Geneva convention, prisoners were entitled to half a day of physical exercise each week. The Vichy armistice Commission felt bound to agree, and Williams obtained entrance to the Fort. Here he found Higginson and the Abbé Myrda. The latter introduced him to O'Leary and his connection with the Marseille organisation began. After the escape from Fort de la Revère, he played the part of guide between Marseille and Canet-Plage where the men embarked for Gibraltar. He was also 'receptionist' at the villa near the Hotel du Tennis, where they were hidden.

On September 13th, 1942, he was evacuated to Gibraltar by the trawler *Tarana* and distinguished himself by swimming excitedly to the dinghy as it came to fetch the party on a clear Mediterranean night. He caused considerable annoyance to the crew, who made loud complaints to Donald Darling when they arrived in port. They claimed that had coastguards or gendarmes seen or heard him in the water, it would have endangered the entire operation, known to Room 900 as 'Bluebottle'.

He therefore arrived in London with a small blot on his copybook.

I met Williams for the first time in the flat in St. James's Street. He was strongly built with a cherubic smile and a sociable manner. He spoke with a slight American accent, and new ideas, especially for naval operations, flowed from him. His boyish enthusiasm impressed me and I was not concerned at his impulsive swim to the dinghy at Canet-Plage. He seemed to have considerable possibilities as an agent for Room 900 in the future, if he were given the necessary training.

He gave an entertaining account of his work for O'Leary. At Canet-Plage he was put in charge of three French Canadians who had escaped from the Germans after the Dieppe raid in August 1942. They were Privates Joly, Lafleur and Vanier, the last two of whom returned to France the following year as radio operators. Williams had taken them to a cinema in Perpignan where they saw a German film portraying the repulse of the Allied landing at Dieppe. A column of prisoners was shown, their hands on their heads, led away under guard. The three Canadians were delighted to recognise themselves in this group, as they had made their escape shortly afterwards.

Throughout the autumn, Williams received special training to organise links between the Paris section of the O'Leary organisation, then still in existence, and Brittany. The final objective was an escape route from the coast to Dartmouth, though at this time the Navy had not decided on a suitable beach.

Langley asked him, "Are you willing to go back?"

"I should be delighted," said Williams with a broad smile.

He was obviously sincere though I wondered if he realised the danger. He was to have several unpleasant experiences in the months to come. Meanwhile, he was keen to start his training and full of determination to get back to France. He reminded me of my student days and the carefree irresponsibility that was only skin-deep. Some of those who took no thought for the future, even voted against 'King and Country', proved very courageous in war. In our work, there were many whose young lives had been spent in harmless dissipation, but once in enemy territory, it was their inner quality which mattered.

Williams was trained in parachuting and night landing by Lysander and took a special course in the organisation of naval rescue from the beaches of occupied France. Since Canet-Plage, we had established an embarkation drill including improved methods of signalling from shore to ship. When he was ready to go to France, the news came of the collapse of the O'Leary organisation in Paris.

At the beginning of February 1943, I was in the flat at St. James's

Street when Williams arrived to discuss the future of his mission.
Langley began with the news of the treachery of Roger le Neveu,
known as Roger le Legionnaire, and the arrest of Louis Nouveau.
He asked Williams if, in spite of these arrests, he was still prepared to
go. He warned him that he would have to start a completely new
line. The original organisation was 'blown' and no contact could be
made with any of O'Leary's group who were still free.

"I will do my best," said Williams.

Langley then gave him orders to go to France and establish a base
in Brittany for sea operations. His mission would have the code-
name 'Oaktree'. Langley spread a chart of the Brittany coast and
an aerial photograph taken by the R.A.F. on the table in the bay
window overlooking St. James's Street. He explained that the Navy
had selected a beach near Plouha, fifteen kilometres from the port of
Paimpol and twenty-five from the railway station at Guingamp.

Williams was to create a new system for hiding men in Paris,
bringing them by train to Guingamp and from there to the beach.
A 'safe house' would be needed near Plouha, where there were a
number of people, including Le Cornec, who had hidden airmen in
the past. The beach itself was shown on the chart at a bay called the
Anse Cochat. The cliff above was patrolled by the Germans and
guarded by a coastal gun and a searchlight which could be seen in
the aerial photograph.

There appeared to be a steep path down to the beach and a cave
where the men could be hidden while they waited to be embarked.
It should be possible to signal from the beach to the incoming ship
without being seen by the Germans on the cliff above. It seemed to be
an excellent place for the purpose but more information was needed
before the Navy would undertake an operation. Williams was to
make contact with François Le Cornec and his friends at Plouha
and organise the despatch of airmen from Paris to Brittany. He
was to take as his wireless operator Signalman Ray Labrosse, a
volunteer recruited by Langley from Canadian Military Headquarters in London, who had just completed his training. Labrosse
was a quiet, tough French-Canadian and a good counterpart for
the volatile and enterprising Williams. He was a man of courage
and good sense who proved an excellent agent for Room 900.

In February 1943, the situation had become serious. With the
O'Leary organisation in ruins, no one could foresee how long

Jean-François Nothomb and Comet would last. Only Mary Lindell was operating in Central France and she had suffered many reverses and misfortunes. Throughout the year, we were continually beset by the need to patch up lines which had been penetrated by the Gestapo. There were few safe contacts to whom we could send agents from England, since after a series of arrests, it was essential to break fresh ground. The duty of Williams and Labrosse was therefore to establish an entirely new base in Paris for hiding and feeding airmen before they were sent to Brittany.

There was the greatest difficulty in getting 'Operation Oaktree' started. An attempt to land Williams by Lysander failed owing to the absence of the reception committee. He was, therefore, transferred with Labrosse to R.A.F. Tempsford, so that they could be parachuted 'blind' to a field near the forest of Rambouillet, fifteen miles from Paris.

Both were equipped with a large amount of money, identity cards, revolvers and two folding bicycles, the first which had been used for a parachute operation of this kind. Several bicycles were damaged before the right method of packing them was devised, and curt minutes on this waste of equipment were received from Crockatt.

During the last fortnight of February 1943, they had the most unpleasant experience. Flying in a Halifax bomber, with all the attendant risks of being shot down over the French coast, they were forced to return to England on nine separate occasions because the pilot could not find the dropping zone. It was seldom that such a series of mishaps occurred, and the weather must have been exceptionally difficult because they had as their navigator the late Colonel Philippe Livry-Level, a famous Frenchman serving in the Royal Air Force. We subsequently learned that the dropping zone was probably obscured by industrial smoke from Paris.

At last their persistence was rewarded, and on February 28th they were dropped near Rambouillet. Langley had almost given up hope that they would ever leave. Each night he awaited the return of the aircraft at Tempsford and, saw, with despair, the two agents climb from it before he joined them in an operational breakfast of bacon, eggs and whisky.

For several weeks we did not know of their safe arrival since Labrosse did not come up on the air. It was not until we received a message from the French intelligence group known as 'Mithridate' that we knew that the set was out of action. Later I was able to reconstruct what had happened.

They landed near a farm at Les Etangs de Hollande, near Rambouillet, Labrosse's bicycle being damaged when its parachute failed to open. The farmer had seen them descend and reluctantly allowed them to hide the containers of cigarettes, tea, coffee, and whisky which they insisted on taking with them, in his barn.

At dawn, Williams pedalled off on the remaining bicycle towards Paris leaving Labrosse to try and make contact with London, which he never succeeded in doing. Williams secured the services of François Campinchi,[1] a Paris lawyer and one of our best agents, to organise the collection of airmen. Within a week of his arrival in France, he was on a visit to Brittany. He made his first reconnaissance at Carhaix, taking with him a large quantity of Players cigarettes for recruiting helpers. Near Paimpol he found what he later described as a 'whole regiment' of American and British airmen, hidden in the Château de Bourblanc, by Comte and Comtesse de Mauduit. Comtesse Betty de Mauduit, a most valiant lady, was American. After a search by the Gestapo at the château, she was arrested on June 12th, 1943, and sent to Ravensbrück concentration camp. There seems little doubt that she was betrayed by 'Roger le Legionnaire', who was now attached to Gestapo headquarters at Rennes. After the arrest of Louis Nouveau in February, the traitor arrived in Brittany, claiming that he had been sent by O'Leary. He invited Le Cornec's group to send airmen to him in Paris but they became suspicious. A number of arrests followed but the main Brittany organisation remained intact.

Williams visited the Château de Bourblanc on April 10th saying that he would return. His intention was to mount a sea operation from the Anse Cochat near Plouha at the end of May, but he was still out of wireless contact with London. Labrosse had 'borrowed' a set from the French intelligence group 'Mithridate', and eventually sent us a message at Room 900 requesting another set. We received this news with many misgivings about the security of 'Operation Oaktree'. How were we to send a set without compromising 'Mithridate' and incurring the wrath of our superiors?

After anxious consultation with 'Monday', we sent a message

Campinchi had been active since the days of Louis Nouveau.

through 'Mithridate' in Paris telling Labrosse that a set would be brought by the Comet line and left in the luggage office at the St. Jean station at Bordeaux. Darling had brought it as far as Seville under a travelling rug. It seemed a very clumsy arrangement, but safer than trying to parachute it through 'Mithridate'. The War Office was already angry that messages were being sent to Williams through another organisation. It was also risky for Nothomb and Comet. It says much for Nothomb's unselfish attitude that he took the risk of carrying the set with him over the mountains into France, where it was duly collected at the station at Bordeaux by Labrosse. It is not clear whether he ever used it, since disaster overtook Williams shortly afterwards.

In May, an abortive operation was planned through 'Mithridate' and using B.B.C. messages, to pick up airmen from the beach, at Le Palus-Plage a few miles east of the Anse Cochat. Williams and his friends waited on the beach, but on the night of May 29th, the message 'Denise est morte' was heard on the B.B.C. indicating that the operation was cancelled. The absence of proper radio communications made it too risky. As a result of this failure, Williams' situation had become dangerous. At least ninety airmen had been collected in Brittany, of whom thirty-nine were hidden by the Comtesse de Mauduit. His only alternative, until a proper sea evacuation could be organised, was to take them through to Spain. He recruited guides and, taking two Polish and two American airmen, travelled by train to Orthez, near Pau, in the frontier zone. On June 4th, the compartment where he was sitting with the airmen was suddenly filled with German police and the party were taken under guard to Pau. This was the last we heard of him until December 1943. He was kept at Fresnes prison in Paris for one month and later taken to Rennes, to be thoroughly interrogated by the Gestapo. Their information was alarming. They had a dossier on him dating from the previous year when, working with Tony Friend, the Monaco official, he took part in the escape from Fort de la Revère.

They also displayed a disconcerting knowledge of Room 900. They had full details of Langley, whom they knew to be a member of Brooks's Club in London. They even had a photograph of him and were aware of our system of training agents in parachuting, night-landing and wireless.

Williams felt compelled to tell them that he had been trained as

'British officer', but he maintained his cover story. As Squadron Leader Valentine Williams of the R.A.F. Ground Staff, he had been persuaded by Langley to volunteer for an escape mission in France. Before he could be transferred to M.I.9 he had flown as a passenger in bomber aircraft which had been shot down. He had then decided to remain in France and join the Resistance.

It did not seem very convincing. But the Gestapo were unable to establish that he had not joined the R.A.F. after his departure from southern France in 1942, and he carried a Service identity card. To extract more information they 'played golf' by striking him on the bottom with a piece of wood while he was handcuffed and, with Teutonic correctness, had him medically examined and declared 'fit to be shot'. They would surely have applied even more gruesome methods had he not made a spectacular escape from Rennes prison on December 20th, 1943.

Williams accomplished this feat with 'Ivan'—a Russian officer named Bougaiev, who had been recaptured after escaping from the Germans while a prisoner-of-war working on the Channel defences known as the 'Atlantic Wall'. Williams, born in Moscow, had the advantage of speaking both Russian and French. In addition to Ivan, other Russians were imprisoned at Rennes whose duty it was to serve the noon-day soup. When his cell-door was opened Williams talked to them in their own language. Ivan was thus able to pass him a saw hidden in a bottle of red wine. But the first attempt was a failure, for Williams was caught trying to cut through a bar in his cell. He was thrown into the punishment cell or *cachot* and left there naked for twenty-four hours. Fortunately Ivan continued to serve the soup and they were able, in Russian, to plan a most daring joint escape.

During an air raid alarm, some days later, Ivan stole the key of the *cachot* and the two men climbed down ladders left behind by workmen, to the moat of the prison. At eight-thirty on the evening of December 20th, 1943, they reached the top of the outer wall and jumped, but Williams, miscalculating the height, fractured his leg. Despite this misadventure, he hid in a hen-house with Ivan till dawn. They were nearly captured by a search party with dogs but employed a useful trick which Williams had learned during his security training in England. As the dogs approached them, they urinated. This, according to Williams, caused the dogs to urinate too and lose the scent. Leaning on Ivan's arm, he hobbled at dawn to a potato field, where they persuaded a farmer to drive them in his lorry under sacks of potatoes to the safe address of Madame Dubois at Bain de Bretagne. Here they remained while Williams' leg was put in plaster. Through Madame Dubois, contact was regained with Campinchi.

The difficulty of getting him to Paris was enormous. It says much for Campinchi's resource that he succeeded. Campinchi arranged that two French gendarmes in his pay should board the train from St. Brieuc at Versailles and 'arrest' Williams. They escorted him handcuffed through German controls at the Gare du Maine.

On arrival in Paris, Williams found that Labrosse, who had fled to Spain after his arrest, had returned from Britain a second time. He was now radio operator to a new chief who was determined that Williams, so recently escaped from the Gestapo, should leave France immediately. The new organisation under Sergeant-Major Lucien Dumais was already preparing a brilliantly successful series of naval operations from Brittany which took place in early 1944.

CHAPTER 19

'Shelburne'

O N HEARING of his chief's arrest at Pau, Ray Labrosse
decided that he could no longer continue to operate without instructions from Room 900, since Williams alone
possessed a code for sending messages. Moreover there was every
chance that he might be compromised. Leaving François le Cornec
in charge in Brittany, he left for Spain in July 1943. His escape was
organised by a Frenchman, Georges Broussine ('Burgundy')[1] whom
he had met at the house of a Madame Mellot in Paris.

Broussine reached Spain through the O'Leary line early in
1942 and volunteered for a secret mission in France. He was recruited by the B.C.R.A.[2] in London that autumn, introduced to
Room 900 and trained in wireless. In February 1943 the aircraft
taking him to France was shot down but he parachuted safely. His
mission was to join the réseau Brandy, of which Maurice Montet,
a French fighter pilot, was the Chief under the pseudonym of Simon
Martel. Montet was killed in action at the end of the war when in
command of a Free French Squadron.

The quality of the Frenchmen recruited by the B.C.R.A. for Room
900 was superb. In addition to Broussine and Montet, they included
Yves de Henaff ('Curacao') whose mission lasted from May 1943 to
February 1944; Pierre Guillot ('Pernod') who organised Lysander
pick-ups from the region of Tours from November 1943 to April
1944; and Jean-Claude Camors ('Bordeaux') who was murdered by
an enemy agent at Rennes after preparing a sea evacuation from
Douarnenez, a small port between Brest and Quimper. After his death,
it was Broussine who took charge of this operation which resulted in
a boat-load of 36 airmen reaching England safely in January 1944.

[1] M.C. [2] Bureau central de renseignments et d'action. The Free French Intelligence
Service.

Broussine was enormously brave. I had given him the address of a chemist but when he arrived there the man had disappeared. Broussine was followed but managed to throw off his pursuers. He took charge of the Brandy organisation when Montet was arrested in June 1943 and sent through several parties of airmen to Spain. In October 1943 he returned to London to report and I discussed a further mission with him which began with his second return to France in December.

Labrosse reported to Langley and myself on his return and we discussed the disappointing results of 'Oaktree'. But Williams' mission, though short-lived, could not be accounted a failure. Most of the airmen hidden in Brittany that summer were taken by guides to Spain. In spite of the loss of the Comtesse de Mauduit and other Breton organisers, the Paris sector under Campinchi remained intact. It had not received the attention of 'Roger le Legionnaire', whose description was now known to all our helpers. Labrosse convinced us that another attempt should be made to bring the airmen by sea to Brittany and he volunteered to return as wireless operator to a new organiser—the redoubtable French-Canadian Sergeant Major Lucien Dumais of the Fusiliers Mont-Royal.

Dumais was asked by Langley to return to France after his arrival on *Tarana* in October 1942, but the plan was reluctantly dropped. It was thought that his French-Canadian accent would betray him. He went to North Africa, as an observer for the Canadian Army and, being an individualist, set up his own 'private army' behind the enemy lines. Such was his success that, on his return to England, he was accepted and started training for Room 900 in summer 1943.[1]

He was short, articulate and very tough. It was he who accompanied O'Leary to the beach at Canet-Plage armed with an iron bar to deal with intruders. His forceful personality contrasted with that of the quiet, unflappable Labrosse. Although uncertain how he would handle the Breton Resistance groups, we thought that he would, after special training in night embarkation, be able to organise successful sea operations in Brittany. Our judgement of both men was fulfilled and they produced magnificent results.

The plan, code-name 'Shelburne', which was also the name of the new escape organisation, involved crossing by Royal Naval motor gun boats (M.G.B.s) from Dartmouth to the beach at the Anse

[1] His accent was no longer an obstacle in Brittany since it resembled the Breton.

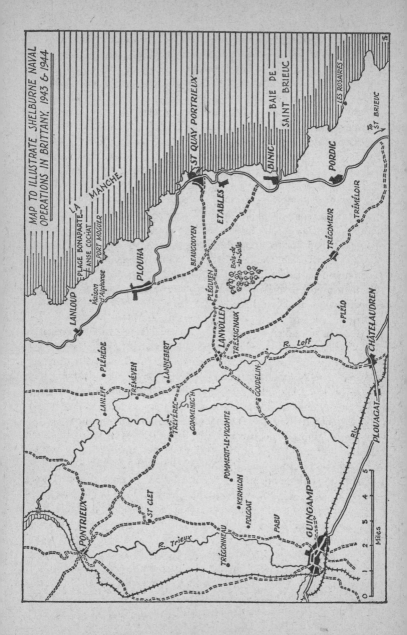

MAP TO ILLUSTRATE SHELBURNE NAVAL OPERATIONS IN BRITTANY, 1943 & 1944

Cochat at Plouha and other operations including rendezvous at sea. The airmen were to be collected from this beach (code-name 'Bonaparte') in small boats and ferried to an M.G.B. standing about a mile off shore. We believed the beach to be secure for it had never been used by Williams and 'Oaktree'.

The M.G.B.s on clandestine work sailed during dark periods. They were about 128 feet in length, carried a crew of thirty-six and were powered by three high-speed diesel engines, cruising at thirty-three knots. They had a six-pounder gun aft, twin turrets on either side and aft of the bridge, and a two-pounder forward.

When Dumais and Labrosse began their training, we were able to plan the evacuation drill and special torches were developed for morse recognition signals from the beach. The escape organisation would first ask for an operation during the dark period by wireless and the date and other details would be confirmed by Room 900. On the agreed date a B.B.C. message would be sent at seven-thirty and nine p.m. meaning that the M.G.B. had already left Dartmouth and was making for the 'Bonaparte' beach. It would then be time to collect the airmen for the embarkation. The message was:

"Bonjour tout le monde à la maison d'Alphonse."[1]

If the operation was delayed by twenty-four hours another message would be sent:

"Yvonne pense toujours à l'heureuse occasion."

When I took charge of Room 900 in the summer, it fell to me, with the aid of Windham-Wright, to put these plans into execution. Dumais, as 'chef de mission', was appointed to command the whole 'Shelburne' network in France, with Labrosse as his second-in-command and wireless operator.

In October 1943, they were landed by Lysander at Chauny north-east of Compiègne.

They were under orders to make no direct contact with either Campinchi or Dr. le Balch in Paris who with Williams and Labrosse formed the 'Oaktree' organisation earlier in the year.

I was much afraid that Campinchi and Le Balch, both valuable agents, might have been endangered by Williams' arrest. On no account were they to be contacted until it was known they were

[1] The messages were changed for later operations and other code-names for particular operations used including 'Waterloo'.

safe. When Labrosse came up on the air in November, I was considerably relieved to hear that they had come to no harm.

I had told Dumais to prepare for the first sea operation in December. Not only was there continued anxiety about the numbers of aircrew in Brittany and Paris who endangered those hiding them, but there was the possibility of an Allied invasion in the spring. It was essential to evacuate as many as we could in the next few months, and he was also to build a line to Spain, which he did with great success.

Labrosse worked his radio set in Paris from the house of a Monsieur Dorré, station master at the Gare La Chapelle and, sometimes, operated from his dining-room. He was assisted by Monsieur Dorré's daughter whom he married after the war.

When a sea operation was due to take place, he would take his set in its suitcase by train to Brittany, where he transmitted from the house of François Le Cornec at Plouha. Later, he had a spare set at Plouha to avoid the dangers involved in taking it by train.

When he made his first inspection of the beach at the Anse Cochat, Dumais was able to meet Le Cornec and inform him of the plans for 'Bonaparte'. He found the Plouha group ready to undertake the hiding of airmen and decided for the sake of security that they should not be brought from Paris until three days before the naval operation was due. The first group arrived in Brittany late in December.

Although I had suffered many reverses and disappointments in my eighteen months at Room 900, and much sorrow at the arrest of so many brave agents, I had the utmost confidence that the 'Shelburne' operations would change our run of misfortune. I hoped that Dumais would be ready for the first operation in December, and I therefore discussed with the Navy a number of details. Among these was the necessity for a 'conducting officer' who would go with the M.G.B. to the beach to meet Dumais or Le Cornec and hand over the money, whisky, cigarettes and other stores which we intended to land.

In September, Langley had been transferred to Beaconsfield and I was now in charge of Room 900. I was therefore ultimately responsible for these plans and wanted to go to Brittany. But M.I.9 were strongly opposed to this, in view of the rule that officers who knew full details of the structure of any branch of secret intelligence should not go into the field. Langley had even been reprimanded for flying as a passenger in a training Lysander by night over the Channel and Darling for going to Perpignan. We were only a few months away from the invasion, and the staff of 21 Army Group were not unnaturally anxious to avoid capture of anyone in a secret intelligence appointment. Langley, Darling and I were once roused at two in the morning when an Air-Marshal was shot down on an unauthorised flight over France in the spring of 1944. Room 900 were instructed to try and find him. Broussine recovered him but he was later captured and liberated during the Allied advance.

I do not pretend that I had any desire to risk recapture by the Germans after my previous experiences. It was not only my escape from Colditz, but the possibility that my name was known to them through the arrest of others, that finally led Crockatt to forbid me to go to Brittany. Later on he relented and allowed me to conduct many exciting operations in 1944. Pat Windham-Wright, despite the loss of his arm earlier in the war, agreed to accompany the M.G.B. and any agents we might wish to send to France by sea. He was to take with him personal messages to Dumais and Labrosse.

At the beginning of December, Dumais signalled that he was ready for his first operation, but extremely bad weather for nine days led to its postponement from day to day until it had to be cancelled. It was not till January, 1944, that the Shelburne organisation had its first success. The date proposed was the 29th of that month. On this occasion the airmen from Paris were met at St. Brieuc by guides and brought to Plouha on a little local train to be hidden in the neighbourhood of the beach.

It was clear from their subsequent interrogations by M.I.9 that the organisation was extremely thorough. They were given false papers in Paris to enable them to enter the forbidden coastal zone and their clothes had the marks of local shops in case of arrest.

Seventy-two hours before the operation I was in constant touch with the Navy at Dartmouth. Conflicting reports about weather and enemy forces in the Channel made it a period of considerable anxiety.

Windham-Wright had already set off for Dartmouth to join the ship, taking with him money, whisky and a spare wireless set for 'Shelburne'. On the afternoon of January 29th I heard that M.G.B. 503 was ready to leave Dartmouth. It was an exciting moment when I informed the B.B.C. and heard them broadcast at seven-thirty and nine p.m.

"Bonjour tout le monde à la maison d'Alphonse."

The 'Maison d'Alphonse' was a primitive Breton dwelling belonging to a sailor called Giquel, a trusted companion of Le Cornec, who lived there with his wife and newborn baby. This tiny stone place was 1500 metres from the cliffs and the rendezvous for the airmen before they descended the steep path to the beach. Its ruins still stand on the cliffs above the Anse Cochat. The Germans destroyed it in July 1944 after the Shelburne organisation had saved no less than 135 Allied airmen who had passed through this humble home. The house had one room where the Giquels slept with their baby, and another where the airmen assembled when the B.B.C. message had been heard. It had a wooden staircase leading to a loft for hay, and in case of alarm the visitors were hidden there.

One evening, seeing lights and hearing noises in the house, a party of White Russians, impressed into the German Army, appeared at the door. They had evidently heard the airmen hurrying to the loft and loudly threatened the Giquels with hiding members of the Resistance. They were drunk, and began firing their automatic weapons in the direction of the house shouting, 'Tommy! Tommy!' and pointing upstairs. In the course of this befuddled action, they shot one of their own men. The situation was saved by the steady nerve of Madame Giquel, who tended the seriously wounded Russian, while her husband improvised a stretcher. This sobered up the rest of the party who then carried off their companion. It was a dangerous moment, for Dumais and Le Cornec had only just delivered the airmen to the Maison d'Alphonse and, hearing shots, returned to the scene, prepared to attack from the rear. They were both armed with .45 colts and grenades, but fortunately there was no need for them to intervene.

On the night of the 29th I sat in Room 900 thinking of the responsibilities that lay upon me for this first 'Bonaparte' operation. It was thought by the more cautious in M.I.9 to be 'extremely risky'. I kept ringing up the Duty Officer at Dartmouth for news but it was not until nine a.m. next day that I heard of its complete success. The M.G.B. had returned with nineteen men. Thirteen were American airmen, four were R.A.F., and two were Frenchmen who wanted to join the Allied Forces. It was a great triumph for Dumais and Shelburne and, at the next opportunity, I sent them warm messages of congratulation. An additional passenger was Val Williams, accompanied by Ivan.

Dumais had persuaded Williams to leave on the first possible sea operation. It was necessary to return him from Paris to Brittany, still on crutches, to an area where he was well-known to the Gestapo. Campinchi again excelled himself. He arranged for two guides to accompany Williams by train to St. Brieuc. He was met there by another guide from Plouha who drove him to a farm where he was hidden in the stables. The train journey had been a nightmare, for he had passed through Rennes, where he had been imprisoned only a month before, fully expecting a search by the Gestapo. On the night of the operation, he was taken with several airmen, in single file, through fields past the village of Plouha to the Maison d'Alphonse which stood alone on the cliffs. On level ground he was able to walk on his crutches, but the pathway to the beach was narrow and steep. Le Cornec obtained a stretcher and with beautiful eighteen-year-old Marie-Thérèse Le Calvez, one of the splendid little band of Plouha guides, carried him down to the beach. The steepness of the path made this an extraordinary feat. The party waited until suddenly the dark shape of a boat arrived from the M.G.B. which had soon the Morse signal flashed from the shore. A group of Commandos, their faces blackened, stepped forward, sten guns at the ready. They helped Williams and Ivan with the airmen into the boats and were soon aboard the M.G.B.

This was the end of Val Williams' picturesque career in Underground France. On arrival in London, he was subjected to a lengthy interrogation on the orders of M.I.9. At the time, he took strong objection to this precaution, but it was essential that an agent who escaped from Gestapo hands should be rigorously examined. Ivan, who spoke nothing but Russian, was detained by M.I.9 at whose headquarters he learned to drink beer and play darts. He was later handed over to the Soviet authorities and never heard of again.

In spite of his many disappointments, Williams was still anxious to return to France, but I felt that this was impossible and M.I.9 supported me. He argued that although known to the Germans in southern France and Brittany, he could still operate in central France. Though enterprising and determined, he had risked his life too often and the extensive Gestapo dossier on him might lead them to others if he were caught again. He was not re-employed and, disconsolate, waited in London till the invasion of France.[1] Before his death in August 1968, he supplied me by letter with many details of his adventures. Secret escape work involved great hazards and, in many respects, Williams was one of our less fortunate agents, though he did much to pioneer the route from Anse Cochat to Dartmouth. But he got away with his life and did not undergo the horrors of concentration camps like Trix Terwindt and Mary Lindell.

The first voyage had gone without incident. The M.G.B. did not appear to have been picked up on the enemy's radar and there had been little difficulty, with good visibility, in seeing the recognition signals and ferrying the men in small boats to the M.G.B. Dumais and Le Cornec were reported in high spirits and ready to continue. A written message from Dumais said that the operation had gone 'a bit slowly' but that the security had been good. This message also referred to the activities of Roger le Legionnaire. Dumais wanted to 'go after him' but was told this was too dangerous. The note continued that Roger, after the arrest of the Comtesse de Mauduit in June 1943 was still attached to the Gestapo at Rennes. There is reason to think that, as late as June 3rd, 1944, he was operating a fake escape route and sent two parties of airmen to Spain. Shortly afterwards, he was liquidated by a Resistance group but I have obtained no further details of his fate.

When the airmen arrived in London, I rushed to the Great Central Hotel and there, in the familiar first floor room, asked them eagerly how the 'Bonaparte' Operation had gone. They knew little of the organisation and its structure, which demonstrated excellent security. The B.B.C. messages were unknown even to Le Cornec and Campinchi. On the evening of the operation, their hosts in Plouha told them excitedly that they would soon be collected by lorry—the same truck driven by François Kerambrun of Guingamp which had met them at the station on arrival from Paris. Some of them had left the train at Châtelaudren, others had come on the 'petit train' from St. Brieuc.

They were impressed by the discipline imposed by Dumais. When they reached the 'Maison d'Alphonse' they waited till midnight when a number of guides arrived, led by Huet, a former officer in the French Fleet Air Arm. In later operations it was he who

[1] He was awarded the British Empire Medal.

armed with a detector, marked the mines which the Germans laid on the paths and beaches to prevent Commando landings. The mine detector was parachuted to Brittany on the night of March 23rd. Whenever he located a mine he marked it, and at dusk covered it with a white rag about the size of a handkerchief. He carried a supply of these in his pocket and removed them on the return journey after the operation had taken place.

Dumais and Le Cornec enforced the strictest silence and at midnight they were with the airmen on the beach waiting for the ship. One additional detail had now been arranged with regard to signals. The morse letter B was flashed every two minutes from a point on the cliff, with a masked torch with a blue light shining on the beach below. The engines of the M.G.B. made no sound as it stood about one and a half miles out at sea out of range of German searchlights. The signals continued from the shore. For some time nothing happened, until Commandos appeared in four rubber boats rowed by sailors. Four or five airmen were carried in each boat and rowed back to the ship, which swiftly started on its return voyage to Dartmouth. Windham-Wright reported that the whole embarkation was completed in twenty-five minutes including the landing of stores.

I fixed the second operation with Dumais for February 28th, 1944. This was carried out with equal success, but in rather shorter time. Over twenty were rescued, including sixteen American airmen. There were no incidents at sea or on shore and no contact with the enemy. There were, however, reports from the airmen of increasing German controls inland. Owing to the curfew, the lorry which collected the men from their hiding-places was used in daylight. François Kerambrun ran great risk of discovery, as he sometimes openly carried twenty Allied airmen. It was his plan, if questioned, to say that they were workmen needed for a 'rush job'. As he said to my wife in 1967, the penalty for transporting two airmen would be the same as for twenty, so he might as well do the whole job at once. Before the February operation a disaster nearly occurred on the road from Guingamp to Plouha, about thirty kilometres from the beach. At a village called Gommenec-h, the Germans had begun the construction of a tank trap, similar to a cow gate, with steel spikes. The work had not yet been completed, and only wooden struts protruded above the surface of the road. Kerambrun's lorry was half over the obstacle before he found one sticking through the steering.

It was a desperate position. The time for the curfew was drawing near and the twenty-one airmen started to lift it bodily off the spike. By great efforts, they had just succeeded when two French gendarmes appeared and questioned them. Kerambrun, a bold, shrewd Breton, made a quick decision. He told the gendarmes everything and, as he later said, "if they were not patriots, we would have killed them with our bare hands." Like many others, the gendarmes were sympathetic to the Allies, and they let the lorry go on its journey to the Maison d'Alphonse. But it had been a terrifying moment, and the airmen were still shocked when they arrived in London.

Shelburne's first March operation was another triumph though not without its dangers.

On March 18th, M.G.B. 503 appeared off the beach at twelve-thirty a.m. and a walkie-talkie sent to Dumais in February was now in use. After passwords had been exchanged, the ship was fired on from a point near Paimpol. The boats were not sent in to the beach, though contact with Dumais was continued. At three a.m. the operation was resumed and twenty-four airmen taken off, nearly all of them Americans. Some of the men were brought on bicycles from Douarnenez. They had been transferred from the Burgundy line under Georges Broussine who had organised the escape of Labrosse to Spain when Williams was arrested.

After his first mission to France Broussine received a well deserved Military Cross from M.I.9 and the French gave him the Legion of Honour. On his second mission, he continued the organisation of the line to Spain with outstanding success and sent 255 airmen over the frontier. Some of these men had been stranded in Brittany after the collapse of 'Oaktree' and the escape of Labrosse. He was nearly arrested in December 1943 on his return from London when the 'safe address' which I had given him proved to be in Gestapo hands. After the Normandy invasion in July 1944 he attempted to get through the Allied lines on a bicycle but was captured by German troops. He subsequently escaped and in consequence one of our ablest and most adventurous French operators has survived the war and is living in Paris.

The Shelburne organisation continued their triumphs. On March 24th, 1944, thirty airmen were rescued, eighteen of whom were members of the United States Air Force. Many had been shot down during the huge daylight raids by Flying Fortresses of the Eighth Air Force on Germany and military installations in occupied Europe, which preceded the invasion. They bombed Kiel on the 13th, Bremen on the 20th and Ludwigshafen on December 30th, 1943. There were also several big attacks in northern France, against flying bomb sites, especially that of December 24th, 1943. A major attack was made on the German airfield at Bordeaux-Merignac by B-17s of the Eighth Air Force on January 5th, 1944. I was able to report to the United States Air Force command that a substantial proportion of those who baled out of their aircraft on these raids were being returned by Shelburne within a month, and sometimes within a few days, of being shot down. The effect on the prestige of M.I.9 was sensational, and what became known as the 'miracle' of Shelburne continued.

The next voyage to the Anse Cochat was on March 30th, 1944. Although only ten returned on this occasion, Windham-Wright was able to have a twenty-five minute conversation on the beach with Le Cornec, who conducted this operation alone. Dumais and Labrosse had returned to Paris to make plans for the increasing number of airmen and to discuss reports of a general 'alert' on the coast. Windham-Wright explained to Le Cornec that as the nights were growing shorter, the operations would have to stop 'for the time being'.

While it was true that it would be more difficult for M.G.B.s to operate on summer nights, my real reason for sending these instructions was the imminent invasion and the need to avoid incidents which would strengthen German coastal defences. The Shelburne organisation had already been an undisputed success, and by March 30th, 118 airmen had returned to their bases.

After D-Day, when German naval and coastal forces were fully occupied in Normandy, we carried out two further operations, after I had gone to France, on July 13th and 14th, 1944. Ten more airmen were brought off, including eight Americans. Shelburne was therefore responsible for the rescue by sea of 128 airmen and seven agents making a total of 135 men and women. Through their system of guides, they sent ninety-eight men to Spain. Another seventy-four were in a group of 132 rescued from the Forêt de Fréteval near Châteaudun in August, who had been sent there by their organisation in Paris. Three hundred and sixty-five airmen therefore owed their liberty to Shelburne.

Later in July, Dumais and Le Cornec, with a group of Bretons, fought off a German battalion at Châtelaudren, killing eighty and taking a hundred prisoners. Earlier in February, Crockatt had supported my recommendation to Canadian Military Headquarters for both French-Canadians to receive commissions. Dumais was promoted to Captain, and Labrosse to Lieutenant. Each received the Military Cross. One-armed Windham-Wright received a bar to his Military Cross and many honours were awarded in Paris and Brittany by M.I.9.

Thus ended one of the most splendid exploits in which the Navy and agents of Room 900, aided by French patriots in Paris and Brittany, took part. While there has been the inevitable post-war discussion as to who should have the most credit for its signal success, I have written the story as I saw it from London in those tense days before the great Allied landing in Normandy in June 1944.

PART VI

'MARATHON'

CHAPTER 20

Before the Bombardment

WITH the appointment of Langley in the autumn of 1943 as joint commander with Lt.-Col. Richard Nelson (U.S. Army) of I.S.9 (Western European Area), our preparations began for the Allied embarkation in France. Though I succeeded him in charge of Room 900, I had also the responsibility for planning underground escape operations before and after the landing had taken place. If the invasion succeeded, what was to happen to the large numbers of evaders and escapers who remained in hiding? I spent much time pondering how large groups of men could be sheltered and supplied by air, if it was impossible to get them over a neutral frontier. But how could we ensure their safety if there were heavy fighting in France?

We knew that plans existed for the destruction by bombardment of rail communications in northern France, in preparation for the invasion. This would make regular journeys by train to the Spanish frontier impossible. With the help therefore of the Belgian Sûrcté and the B.C.R.A., I secured a magnificent group of agents to organise concentrations of airmen away from the battle zone. The whole scheme, known as 'Operation Marathon', covered Holland, Belgium and France. The principal areas selected for hiding the men in large groups of 'camps' in France were Rennes and Châteaudun and, in Belgium, the Ardennes. My idea was to transfer airmen who could not be evacuated to Spain from Paris and Brussels, to organised camps in rural areas where food and other necessities could be dropped to them by parachute. This would involve the selection of suitable sites, preferably in heavily wooded regions where the men could be liberated by the Allied advance. Since I expected that 400 or 500 airmen were involved, the operation required a highly trained team of organisers and wireless operators and I felt that the camps should be established before the battle began.

There was much discussion in M.I.9 about this plan. It was considered imaginative but 'too risky' and many meetings with Crockatt took place to discuss its hazards. It was argued, on the one hand, that if rail communications were cut by bombing, immediately before and after the landing in Normandy, the men would be safer where they were already hidden. This was, generally, in Paris, Brussels and other large towns. I felt, from the beginning, that not only would food be scarce, but it was too much to ask individual families to run the risk of hiding the men until the Allied Armies arrived. No one could foresee what progress they would make, nor was it possible to tell whether the Germans would defend Paris and Brussels. I also expected an outburst of S.S. and Gestapo activity against our agents.

There was the obvious danger that an Allied airman with false identity papers in civilian clothes would not in the future be treated as a prisoner-of-war. In the panic-stricken state of many German troops, harassed by the Resistance, they might be shot out of hand, with those who helped them. Airmen might also take up arms and join Resistance groups as the Allies drew near them, thereby running every chance of massacre by the S.S.

I was sure that the safest plan was to evacuate the men, especially from Paris and Brussels, and hide them as far as possible away from German troop concentrations. The places selected should be sufficiently near railway stations to bring them to the camps, in regions where well organised Resistance groups were known to exist. This latter view prevailed against much opposition. I knew that it was fraught with many risks, but if we could find the right sites for the camps, it was the best chance of saving these men from capture or summary execution as partisans. At Room 900, I was aware that the destruction by bombing of railway lines, especially in Belgium and France, would make evacuation to Spain difficult, if not impracticable, after April 1944. It was therefore necessary to train the special team for 'Marathon' and begin preparations well in advance. Since it was impossible, at this time, to give any indication of Allied invasion plans, I could tell the agents little about 'Marathon'. Their duties would be to keep the escape lines in operation until the time came to form the camps.

The first section consisted of Georges d'Oultremont ('Ormond'), a survivor of the Maréchal affair, and a French-Canadian wireless operator, Corporal Conrad Lafleur, ('Charles') who had escaped from Dieppe with Dumais. Their mission was to organise 'pick-up' operations by Lysander with headquarters at Reims, and make contact with Nothomb and Legrelle in Paris. In reserve were Baron Jean de Blommaert ('Rutland') and Lemaître ('London'), his Belgian operator, and Capitaine Dominique Edgar Potier ('Martin'), a Belgian Air Force officer who was already in France.[1] To organise the camps in the Belgian Ardennes, I had in training Albert Ancia (code-name 'Daniel Mouton'). I planned that he should be parachuted to France, but would make his way to Belgium and link up with Comet in Brussels. In the early part of 1944, I decided that the maintenance of large numbers of men in rural areas, perhaps camping in forests, would need the strictest discipline. The Sûreté therefore found for me a Belgian in the R.A.F., Squadron-Leader Lucien Boussa ('Belgrave'). This was a group of the highest quality. Room 900 were now able to recruit agents and radio operators who, by their character and training, had the best qualifications for this work. It was a tribute to the successes of O'Leary, Dédée and earlier leaders that I was able to command such support. It was also the reason for the successful outcome of most of 'Operation Marathon'.

Many of our conferences with the Belgians took place at 22, Pelham Crescent where d'Oultremont and de Blommaert lived in London. In these civilised surroundings, we planned one of Room 900's best schemes. Over all of us hung the fear that if the Germans knew that they were losing the war, they would turn to brutal methods and spare no one, even in uniform. The hundreds of Allied aircrew who remained in Belgium and France would still be needed for the war effort. It may have been for this reason that we had greater support from the Air Ministry than before. 'Marathon' would involve more sorties by the R.A.F. for parachuting agents and supplies than Room 900 had ever planned in the past.

I did not know how long we should have to wait for the actual landing. I had to assume that it would come some time in the late spring. It was also impossible to tell when our forces would reach the areas of France and Belgium which we had selected for the camps. Even if the lines to Spain and the Shelburne sea evacuations continued until April or May 1944, the number of R.A.F. and American

[1] He parachuted in July 1943.

aircrew shot down would inevitably mean that several hundred would still be at large after D-Day.

On October 21st, 1943, Georges d'Oultremont and Lafleur were sent to France. D'Oultremont, as always, was in high spirits. On the evening before he was due to parachute to Fismes, near Reims, I held a party for him at the Embassy Club in London which went on until the early hours. Such was his exuberance that he climbed on one of the tables and hung from the chandelier. We left the Embassy Club at three in the morning and returned to Pelham Crescent. No one would have supposed that d'Oultremont and Lafleur were due to leave for enemy territory next evening and risk their lives a second time. But we could not know the real, sad irony of our celebrations. For at dawn that morning of October 20th, the members of the Swedish Canteen who had worked with Jean Greindl were being taken to their place of execution in Brussels. None of us ever forgot this grim coincidence.

Although I had come to realise the dangers of interfering in the control of the Comet line, I knew that d'Oultremont would act with discretion if he were to make contact with Nothomb and Legrelle in Paris. Jean Masson was sure to strike again, as he did in January 1944, when Nothomb was arrested. D'Oultremont had been a reliable assistant to Jean Greindl and I was confident that he would manage Lysander receptions efficiently and I hoped that he would remain in France until 'Marathon' began. Next afternoon, I gave him a final briefing, with Lafleur. He was to find a suitable landing ground near Reims for Lysanders to pick up agents and airmen. He was also to organise the parachute reception of de Blommaert in the following month. Both men had received training in laying a flare path and giving the necessary signals. D'Oultremont had false papers in the name of Laporte, with a cover story as a lawyer. I was afraid that as a Belgian he might be suspect in Reims or Paris, but this was a relatively minor risk for him to take, compared with returning to Brussels, which he was strictly forbidden to do. Lafleur was a small, dark French-Canadian and extremely tough. The risk of detection through his accent was discussed as it had been in the case of Dumais. But radio operators were always briefed to keep out of sight and conduct their lonely activities moving from house to house. In many ways, it was the most perilous job of all. Both were well-armed and took with them plenty of whisky and cigarettes. They were safely dropped to a field near Fismes early on October 21st.

Lafleur soon came up on the air and reported their arrival at Reims. They had made contact with safe addresses in the area. D'Oultremont then made for Paris, where he was able to meet a number of French girls who were ready to act as guides and an accommodating banker who was prepared to keep the three million French francs which I had given him. He told me, afterwards, of a dangerous moment when a friend of the banker questioned his forged papers and suggested that he was a Gestapo spy. The banker was advised to shoot him, but d'Oultremont was, at all times, a lucky man. Eight days before he had parachuted to Fismes, an S.O.E. agent had arrived in Paris. This man, who had met d'Oultremont in London, was able to identify him. The whole affair ended in an excellent Belgian restaurant in Paris which, d'Oultremont was astonished to find, still existed after three years of German occupation.

He next set about finding suitable landing grounds for Lysanders and selected a spot near Coucy-le-Château in the Aisne, where it was possible to arrange for two Lysanders to land in one night. I received a message from Lafleur describing the field, its measurements and other features. It was then photographed from the air by the R.A.F. and I obtained approval for an operation to bring out a number of airmen whom d'Oultremont had collected from Paris.

Although night landing operations using Lysanders and even twin-engined Hudson aircraft had by now become a commonplace for S.O.E. and other Intelligence organisations, Room 900 had little experience of them. Lysanders with only three passengers were considered more suitable for the despatch or return of agents or political leaders than for evaders. In view of the large numbers in our hands the Air Ministry was not prepared to risk many aircraft of this type and our primary method of rescue remained the sea operations and the passages to Spain.

Nonetheless two Lysanders went to Coucy-le-Château at the beginning of November and returned safely, bringing out five pilots, three of them American. The reception arrangements and signals from the ground had been efficiently made, but despite the goodwill of Lysander pilots, the Air Ministry did not look upon such operations with enthusiasm. It seemed that d'Oultremont and Lafleur could be better employed in maintaining a parallel escape line to Comet and making preparations for the camps.

De Blommaert had, since 1942, been one of the leaders of the young Belgian group at 22, Pelham Crescent. He had been recruited from the Belgian Army and proved to be an exceptional organiser. He was tall, blond, and thoughtful. His reticence and thoroughness commanded respect especially with the French Resistance. In August 1944 he made a magnificent success of a plan for hiding airmen in the forests near Châteaudun.[1] Capitaine Edgar Potier, who had been conducting Lysander pick-ups since the summer, was a regular Belgian Air Force officer. Though over forty, he volunteered to go to France to take part in escape work. He was a man of deep religious feeling and I was sure that, if in danger, he would see things through to the bitter end. I was certainly right.

De Blommaert was to parachute to France at the end of November with Lemaître, a good Belgian wireless operator. With Lafleur, still operating from Reims, a reception committee, led by d'Oultremont, was engineered at the same field near Fismes where both had been dropped a month before.

A password had also been arranged between de Blommaert and the reception committee. At the party at the Embassy Club on October 20th, I had first received the surprising nickname from the Belgians of 'Napoleon'. I therefore told d'Oultremont that, on landing, de Blommaert should say 'Napoleon' and the reply from the reception committee would be 'Marie-Louise'.

At the end of November, de Blommaert and his party descended out of the darkness near Fismes about three o'clock in the morning. As he landed he cried, 'Napoleon'. Instead of the reply 'Marie-Louise', he recognised the voice of d'Oultremont.

"Blom, what on earth are you doing here?"

"Nom d'un chien, fermes-la! On n'entend que toi ici," growled de Blommaert.

The two friends were delighted to meet again, and embraced.

Next day he began his task of making new contacts, and the two agents soon separated. While I was preparing a new parachute operation, Lafleur went off the air. I have said that he was well-armed. One evening, the German radio detector vans, which had

[1] See Chapter 22.

been listening in for some weeks, surrounded the house where he was transmitting at Reims and caught him in the act. The daring young French-Canadian immediately opened fire, killed or wounded two of them and jumped out of the window. He fled from Reims and made contact with the Comet line, which brought him safely back to Britain. He received the Distinguished Conduct Medal.

Left without a wireless operator, with the Gestapo on his trail, d'Oultremont made for Paris, where he met Nothomb on January 17th, 1944—the day before the latter's arrest. He had already obtained new papers through his banker friend to travel to Spain. Before he left he was able to warn de Blommaert of Nothomb's arrest and the renewed activity of Jean Masson who had lain low since the arrest of Frédéric de Jongh in June 1943. The line which took him to Spain was run by a French information réseau, and he passed the frontier at Mauleon in March 1944.

On arrival at Pamplona, he met 'Monday' with Albert Greindl, on his way back to Paris on a special mission for another service. D'Oultremont later described to me how, with their usual high spirits, they exchanged hats. Albert Greindl had evidently arrived wearing an 'Anthony Eden', which seemed unsuitable for crossing the Pyrenees in rough weather. D'Oultremont, therefore, took it back to England, giving Greindl a hat he considered more appropriate, bought in the Boulevard de la Madeleine in Paris.

Messages received after the arrest of Nothomb showed that de Blommaert was also in danger. I telegraphed 'Monday' that he should return, leaving Lemaître in France, so that we could reshape our plans for the next two or three months. By this time, it had become important to preserve all our best agents for 'Marathon' and the invasion scheme. I knew we could wait no longer to set it in motion.

The message to return was brought to de Blommaert by Micheline Dumon ('Michou') of the Comet line from Spain on February 28th. He crossed the frontier on March 2nd with Lafleur, still limping after his jump from the window at Reims, and arrived in London on March 9th. Micheline Dumon was herself forced to flee in May for she was also in the greatest danger from the Gestapo. This diminutive girl of twenty, known always as 'Michou', had worked in the Comet line since the earliest days, usually as a guide between Brussels and Paris, or Paris and the frontier. She escaped literally by the skin of her teeth, and among her many gallant services she brought ten men over the frontier between December 1943 and May 1944. 'Michou' received the George Medal after the war and is now Madame Pierre Ugeux.

CHAPTER 21

The 'Sherwood' Plan

THE message which I sent to Jean de Blommaert through 'Michou' in February 1944 was urgent. On the second Brittany sea operation, Dumais submitted a written report warning that de Blommaert was known to the Gestapo in Paris. This report could not be ignored though it was not known that Jean Masson was involved. Shortly after his return to France in November 1943 de Blommaert had been in touch with a man who called himself Pierre Boulain of 13 rue de Bourgogne, Paris, and claimed to be a Belgian. A meeting was arranged between them in the belief that Pierre Boulain had been a genuine helper of Nothomb before the latter's arrest. He now offered to create a new line from northern France to Paris and received 20,000 francs.[1]

After de Blommaert had left for England in March, Michou discovered that Pierre Boulain was a Gestapo agent. The arrest of a number of helpers in Paris, including a French woman dentist, had made her certain that there was a traitor in the line. The method which she adopted to find the name of the traitor was characteristic of this extraordinary girl. She went straight to Fresnes prison and stood outside the walls, where she could observe the women's quarters. She did not know the position of the cell where the woman dentist, named Martine, was imprisoned, but she cried out:

"Martine! Martine!"

A voice answered from within the prison. It was Martine.

Then Michou cried again: "Who is the traitor? Who has betrayed you?"

The voice called again: "It is Pierre! It is Pierre Boulain!"

The incident reminded me of François Dissart as she stood outside the prison at Toulouse in 1943 trying to reach O'Leary.

[1] The author is indebted to M. Jean-Pierre Mallet, who worked for Comet, for much of this information.

Michou was able to alert de Blommaert when he returned to France in April and he escaped from this dangerous enemy. But who was Pierre Boulain? Could he and Jean Masson be the same?

The traitor, whoever he was, belonged to a Gestapo team headed by a man named Prosper Desitter. Desitter had appeared in reports to Room 900 for some months. He was known as 'the man with the missing finger' and was suspected of several denunications. All underground services had been warned against him. It was impossible at the time to unravel the full particulars of the latest Gestapo attempt to destroy the organisation in Paris but the position was extremely serious.

On arrival in London on March 9th, de Blommaert spent two days at 22, Pelham Crescent writing his report. We then began urgent discussions about his future and whether it was safe for him to return to France. There was no doubt that he had been extremely lucky, but I felt that if he were able to establish a camp in the country-side and remain as far as possible from Paris and Pierre Boulain, he had every chance of survival. Taking a map of the region Chartres—Châteaudun—Orleans, we selected the extensive and thickly wooded area between Châteaudun and Vendôme known as the Forêt de Fréteval. The forest, near the small town of Cloyes, was dense and intersected by rides. Surrounding it were many open spaces suitable for parachute operations.

Our first proposal had been for a series of 'mobile' camps, as far as the Spanish frontier. The airmen would be carried in lorries by road from camp to camp, organised by local resistance workers. They could also move by bicycle. But this scheme was far too elaborate and dangerous. Large numbers of German troops were now travelling by road, owing to our fierce bombing of the railways.

Our later talks developed the principle of 'static' camps, and they determined the final shape of the plan for the Forêt de Fretéval. I gave it the code-name 'Sherwood' after Robin Hood and Nottingham Forest. It was here that airmen and others hidden in Paris would be concentrated. Those who had not been taken off by the Shelburne organisation from Brittany would be hidden near Rennes. Those in Brussels would, as before, be moved into the Ardennes under Albert Ancia. At my final conference with de Blommaert, I proposed to send Squadron Leader Boussa with a new Belgian radio operator,

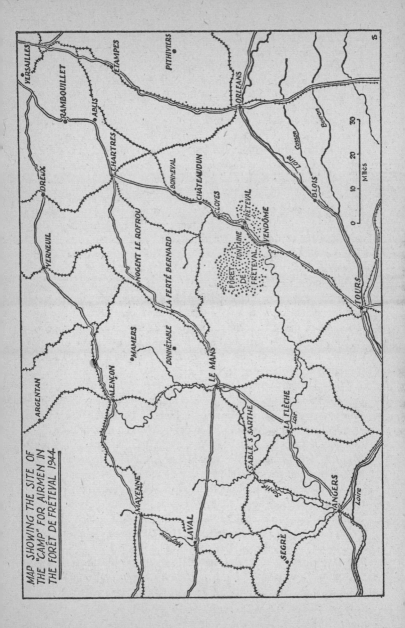

MAP SHOWING THE SITE OF
THE "CAMP" FOR AIRMEN IN
THE FORÊT DE FRETEVAL 1944

VERSAILLES
RAMBOUILLET
ABLIS
ÉTAMPES
PITHIVIERS
ORLÉANS
Buron
DREUX
CHARTRES
BONNEVAL
CHÂTEAUDUN
CLOYES
FRETEVAL
Cosson
BLOIS
VERNEUIL
NOGENT LE ROTROU
LA FERTÉ BERNARD
FORÊT
DE
FRETEVAL
FONTAINE
FRETEVAL
VENDÔME
Loir
ARGENTAN
MAMERS
BONNÉTABLE
LE MANS
TOURS
ALENÇON
LA FLÈCHE
Loir
SABLÉ S SARTHE
Sarthe
MAYENNE
Mayenne
LAVAL
ANGERS
Loire
SEGRÉ

0   10   20   30
Miles

Toussaint ('Taylor') to assist him once the camp had been made ready.

I was well aware that this plan, though original, involved great risks, especially if a large number of German troops were stationed in the neighbourhood of Cloyes, a small market town, three miles from the forest, In spite of the bombing, de Blommaert would have to organise the transfer of the men from Paris by train to Châteaudun. Then they would have to be escorted along country roads for about ten miles to the forest. There was also the crucial problem of feeding them in a forest without discovery. But Free French services reported there were strong Resistance parties in the area and that local farmers and priests were loyal to the Allies. It seemed a good choice for a hiding-place. My main anxiety was that airmen might be involved in a battle if German troops took cover in the forest. Much depended on where the battle for Paris and the Seine took place.

I could see that de Blommaert was excited by the prospect of this operation and that he believed it to be practicable. Ancia, too, seemed shrewd and dependable and I felt I could count on him to organise his camp in the Belgian Ardennes. Thus far, our calculations depended on a study of the map. De Blommaert's first duty would be to make a reconnaissance of the forest and recruit agents in Cloyes and the surrounding villages. He had also a difficult diplomatic task to undertake in dealing with escape lines still in operation.

As the airmen would have to be transferred from Comet, and probably Shelburne, I realised that much would depend on his ability to persuade their leaders of the logic of the plan. In the event, he and Ancia had great difficulty in doing so, though I sent messages by 'Monday' to Madame de Greef at St. Jean de Luz and Yvon Michiels ('Jean Serment') the chief in Brussels, explaining its purpose. It was inevitable that a certain rivalry should grow up among those who had stuck it out in occupied territory throughout the war, and the new arrivals. The landing in France would completely alter their situation. I told de Blommaert to exercise great tact. He was to hand over a sum of money to Comet, explain to them the plan, then avoid Paris and make for the Forêt de Fréteval.

On April 9th I was with de Blommaert and Ancia at R.A.F. Tempsford before they were parachuted to France. The calm and poise with which de Blommaert set off on this second mission after his narrow escape from treachery a month before, won my deepest admiration. Somehow I felt certain that he would survive and that we should meet again, for after the invasion, I planned to lead the expedition to liberate the party in the Forêt de Fréteval myself.

The two Belgians landed on a field at St. Amboise, near Issoudun at two a.m. on April 10th. De Blommaert's parachute became entangled in an overhead electric cable and he had to abandon it. They lay up in woods until five o'clock and saw a man stop and look at the parachute hanging above him. By eight-thirty that morning they were in contact with friends in the neighbourhood who had worked with de Blommaert on his previous mission. Next day they reached Paris where they were able to hide the two million French francs which I had given them. Most of de Blommaert's previous helpers were safe, and he found his flat untouched. I had sent a B.B.C. message to announce his imminent arrival and it was understood by his contacts.

When they made enquiries about Comet, they found that a number of helpers in Belgium had been arrested. Only in the south, where Madame de Greef still held sway, was the line intact. The convoys of airmen from Brussels to Paris soon began again but the number of trains was severely limited by bombing. The moment had clearly come when the camps should be prepared. But the underground conflict with Gestapo agents still continued. In de Blommaert's absence in England Prosper Desitter, 'the man with the missing finger' and Pierre Boulain had remained at large, pretending to be agents of Comet. At the beginning of May, Pierre Boulain arrived without warning at a secret rendezvous used by de Blommaert, and known only to his closest friends. Providentially, Michou appeared and made warning signs. Convinced that Pierre Boulain was a danger to his whole organisation, de Blommaert made plans to liquidate him. He invited a Free French group to assist, but the man who they claimed to have tortured into confessing that he was Pierre Boulain did not correspond with the description of the man known to de Blommaert and Michou. Was it possible that the Gestapo were employing another Pierre Boulain?

The second phase of this tortuous and risky affair took place in Paris on May 16th, 1944. Pierre Boulain reappeared and, like several traitors at the end of the war, offered to turn double agent. Ancia, accompanied by a Free French 'executioner', asked him to take

500,000 francs to Comet in Brussels, the money to be handed over next day. Pierre Boulain accepted but he was heavily guarded by Gestapo agents who stood in the background. The Free French now asked for freedom of action to dispose of him through their special 'liquidation group'. On May 22nd, de Blommaert, who had left Paris for the forest after his narrow escape, received a laconic message from Ancia:

"Le coup est fait mais ça chauffe."

It was later alleged that Pierre Boulain had been shot in the street from a 'liquidation car' which was then chased by the Gestapo. But the same man was also seen a week afterwards.[1] It was not till the liberation that it became clear that Pierre Boulain was the same man as Jean Masson who later, under his real name, Jacques Desoubrie, was tried and executed at Lille. The identity of the man who was shot in the street is a mystery.[2] It was time for Ancia to leave Paris and he left to start work in the Belgian Ardennes, while Michou reluctantly fled to Spain. On arrival in London she pleaded with me to send her back to France, but I firmly refused. Had she been captured, she would have certainly suffered the fate of her father and sister.

De Blommaert had already made visits to the Forêt de Fréteval and he now took up his headquarters near Cloyes. Before leaving Paris, he made arrangements with Philippe d'Albert Lake of Comet for a system of guides by train to the camp. His contacts with the Resistance at Cloyes, made in April, were of the greatest value. As we had foreseen, he found that farmers, bakers and other tradesmen were willing to supply food for the airmen on the black market. He also reached agreement with the Resistance that there would be no sabotage or other subversive activity against the Germans in or near the Forêt de Fréteval. It was his hope that the German Army would eventually be forced to retire towards the Seine leaving the forest in a no-man's-land between Le Mans and Châteaudun. This was exactly the position when I liberated the camp in August 1944 and the airmen had hidden beneath the thick foliage for over three months.

On May 13th, Boussa, with his wireless operator, Toussaint, arrived at the forest, having travelled overland from Spain. They

[1] By Jean-Pierre Mallet.
[2] See Chapter 25.

brought my orders to proceed with the Forêt de Fréteval and other camps as soon as possible. Information which I received from the War Office suggested that, if the landing succeeded, the Germans might be falling back on the Seine in a few weeks. I knew that, with difficulties of rail transport, it would take a considerable time to bring airmen from Paris where over a hundred were reported in hiding. Boussa was nearly forty, spare, energetic and amusing. He had already been chosen to maintain discipline and morale. To keep a large number of airmen of different nationalities in a forest for anything up to three months would be a difficult assignment. As he was a serving R.A.F. Officer of senior rank who had distinguished himself in air combat he would be able to enforce the rules of the camps.[1] He had a strong personality and a sense of command. Since he spoke English well, he was given instructions in security and interrogation of airmen on their arrival from Paris. Success for the 'Sherwood' plan depended therefore on the personal leadership of de Blommaert and Boussa. Their principal problem would be to keep order in the forest and prevent the men, through impatience or claustrophobia, from making attempts to escape on their own.

On May 16th I receive a message on Toussaint's radio set, apparently from the Châteaudun region, announcing his safe arrival with Boussa. He gave details from de Blommaert of a dropping zone near the Forêt de Fréteval for parachuting supplies of food and arms. The latter were on no account to be given to the airmen, who would certainly have been shot as members of the Resistance. The 'Sherwood' group were lucky in the high quality of the local Free French Forces of the Interior based on Châteaudun. One of the leaders, Omer Jubault, was a gendarme from Cloyes. It was at Cloyes, at the Hotel St. Jacques, that Mary Lindell had stayed the night with Windsor-Lewis on their celebrated journey to the demarcation line three years before. Jubault, shrewd and devoted, had already risked arrest for his aid to the Resistance and had now disappeared from the police force. Taking two foresters into his confidence, he selected a site among the trees, well-concealed from the Cloyes-Vendôme road along which German military transport was passing at all hours.

The first airmen were brought by train to Châteaudun on May

[1] He won the D.F.C. in the Battle of Britain and was promoted Wing Commander for this mission.

20th and taken ten miles across country to Cloyes, in spite of frequent bombing on the journey from Paris. They were hidden in neighbouring villages for the next two weeks.

On June 6th, the day of the invasion, thirty Allied airmen were moved into the forest and the camp began.

The 'Sherwood' plan was now in operation, but the difficulties were enormous. For those who did not experience it, it is difficult to imagine life under German occupation at this period of the war. Rationing was extremely strict, and there was virtually no coffee, rice or chocolate, except on the black market. Wine was only available for those doing heavy work. There was practically no fuel or petrol. Nonetheless, local farmers supplied the camp with fresh meat, vegetables, butter and eggs. Monsieur Viron, a miller, organised the delivery of fresh bread, brought by a young girl in a horse-drawn cart. She made the journey through the forest rides for several weeks, in spite of being machine-gunned by Allied aircraft in mistake for German transport. Two airmen were selected as cooks and worked with charcoal fires which gave little smoke.

The organisation already had a number of tents to shelter the men, but they had been obtained only with the greatest difficulty. One had come all the way from Dunkirk. In the middle of June, I arranged to parachute more at Issoudun, but owing to a misunderstanding, the aircraft returned without dropping its load. For some reason, de Blommaert did not receive the message until too late and there was no reception. A second supply operation (code-name 'Jupiter'), on the night of July 6th/7th, was successful. Fifteen containers were dropped containing tents, food, medicines and clothes.

One of the weaknesses of de Blommaert's position lay in poor radio contacts with Room 900. His own operator, Lemaître, remained in Paris at the service of Comet and seems to have had considerable difficulty with his set, though he did everything possible to maintain contact. He was needed in Paris, where Philippe d'Albert Lake was in charge of the reception and dispatch of evaders to the Forêt de Fréteval, a delicate and essential operation. I also remained in communication with Dumais and Labrosse. After their last sea operation in July from Brittany, airmen held by 'Shelburne' were also sent to the camp.

The second operator, Toussaint, had his set at a village near the forest. He had left a spare set and crystals at Bayonne with the

Comet organisation on his journey from Spain. I was not aware of this at the time, and it meant that de Blommaert and Boussa were never quite sure whether their messages were being received by Room 900, and we were often unable to 'raise' Toussaint. Spares were dropped to him on the supply operation 'Jupiter', but there was little improvement in the links with London. It transpired that Comet in Bayonne had sent the spare set for Toussaint by train to Paris. After the camp was liberated, de Blommaert reported that it was either destroyed or stolen when a train was bombed while en route to Châteaudun.

In desperation, Boussa recruited a French operator who claimed to have been trained in England, but had lost touch with his organisers. However, he also failed to make regular contact with Room 900. In spite of this inadequate radio network, the two Belgian organisers set about the establishment of the camp and its administration with remarkable efficiency. Provided the tents were concealed deep in the forest and away from the rides, the Germans were unlikely to see them. It seems probable that they knew that people were in hiding there, but believing them to be armed Resistance forces, were reluctant to enter.

As the camp grew in size, provisions became de Bommaert's most serious headache. After the operation was complete in September 1944, he made a report on the minimum rations required for such an exercise:

> "500 grammes bread per man per day
> 1 kilo of butter for 12 men each day
> 1 litre of milk per man per day
> 2 eggs   ,,   ,,   ,,   ,,
> 400 grammes potatoes per man per day
> 100 grammes meat   ,,   ,,   ,,   ,,.
> 8 cigarettes   ,,   ,,   ,,   ,,
> If possible, fresh fruit and vegetables, coffee, tea and sugar."

He managed to obtain most of these quantities locally, supplemented by food dropped by parachute. Among his other recommendations were:

"If there is any alcohol, entrust it to a man who will keep it under guard.

"In the absence of potatoes, dried beans are useful.

"Flour is essential and also sugar, which was very difficult to obtain, but I managed to obtain some honey."

It seems incredible that by the middle of August, 152 men were being fed in the forest, largely from local supplies. French patriots even risked the curfew to obtain fresh fish for the airmen at night from the river Loir. De Blommaert has also left some interesting comments for future guidance on the security of the camp. It was necessary to have as few people as possible who knew of its existence, and to have agents to report rumours, and enemy movements. Sentries should be posted at all times, especially at dawn and throughout the day, at the entrances to the forest. In the event of an alarm, he had a plan for speedy escape. Each man had an 'escape kit' ready prepared with rations and a small sum of money. These precautions were similar to those of partisans and 'maquis' in other theatres of war. The main difference between such partisan activity and the 'Sherwood' operation was the presence of over a hundred valuable, unarmed aircrew. It made the task of the organisers exceptionally delicate and they felt the strain of their protection.

At the end of July, the camp numbered over 100 and some were wounded and sick. A male nurse was appointed from among the airmen whose duty was to look after the lightly wounded in an ambulance tent. Severely wounded were hidden by an aged Frenchwoman in her house on the edge of the forest, which served as a hospital. They were treated in secret by a doctor from Cloyes and an American pilot had a successful operation for appendicitis. On the Jupiter supply operation I sent drugs and D.D.T. to disinfect the straw of which the men made beds. Apart from his immediate entourage, de Blommaert allowed only the doctor and a hairdresser to enter the site. He still found great difficulty in obtaining medicines locally. Had there been better radio contact, I should certainly have been able to send more supplies to him. The sick and wounded suffered in consequence, despite the devotion of their French helpers.

Other administrative problems were stoves, plates and saucepans, some of which were dropped by parachute, others lent by farmers. The tents, dropped on Operation Jupiter on July 6th/7th, were most successful. Prior to this date, many men had been obliged to sleep under cover of parachutes slung over branches or in the large

British Bell tent, a relic of Dunkirk and bought at black market price. When the camp had grown to twenty-five tents, it was decided to create a second on the same model at the edge of the forest at Richeray, six miles away. This was a good site, although there were a number of German ammunition dumps close by. De Blommaert considered that the presence of German guards was an advantage since it kept away the curious and the enemy would never suspect his choice of a hiding-place. Boussa remained in charge of the first camp while de Blommaert took command of the second. When airmen arrived from Paris they were brought to the first camp and interrogated by Boussa. They were then transferred through the forest to Richeray.

Boredom and anxiety were extremely difficult to combat. The men passed their days, thanks to fine weather, sun-bathing and talking. From logs and branches they made themselves tables and chairs. They also created a primitive golf-course but their greatest relaxation was to listen to wireless announcements of the progress of the battle. Important news was posted on a tree which served as a notice board. Senior officers maintained a degree of military discipline. The men rose at six a.m. for breakfast. Then they made up their beds of straw and camouflaged the tents with branches. In this way their morale and health were maintained until their liberation on August 13th, 1944. But their lives were not without dangerous incident.

When bombing and troop movements finally stopped the line to Spain, de Blommaert recruited a number of guides from Comet, among whom was Virginia d'Albert Lake, an attractive American, whose husband Philippe was the chief organiser in Paris. On June 12th, Virginia and her husband attempted to reach the camp with eleven airmen, some on bicycles and some in a farm-cart. On the way from the station at Châteaudun, she was stopped by a German patrol whose officer, speaking in perfect French, recognised her American accent. The remainder escaped, including six airmen in the farm-cart, though they were only fifty yards away from the German troops.

Virginia was taken to the Feldgendarmerie at Châteaudun and interrogated.

She explained that she was bicycling towards the Spanish frontier with a friend and this accounted for 127,000 francs and a pencil sketch of the route to the camp which were found on her. The Germans did not appear to have noticed the escape of the rest of the party, who scattered and were later found by de Blommaert hiding in farmhouses. But the Gestapo intervened, and, not believing her, sent Virginia to Ravensbrück concentration camp where she suffered until her release in 1945. After her arrest, Philippe d'Albert Lake returned to Paris and was able to make contact with another organisation which brought him by Lysander to London. He impressed upon me that de Blommaert was wanted by the Gestapo and known to them as 'The Fox'. Three weeks had now passed since Allied troops had landed on the Normandy beaches. They were now held down by the Germans but sooner or later they would break through and pursue them towards the Seine. I therefore prepared to leave for France, with the rescue of the men in the 'Sherwood' forest as my first objective.

There were more alarms and occasional arrests of guides and other helpers but the camps contined to grow in size without the loss of any airmen. As part of the 'Marathon' programme, smaller camps had been organised in Brittany and northern France. De Blommaert reported that there were fifty hidden in between Chartres and Paris, and sixty between Mantes and Beauvais. Thirty of these were in a camp organised by him at Auneuil near Beauvais. The efficient Paris staff, under d'Albert Lake, had recorded all their names. Lieut. Patrick Hovelacque (Kummel), recruited from the B.C.R.A., who had parachuted to France earlier in the year, reported over fifty in his hands at Chantilly.[1] All these camps were liberated but meanwhile they stood at great risk. I was determined to carry out their rescue in person and Langley agreed that the Anglo-American I.S.9 (Western European Area) should train for this operation. It was now essential that I should be in Normandy, and, after handing over Room 900 to Darling,[2] who had been transferred from Gibraltar, I set sail for France. I landed at Arromanches from a motor torpedo boat and established myself not far from Caen. I had a month to wait before the great break-through from the beach-head began and I could start the expedition to the Forêt de Fréteval.

[1] He received the M.C.
[2] In 1944 and 1945, Major Brinsley Ford and Major John Banks also served at Room 900.

CHAPTER 22

The Race to the Forest

WHEN I left for France, mystery surrounded the fate of Capitaine Potier, the modest, Belgian Air Force Officer who had parachuted in July, 1943, to organise Lysander operations. It was not until after my meeting with de Blommaert at the Forêt de Fréteval that I heard his story. Potier had visited an address in the control of the Gestapo and was arrested. No doubt this was the work of our enemies Prosper Desitter and Jacques Desoubrie alias Jean Masson and Pierre Boulain. Potier was taken to Fresnes, subjected to appalling tortures, and was heard by other inmates groaning in his cell. A man of deep Catholic conviction, he threw himself over a balustrade in the prison rather than give away his friends in his agony. His suicide, contrary to his piety and conscience, left a lasting impression on me. The sacrifice of his life must, I felt, have been preceded by an inner struggle with his profound religious feeling. It was both a personal tragedy and an act of faith. He was one of the bravest of all the agents under my charge, and his contribution to the moral forces behind the escape movement, to which many members of the Catholic faith belonged, set an example of steadfastness and loyalty to all of those who in that summer of liberation set out to wind up the escape organisations.

My intention, on arrival in Normandy, was to rescue as many lives from the Germans as possible, especially of those who now lay at the mercy of the embittered and defeated Secret Police. From this time until the end of the war, the Gestapo behaved with vindictiveness and purposeless brutality, knowing that Germany had lost the war. In this objective of preventing both airmen and agents from falling into their hands I had, as on many other occasions, quite remarkable good fortune.

I.S.9 (Western European Area) or I.S.9 (W.E.A.) was attached to the intelligence staff of Field Marshal Montgomery's 21 Army

Group. Langley had been appointed a General Staff Officer (Intelligence), or G.S.O. 1 (I) and I became the G.S.O. 2 (Planning) of I.S.9 and therefore a G.S.O. 2 (I) of 21 Army Group. These high-sounding titles disguised my real underground activities. At no time did I venture near 21 Army Group, leaving the links to Langley. I concerned myself entirely with rescue operations until the British Army reached Holland and finally liberated that country in May 1945.

I.S.9 (W.E.A.) was a curious body of men. Langley, and the American Colonel Richard Nelson, had a headquarters staff at Bayeux in Normandy. Under them was a British and an American interrogation section. Then came four small field sections, one British, two American and one Canadian, led by officers and N.C.O.s equipped with jeeps. The role of these sections took some time to devise. Until the Americans broke through and started the pursuit of the enemy towards the Seine, they had little to do. They were inadequately armed for protecting airmen or others cut off by the enemy. After the break-through, it was necessary to persuade other troops, especially S.A.S. and commando units, to give them the necessary support.

It would have been better to create armed formations at the start to operate, if necessary, behind the enemy lines, but M.I.9 in Britain was essentially a staff organisation, chiefly devoted to the collection of intelligence about prisoners-of-war. Room 900 remained secret and remote from the Army in the field, though in Normandy I was in wireless contact with Darling. Little thought however had been given to how the scheme for the camps could be brought to a safe conclusion without specially trained and equipped troops. This defect in our planning had long been obvious to me, but despite the efforts of Crockatt and Langley, the role of such rescue units was not understood at 21 Army Group. It was a concept new to conventional military intelligence and no suitable forces existed except S.A.S. and the Commandos who had other parts to play. In consequence, the chances of saving people from capture in the battle zone or behind the lines depended more on luck than planning. Our sections had neither the training nor equipment for this type of operation.

While the battle blazed in the Normandy beach-head, there was little that I.S.9 (W.E.A.) could do. Its staff sat in the British or

American Zones wondering what would happen next. Before I left Room 900, leaving that diminutive organisation under Donald Darling, I had proposed Operation 'Labyrinth', a scheme to send French and Belgian guides in civilian clothes through the German lines in Normandy to contact airmen. They were to be known as 'Retrievers' and if combat conditions permitted, they were to try and bring the men back to safety. A number of these 'Retrievers', including d'Oultremont, who had remained in London after his last mission, were stationed at Bayeux.

It proved a thoroughly impracticable plan. The concentration of troops on both sides was so dense that the risk of sending an agent in civilian clothes across the lines was unjustified. Only when the Germans began to retreat and large areas of France were in no-man's-land was this form of infiltration possible. Other intelligence branches tried it, with disastrous results. Realising that 'Labyrinth' in such conditions was murderous, Langley agreed that the 'Retrievers' should be released to England for other services. D'Oultremont returned to London where he joined the Belgian S.A.S. Regiment and, on later operations, added the Military Medal to his decorations.

The interrogation section of American and British officers was designed to question all evaders and escapers on their liberation and to make preliminary reports before they were sent home. It was able to collect useful tactical information. During the German retreat, many men were picked up by individual fighting units and returned to Britain, where, no doubt, they were questioned at the Great Central Hotel.

At Bayeux, Langley was handicapped by having to send all messages to M.I.9 through conventional military channels, whereas I had the advantage of direct communications with Donald Darling at Room 900 through another intelligence unit. This contact was maintained with de Blommaert and other troops in enemy territory until, a few weeks later, I found myself miles away from Normandy during the American advance on Le Mans without any radio links at all. This division between conventional military intelligence in the combat area and clandestine operations by Room 900 led to misunderstanding. It provoked the frequent comment from staff officers, both British and American, that I.S.9 (W.E.A.) was a 'private army' and not their affair.

For three weeks life in the Normandy beach-head was uneventful and frustrating. I was in continuous anxiety about the fate of the camps. It did not seem possible that they could hold out for much longer. Of the plan for the Belgian Ardennes to be carried out by Ancia there was no news at all. Coache, the Comet radio operator, had been off the air for weeks in Brussels and it was probable that he had been arrested, though I knew from 'Monday' who was able to keep in touch with Madame de Greef that Comet was still in existence. A thin trickle of airmen, some guided and some on their own, was still crossing the Pyrenees as late as July. I therefore had to wait, occupying the time by paying visits to the front line at Caen and listening to the pounding of artillery and tanks by day and night.

The B.C.R.A. had attached to me, as liaison officer, Capitaine Gilles Lefort, a cool and most able French officer who calmed my impatience and dissuaded me from impulsive schemes. Major James Thornton, a Canadian, serving in the American section of I.S.9 (W.E.A.) also joined me in making plans for the liberation of the camps. Having initiated what many staff officers considered to be a wild-cat plan for the camps, I felt responsible for their safety. I was determined that as soon as a break-through occurred on any part of the Allied Front, I would make a dash to them. Lefort and Thornton agreed to accompany me.

At the beginning of August, the Americans pierced the German line at St. Lô and attacked north, towards Cherbourg. They followed with their famous break-through into Brittany at Avranches. I packed my jeep, in high elation, and led the American sections of I.S.9 (W.E.A.) to Rennes where we expected to find a group of airmen. The road to Avranches was a terrible mêlée of German dead and broken transport, the corpses of mules and horses, shrouded in fine summer dust, blocking the way. We drove through the villages, narrowly avoiding ambush by the retreating enemy, and we were often cut off from American forces. The exhilaration was unforgettable. The restraints of London and the beach-head were past and the smell of pursuit was in the air.

At Rennes, to my mortification, the camp of evaders had already dispersed. I stayed there long enough to send a party of French 'Retrievers' towards Plouha to make contact with Dumais and 'Shelburne'. Leaving an American section to look after any airmen who might be left in Brittany, I turned about to follow General

Patton's American Third Army towards Paris and the Forêt de Fréteval. I knew that de Blommaert and Boussa and more than 150 men were waiting impatiently. Lefort, Thornton and I were back at Avranches on August 8th, but our road to the camp was blocked by an enemy counter-attack at Mortain. We therefore summoned all available sections of I.S.9 (W.E.A.) and by-passing Mortain followed Patton's thrust along the road to Laval and Le Mans.

It seemed that my calculations were justified and that Patton's troops were moving rapidly towards the Forêt de Fréteval. From Le Mans the camp was forty-seven miles in the direction of Châteaudun. I arrived in Le Mans on August 10th confidently assuming that American Third Army would attack towards Chartres and Vendôme. I was disconcerted to hear from the staff of an armoured division that they intended to attack north of Alençon and close the 'Falaise Gap', a manoeuvre which destroyed much of ʰ.. ..rman army west of the Seine. It was a serious position for me. I had counted on tanks and armoured cars to help me recover the airmen. I did not possess sufficient fire power to deal with any large body of Germans. I had only half a dozen jeeps and a few automatic weapons to effect the rescue of at least 150 people in enemy-held territory. Nor was there any clear information about a German withdrawal from the Fréteval area. German battle-groups were reported between Le Mans and Châteaudun, and I had no direct communication with the camp.

After a rapturous reception in the main square of Le Mans, I made my headquarters at the Hotel Moderne which the Germans had just left, to find an excited mass of war correspondents and Free French with rifles. The only thing to drink was cheap white wine which did not seem to prevent an atmosphere of rejoicing. But I was worried and alarmed. I sat in the dining-room with Thornton and Lefort with a map of the region, planning the route to the forest. I was going to be responsible for a terrible tragedy if things went wrong, and I began to search around for means of obtaining transport and armed protection.

In the afternoon, Thornton and I drove to the headquarters of American XV Corps, north of Le Mans, and begged a worried Staff Officer for a few trucks and armoured cars. I explained that half the men in the camp were from the American Air Force and I feared a tragedy if they waited any longer. I believed that, hearing the sounds of battle, some of them would break away and join Resistance forces in civilian clothes. We had heard grim stories of massacre by the S.S. and seen evidence of it on our way. In some cases whole families had been shot and their houses burned. The Germans were in a mood of panic. They were harassed in their retreat by the French underground who mined the roads, threw petrol bombs at tanks and sniped at them all the way to the Seine and beyond.

These arguments failed to convince the American Staff and their Corps Commander. They had their orders to wait for a move on Alençon and they could spare neither troops nor transport. They declared the rescue operation to be impossible without light tanks. We returned to Le Mans greatly depressed, but in the courtyard of the hotel found a large number of armed jeeps. Standing by them were troops in maroon berets. This was a remarkable piece of luck for me and even more for the inmates of the Forêt de Fréteval. They were an S.A.S. squadron under the command of Captain Anthony Greville-Bell and consisted of four officers and thirty-four men. They had completed their mission in Brittany but, finding little to do there after the German withdrawal on Brest, had decided to move east and await orders at Le Mans.

In high spirits, I hurried into the hotel and found Greville-Bell in the lounge. He was a dashing young officer with a D.S.O., ideally suited to 'private warfare', and no respecter of red tape. I could not have found a more suitable person to help me in this advanture. His troops would be a great advantage if we met opposition on the way to the forest and most important of all, he had his own radio communications with London. To add to these welcome friends, a group of twenty-three Belgian S.A.S. arrived that evening from south of Le Mans. Greville-Bell sent a signal to S.A.S. headquarters in London asking for permission to take part in the operation, which he received the following day. S.A.S. headquarters also provided indirect communication with Darling at Room 900, which was without news of me. For several days messages from London had arrived in Normandy, demanding the whereabouts of 'Saturday'. Without the aid of S.A.S., the operation would have been impossible.

On the following morning, August 11th, I was studying the map at the Hotel Moderne. Like all those days of liberation, it was fine and hot. The war correspondents had left to report the battle of the

'Falaise Gap', and the S.A.S. were cleaning their weapons and checking ammunition in the courtyard. There was still no transport for
the airmen. I sent Thornton and Lefort into Le Mans to French
Resistance headquarters in the hope that we could requisition local
buses. It seemed an unmilitary request, but the Resistance were
delighted to help. They scoured the town and found a few large
coaches painted grey which had been left behind by the Germans.
We were again lucky, for in their hasty retreat the Germans usually
commandeered all they could find, including horse-drawn vehicles.

The buses were fitted with the familiar charcoal burners to supplement the absence of petrol and needed considerable maintenance.
The possibility of a breakdown between Le Mans and the forest
was not pleasant, but there was no alternative. Later in the morning,
Thornton and Lefort returned with local Resistance leaders and we
sat down to a discussion of the rescue plan in the hotel dining-room.
We were interrupted by a commotion in the lobby and the appearance in the dining-room of Boussa and M. Viron, the miller who
had been supplying bread for the men. Running the gauntlet of
German patrols and trigger-happy partisans, they had driven from
Fréteval. I was delighted that Boussa was safe, but somewhat
anxious at this exploit.

"You must come and fetch the men immediately, mon Commandant," said Boussa.

He was strained and excited, and I felt much sympathy for him.

"There are no Germans at the forest. They have pulled out towards Chartres. It is quite safe for you to come. If you do not, the
men will start escaping on their own. Already some of them have
gone, and are in surrounding villages. Many of the local people are
already showing the French flag. It will be dangerous if the Germans
come back and take reprisals."

The dangers of the situation were obvious to me, but the French
leaders explained that the transport was not yet ready. They had
evidently been over-optimistic.

"Where are these vehicles?"

Volubly, they gave a number of garages in the town and the names
of the proprietors. They had not yet found the drivers, though, in
the state of confusion which reigned in Le Mans, this was under-
standable.

"How long do you need to get everything ready?" I asked.

"At least twenty-four hours, mon Commandant."

I turned to Boussa. I fully shared his impatience.

"Our main difficulty is that we have not been able to obtain American transport and troops as they are advancing towards the north. I think you must go back to the camp and tell the men that they will have to wait at least forty-eight hours. There might be a disaster if we appear without sufficient transport, and you must give direct orders that they are on no account to leave the camp."

Boussa looked crestfallen.

"The men are very excited and Jean de Blommaert and I are finding it very difficult to keep them calm."

I was embarrassed at having to show such caution. Captain Peter Baker, a young officer of I.S.9 (W.E.A.), volunteered excitedly to go to the camp. I knew that he had visions of changing into civilian clothes and making his way to Paris to write an article for an American newspaper. It was no time for heroics and there would be serious trouble if these unarmed pilots were captured or wounded. We talked for some time about his proposal. I was anxious not to restrain such dash and enthusiasm. The French were declaring that they 'controlled' the road to the forest, but it seemed that, if Baker could get through, he might be able to explain the situation to the men. I let him go with five S.A.S. troops under an officer. They were fired on by a small group of Germans and one man was slightly wounded but they reached the camp that afternoon and helped to sustain morale. Boussa and the courageous M. Viron in his baker's van returned at the same time.

I said to Boussa in the courtyard of the hotel that we would try to get to the forest on August 14th. We had already decided on a rendezvous with the party at a point on the edge of the forest on the road between Vendôme and Cloyes. There remained considerable difficulties. Only half the buses had drivers. Nearly all the young men of the town had joined the Resistance and were far away or had been deported for work in Germany, and the vehicles still needed mechanical attention.

Next morning further efforts were made to obtain American military transport, which remained standing outside Le Mans waiting for orders. It was maddening to see rows of lorries and trucks parked at a Divisional headquarters, but the American commanders were suspicious of the exotic crowd of armed patriots who accompanied me. They were not prepared to risk their vehicles on so long a journey into country which had not been cleared of the enemy without the use of tanks. There was nothing to be done except return to the hotel. The airmen would have to wait another day.

At noon, as I was preparing to send another officer to the forest, de Blommaert appeared, smiling, but impatient. He had come from the forest with Monsieur Viron. My delight at seeing him safe was sadly affected by what he had to say.

"The men are terribly disappointed that you have not come. I assure you that it is safe. This morning several of them have broken away from the camp and are celebrating with the inhabitants of the village of St. Jean-Froidmentel. All the flags are out and people are bringing their best wines out of the cellars."

I could picture what was happening, and my anger mounted against the Americans. It was obvious that with S.A.S., I could have moved to the forest and remained there overnight. Without the transport, however, we could not have brought the men to safety. Our presence in the forest would certainly have alerted the Germans. The prudent course was to make a dash there when the buses were ready and get the men back before anything happened. The Americans continued to report German rear guards in the neighbourhood. A fight between these rear guards and the S.A.S. would obviously put the airmen in extreme danger. They would probably scatter and be difficult to collect. I was now determined to do the operation in one piece, though the reproachful looks of de Blommaert were hard to bear. He insisted on returning to the camp for the night.

We sat down to a lunch of American rations and white wine, gloomily uncertain about the buses. In the afternoon, I received a message to go to one of the main squares in Le Mans. There, decked with flowers and French flags and guarded by civilians with rifles, was a collection of sixteen coaches and trucks. I was assured that they were all in working order and though the operation seemed comic, I decided that we could wait no longer. The whole party would leave the following morning.

My varied collection of 'troops', some in uniform, some with Free French armbands, assembled at eight a.m. on August 14th outside the hotel. They numbered about 100. It was a fine, hot morning and in high spirits we set off along the road to Vendôme with a patrol of S.A.S. ahead of us. I had given orders to travel as fast as possible. Within three-quarters of an hour, despite much spluttering from the 'buses' we turned off through gay villages towards Cloyes and up the road through the forest to the rendezvous. It was easily found. At a clearing beside the road, we found de Blommaert and Boussa with a large crowd, cheering and waving. It was far more like the departure for a seaside outing than the end of the extraordinary 'Sherwood' plan. The airmen were lean, bronzed and dressed in rough French working clothes. Some were angry and impatient. A few had disappeared and ten were taken off by two American tanks on the edge of the forest. I shook hands with Omer Jubault, the gendarme who had done so much to make the plan a success. I could only apologise for our failure to arrive before. Then we turned round and set off at a hot pace back to Le Mans.

The S.A.S. searched the villages en route and picked up a few tattered and demoralised German prisoners whom they pushed into the coaches beside the airmen. It was hard to believe that this was the end of operation 'Sherwood'. In my jeep were de Blommaert and Boussa and I could see that they could hardly realise that their extraordinary feat had been accomplished, after three months of suspense. It was fortunate that we had not delayed the expedition longer. That evening German patrols were reported in the forest, alerted, apparently, by the activities and rejoicing on the road to Cloyes.

Just before noon, we were back in Le Mans where a meal had been organised with American rations at a former French Army barracks. The Americans seemed to have realised the significance of the arrival of a large number of their airmen, who loudly demanded transport back to base. Army trucks and lorries at last appeared outside the barracks and after lunch the whole party left along the road to Laval where, sad to relate, some of them were injured by the overturning of one of the vehicles.

In a signal to Donald Darling on the S.A.S. radio set, I stated that the total number of men collected was 132. They were Americans, Canadians, New Zealanders, Polish and British. De Blommaert stated that the total roll call of the camp the day before had been 152, and it was assumed that those missing had either been collected by American tanks or were hiding in villages. Nearly all went back on flying operations and thirty-eight of them were killed in action before the end of the war.

To have planned and executed a scheme to hide and feed 152 airmen under the noses of the German Army and the Gestapo was an outstanding achievement. In a personal signal to Crockatt at M.I.9 that afternoon, I recommended de Blommaert for the D.S.O., since he had begun the camp and had already done great service for the Comet line, and Boussa for the M.C. They both received immediate awards as well as the French and Belgian Croix de Guerre. Omer Jubault and members of the Paris organisation of Sherwood and Shelburne were also decorated.

For many years Operation 'Sherwood', except to those who had taken part, remained an unknown story of the French Resistance movement. In 1966 a committee was formed under Omer Jubault, now retired from the French police, to erect a memorial at the place where my 'army' had collected the airmen over twenty years before. Funds were raised to which the Royal Air Force Escaping Society and many other organisations contributed. On June 11th, 1967, at an official ceremony, Jean de Blommaert and I laid wreaths on the grave of Lucien Boussa at Cloyes. He had died suddenly at the Hotel St. Jacques in March. The same afternoon, in the presence of a crowd of five thousand and full military honours, Monsieur Duvillard, the Ministre pour Ancien Combatants, unveiled a plain stone column at the edge of the forest with the inscription:

"Ici vécurent sauvés par la Résistance 152 aviateurs alliés. Mai-Août 1944."

PART VII

OCCUPIED HOLLAND

CHAPTER 23

After Arnhem

THE 'Sherwood' expedition, sometimes known as 'Rapière' or 'rapier-thrust', had its own unregimental character and romance. I shall always recall with pleasure our high-spirited journey to the Forêt de Fréteval. Viewed as a military operation, it can only be regarded as a calculated risk, but as an exercise in underground war, it was a major success. Though in no way to be compared with the exploits of the Long Range Desert Group in North Africa or S.A.S. in Europe, the results were none the less impressive.

On August 14th Peter Baker, de Blommaert and a group of S.A.S. returned to the forest to recover ten airmen who might still be hidden in villages or farms. They were fired on by French resistance workers in mistake for Germans, without suffering casualties, and found that nine of the airmen for whom they were looking had been taken away by American tanks, which caused them no little annoyance.

In Le Mans, I discussed how I could take the whole of my 'private army' to Chartres, about twenty-two miles beyond Châteaudun in the direction of Paris. My purpose was to recover more airmen known to be hidden in subsidiary camps which were in effect groups of farmhouses and barns near Mantes and Beauvais.

I was also thinking of the situation in Paris about which wild reports of 'revolution' and 'massacre' were reaching me. A number of French people belonging to our organisations might still be in danger and it was our duty to reach the city as quickly as possible to see if they were safe. Though the Germans were withdrawing to the Seine under heavy air attack, the military situation around Chartres was officially described as 'fluid'. I was obliged to spend a great deal of time arguing with the American staff in Le Mans who were reluctant to give permission for any troops to go ahead of the main advance, and spoke of me as a 'bandit'. This may have been due to my irregular appearance and dress, since I had lost my steel helmet and wore corduroy trousers.

The battle of the Falaise gap was barely finished and the American 3rd Army was preparing for the capture of Paris. I was nonetheless impatient, fearing that the remaining organisers and airmen might be overrun or taken prisoner. It was still not known whether the Germans intended to defend the city. If they did, it would be difficult to extricate the airmen. On August 17th, Peter Baker, de Blommaert and Belgian S.A.S. left for Chartres, but were unable to make further progress until the next day when the Americans attacked along the road to the north from Nogent-le-Roi. When I arrived, Chartres had been cleared, but there was still minor fighting outside the town on the road to Paris.

At the village of Jouy, six miles from Chartres, where we were guests at a feast in the village hall, I divided the rescue forces into two parties. One, under Baker, was to infiltrate as far as Rambouillet, in which they succeeded next day, receiving a royal welcome from the inhabitants. Since de Blommaert had reported a camp near Mantes, I took a second party to Dreux where we picked up a handful of airmen and handed them over to an American division. I continued to Mantes to find a pontoon bridge over the Seine, but there was fighting on the east bank. It was impossible to send through a courier on a bicycle to contact a camp of thirty-two men at Auneuil near Beauvais. I returned to Chartres as there appeared to be no more in hiding west of the Seine.

Our operations continued to be of a character best described as 'para-military'. In jeeps loaded with flowers and champagne we drove gaily from village to village, careless of German snipers and excited French riflemen.

At Rambouillet, I found Baker and de Blommaert and a huge crowd of excited war correspondents and photographers, dominated by the vast figure of Ernest Hemingway, which had gathered for the liberation of Paris. The American troops had now withdrawn to allow the French Division Leclerc to lead the triumphal entry. The French had not yet arrived at Rambouillet and an expectant lull descended on the battle. I spent my time debating with French and American officers whether it was safe to send couriers through to Paris in civilian clothes to contact our helpers.

The liberation of Paris has been described by some as a serious

battle, by others as a fiesta, but for me the period of waiting for the
French division to arrive and capture the town was one of irritation.
I pictured the arrest and deportation of our helpers at the last moment.
When Langley and his staff reached Rambouillet, we drew up a list
of addresses of the Comet and Shelburne organisations. The desire
to be first in the city was mingled with the more responsible objective of getting them out of danger. I was also anxious to reach Patrick
Hovelacque and his réseau at Chantilly, who were still in radio
touch with Room 900. Anyone in uniform had strict instructions
that they must wait for the French troops. My voluble impatience
was allayed next day by their arrival.

On August 25th, the Division Leclerc encountered heavy opposition in parts of the city, but Thornton and I managed to drive from
Rambouillet to Versailles, enter Paris by the Porte d'Orleans and
race up the Champs Elysées. As we rounded the Arc de Triomphe a
scattered fusillade from windows and rooftops, mainly from French
sources, made the journey one to remember. At the Hotel Windsor,[1]
I made a headquarters and interrogation centre, and after rescuing
two Germans from an angry crowd, sat down to study the map of
Paris, while the hotel cellars were searched for booby traps.

Much to my relief I found, as I toured the city, that most of our
helpers, whom twenty-four hours before I had thought in mortal
danger, were safe and well. The next day was spent amid the
wildest scenes of jubilation, shooting and drinking. Into the hotel
walked Albert Greindl, brother of the Comet chief who had died
so tragically from Allied bombing in Brussels. After his meeting
in Spain with Georges d'Oultremont, when they exchanged hats,
he had been working for an underground service in Paris. Captured
by the Gestapo, he was about to be taken by train to Germany and
liberated at the last moment.

Others who sought me out included the Reverend Donald Caskie
of the Seamen's Mission at Marseille, thin and pale after years in the
hands of the Gestapo.

It was difficult to compose one's thoughts in the bedlam of the
next few days. Large numbers of Resistance workers called at the
Hotel Windsor. They imagined me to be 'the Chief of the British
Secret Service'. Some wanted food, some to enrol in I.S.9 (W.E.A.)
and others put in claims for British decorations. I soon saw that if I

[1] Now the Hotel Windsor-Reynolds.

stayed too long in Paris, the Allied advance towards Belgium would outstrip our efforts to make contact with the camps which I assumed to have been organised in the Belgian Ardennes. Langley and his staff began to conduct interrogations and collect the names of hundreds of people who had helped airmen. A few weeks later, Crockatt set up 'Awards Bureau' to register these names, and make recommendations for honours, that in Paris being in the charge of Darling.

I was now without the S.A.S. and ill-equipped to conduct rescue operations. None in fact took place in the Belgian Ardennes, though I saw plenty of action. As part of the 'Marathon' project for Belgium, the camp should have been near Bastogne, scene of a heroic stand in December 1944 by American paratroops.[1] I searched for them with a small group from I.S.9 (W.E.A.) in the wake of the American advance, but they were nowhere to be found.

The mystery was explained when I reached Brussels on September 3rd. On his arrival there in May, Ancia had experienced great difficulties with the Comet organisation. They were unenthusiastic about the 'Marathon' plan and reluctant to establish a camp in the Belgian Ardennes. Moreover they were suspicious of Ancia's identity, with the result that he was unable to do much useful work. Comet retained the fierce spirit of Belgian independence and the majority of the airmen hidden in Brussels remained there. I reached the town as it was liberated by the Guards Armoured Division. Their tanks moved inch by inch through a solid mass of wildly cheering Belgians. So excited was their welcome that it was with difficulty I reached the Hotel Metropole where families hiding airmen had been ordered to collect so that their names could be registered.[2] They sat together in the lounge. They were already drinking champagne in large quantities when an American Colonel connected with S.H.A.E.F. General Eisenhower's headquarter's, announced:

"Drinks on Uncle Sam, boys!"

They needed no second invitation. A very large bill, sent to Langley by the Hotel Metropole, was only paid by S.H.A.E.F. after a long correspondence. On the following day, there were at

[1] 101st U.S. Airborne Division.
[2] Anne Brusselmans, M.B.E., *Rendez-vous 127*, Ernest Benn, 1954. She had sheltered evaders since 1941.

least 100 airmen and quite as many Belgians who had worked for Comet in the rooms of the hotel. I found it moving to see them celebrate and later take leave of those who had risked so much for them.

A pale and anxious figure made his appearance amid these festivities, having by a miracle avoided being sent to Germany after his arrest. It was René Coache of Asnières, the French radio operator in Brussels. He had spent several weeks in detention by the Gestapo, and he was lucky to escape with his life. In the confusion of the German withdrawal he had managed to escape. I was overjoyed to see him safe, but it was impossible to wait long in Brussels. The British Army were already advancing to the Dutch frontier and I was anxious to make contact with the organisation which I had set up in Holland.

Despite the terrible story of Trix Terwindt, in February 1943, I had sent several men to Holland. The first was Dignus Kragt, known as 'Frans Hals' or 'Dick'. He was a British subject with a Dutch father and English mother, born in England in 1917. He had worked as a radio engineer for Phillips at their Mitcham Works in England before the war and, in 1942, volunteered to parachute to Holland, to set up an escape line for Room 900 over the Dutch-Belgian frontier.

Dick Kragt was a brave and persistent agent, and a trained radio operator. He knew Holland reasonably well but had not been there since the death of his father some years before. He was to be dropped near Epe and establish contact with Comet so that airmen shot down in Holland could be transferred to them in Brussels. In June 1943 Comet seemed once more secure and, in this high summer of Nothomb's success, parties were travelling regularly from Brussels to Spain. Though comparatively few aircraft were shot down in Holland, we needed an organised route for them. Realising that all our previous contacts in the country were blown, it was some time before I secured a safe address for Kragt. Nor was the War Office easy to persuade that he should take a wireless set to Holland. They were now convinced that nearly the whole S.O.E. system—and its wireless equipment in Holland—was in the control of the Germans and history was to prove them right. They were afraid that no wireless operator, even if unconnected with S.O.E. would survive the efficient direction-finding equipment of the Germans. But it was impossible to send Kragt without communications in case there were further catastrophies in Brussels or Paris. I was therefore permitted to send him alone with his own radio equipment. This had many disadvantages.

In the first place, I was opposed to any escape organiser working his own wireless set, which put him at great risk, and I promised Kragt that another operator would be parachuted to him later in the year. Such was the uncertainty surrounding conditions in Holland that it was November 1943 before I was able to send one. During 1943, the Dutch Intelligence Bureau in London was being reorganised under Dr. J. M. Somer.[1] It was difficult to obtain recruits for escape work, about which the Dutch, at this time, were un-enthusiastic, though, after Arnhem, they gave me all possible help.

Kragt was dropped without a reception committee, for none existed, at Vaassen near Apeldoorn on June 23rd, 1943. Vaassen was eight miles from the agreed target, the Wesselse Veld west of Epe, so he had good reason for complaint. The aircraft had returned on three nights as the pilot could not find the dropping zone. On the third occasion, I watched the aircraft crash-land at Tempsford after it had been severely damaged by canon-fire. I was astonished at the courage of agents, who not only had to endure the tension of waiting to drop, but the chance of being shot down as well.

In 1968, Kragt recalled to me his unnerving arrival in Holland. On the fourth trip he found himself at two-thirty a.m. in the garden of a house at Vaassen. His baggage parachute, containing his wireless set, clothing and money, landed in a tree in an adjacent garden beneath the bedroom window of a Dutch quisling. While he laid low, he saw figures moving with blue torches, and it was useless to attempt to recover his equipment. Anxious to get clear of the area before the curfew ended at four a.m., he struck across country, after hiding his parachute in a ditch. He had with him a map, compass, .38 automatic, identity card and 500 guilders. All the rest of his stores were suspended in the tree in the quisling's garden. They were discovered next morning and handed over to the Germans, Kragt's parachute being found two days later. As a result he had no wireless set of his own for several months.

Throughout June 23rd, the weather was dry and he was able to hide in the tall grass of a field by the road to Deventer, still unsure

[1] Bureau Inlichtingen or B.I.

of his exact position. At midnight, braving the curfew, he set off
to find the safe address. Three months before, a Dutchman who was
Jewish had been sheltered and helped to Brussels by Mr. J. J. van
den Boogert, known as 'Koos,' who lived in a village near Epe. The
man escaped safely to England where he gave me the address of
Koos and a password. Kragt was to say that he came from the
'black cat'.[1]

Using his compass, he reached the village at dawn. As he shivered
in the morning dew, he heard a voice singing 'God save the King'
in English from a farm near the house of Koos. Encouraged by the
sound, he waited in some bushes near the house till seven o'clock,
then knocked on the door and gave his 'black cat' password.

Koos, a kindly Dutch official, who was shot by the Germans in
1944, exclaimed:

"I suppose it was you who lost your luggage in Vaassen the night
before last?"

Though in the hands of good friends, Kragt was without direct
communication with Room 900. He nonetheless passed messages
through a secret intelligence agent who had landed safely with his
set in the same month, a circumstance that did not endear Kragt
to the War Office. These criticisms were harsh and unreasonable.
I tried to persuade my overseer to put himself in Kragt's position.
The loss of the set was not Kragt's fault, for had he been dropped
by the R.A.F. in the right place near Epe, an expanse of open
ground, he would have had his own links with London.

Although Kragt had cause to be disgruntled, he nonetheless
established a line to Brussels and sent through over 100 airmen
before the airborne attack on Arnhem in September 1944. In November, 1943, I parachuted a young Dutchman of nineteen named
Temmerman ('Timon') as a wireless operator and a spare set to
him and later three more sets which he either operated himself or
was assisted by a Dutch Merchant Navy operator, Dirk Last, known
as 'Zwarte Kees'. He also organised the reception in October 1944
of two other Room 900 agents known as 'Ham' and 'Bacon' who
later fell into German hands.

This was the Room 900 organisation in Holland before the
famous attempt to capture Arnhem. It was to play a leading part
in escape operations in the months ahead.

[1] The 'black cat' was Maurice Kiek, a wireless operator for Room 900 in June 1944.

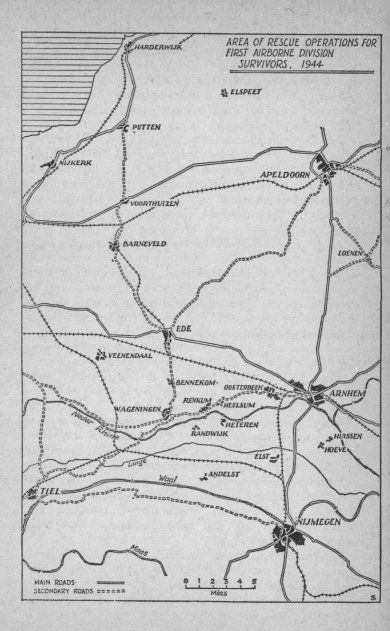

AREA OF RESCUE OPERATIONS FOR
FIRST AIRBORNE DIVISION
SURVIVORS, 1944

HARDERWIJK

ELSPEET

PUTTEN

NIJKERK

APELDOORN

VOORTHUIZEN

BARNEVELD

LOENEN

EDE

VEENENDAAL

BENNEKOM

OOSTERBEEK

ARNHEM

RENKUM

HEELSUM

WAGENINGEN

Neder Rhine

HETEREN

HUISSEN

RANDWIJK

HOEVE

Linge

ELST

ANDELST

Waal

TIEL

NIJMEGEN

Maas

MAIN ROADS
SECONDARY ROADS =====

0 1 2 3 4 5
Miles

The failure of the airborne landing at Arnhem on September 17th forced me to alter all my plans for Holland. Much of the British Army was held down in the low-lying region, between the Rhine and the Waal, for the rest of the war. Instead of a small group of airmen hiding in the Hague or Amsterdam, several hundred parachute troops who had not been evacuated after the battle, but had evaded capture, were hidden by the Dutch Resistance and many were said to be wounded.

Kragt under his pseudonym of 'Frans Hals', 'Fabian'[1] Belgian Commander of an S.A.S. troop, who had arrived in occupied Holland some weeks before Arnhem, and later, 'Ham' who had his own radio set, were our means of communication with them.

In the first week in October, I established headquarters on the outskirts of Nijmegen not far from the banks of the River Waal. I could see the gaunt structure of the Nijmegen Bridge over which the British Army had raced a few days before to save Arnhem without success. The bridge was a nightmare to me and many others, for day and night, it was under heavy shellfire. It was a terrifying experience to cross it. I could also recall the hot day in July 1940 when, herded with other British prisoners in a coal barge, I had passed beneath it on the voyage to Germany and Colditz.

In the first few days at Nijmegen, I made a discovery which revolutionised the situation of the airborne survivors. Not far from the bridge was the Nijmegen Power Station, linked by a direct telephone line across the Waal and the Rhine to transformers in enemy territory. One of these was at Ede, twenty miles from Nijmegen power station and about six miles from the German bank of the Rhine. Dutch Resistance workers assured me that this link was intact; they were already using it to talk to their own organisation on the other side. This gave me the idea of communication with the men themselves, reported to be hiding round Ede.

When they heard of this plan the 'cold feet department' were horror-struck. The idea of telephoning across the enemy lines was regarded as lunacy. But I was assured by the power station engineers and staff that it was safe and there was no reason to think that the enemy could tap it. Langley secured the agreement of 21 Army Group to use it, though I.S.9 (W.E.A.) were not the only intelligence organisation to do so.

At first, it was simply a question of waiting each night for the

[1] Gilbert-Sadi Kirschen D.S.O.

telephone to ring, and hearing a British officer's voice reading a long list of names. In this way, reports of casualties and the names of those who were still in hiding were reported back to their families. It was a strange sensation to hear 'The Voice' from behind the enemy lines —an experience which I shared with Major Hugh Fraser[1] of S.A.S. who had now joined I.S.9 (W.E.A.) in Holland as second-in-command. Fraser and I went there at six o'clock each night as shells burst round the Nijmegen bridge and shook the power station. Gradually, a plan was formed for the Dutch underground to escort the men to the bank of the Rhine near Wageningen. From the Allied bank we would go across to collect them in assault boats. This plan, was known as 'Pegasus' and was certainly the boldest of all the rescue operations that we had undertaken. 'The Voice' also provided useful targets for British gunners and the R.A.F.

While these strange talks continued, accompanied by conferences at the headquarters of 30 Corps commanded by General Sir Brian Horrocks, I sought to establish an escape route west of Arnhem over the river Waal at Tiel. 'Pegasus' might fail, for the crossing of the Rhine by a large party would be hazardous, and it might only succeed once. It might also be possible to establish a route further away from the main concentration of enemy forces round Arnhem and bring the men across the Waal in canoes or other small craft.

The area west of Nijmegen on the south bank of the Waal was largely in British hands, but much of that between the two rivers was held by the Germans. The plan was later consolidated by the lone escape of Colonel David Dobie,[2] commanding the 1st Parachute Battalion across the Waal at Tiel, and given the code-name 'Windmill'. Dobie had been rowed across in a small boat by a young Dutchman and on the day after his escape, Hugh Fraser and I studied the river bank in the desolate no-man's-land opposite Tiel. Here the Waal curved towards the sea. The current, though fast, left the river navigable for small craft and its width at this point is about 600 yards.

The young Dutchman who had brought out Dobie was kept at Nijmegen while I discussed the first part of 'Windmill'. This was to send a British officer across the river to Tiel. Each night

[1] The Right Hon. Hugh Fraser, M.P.
[2] D.S.O.

there were two or three clandestine passages over the Waal, unknown to the Germans. The Dutchman agreed to return and bring back two men whom he described as 'very important'. He would then row the British officer across to Tiel, and take him to the address of a family named Ebbens in the town to set up a chain of guides. This would be called the 'Windmill Line' and bring the paratroops in small parties down from Ede. It was clear that both 'Windmill' and 'Pegasus' must be organised before the rivers became too high with the approach of winter.

On October 6th I wrote to Langley in Brussels asking for permission to send the officer (codename 'Harrier') across, on condition that he should remain in uniform while in enemy territory. Langley replied agreeing, provided Harrier wore uniform at all times. In the light of after events, it was as well that this correspondence took place, for Harrier disobeyed our orders.

The road which we had chosen to the crossing point opposite Tiel ran beneath a dyke or river wall, through villages frequently raided by parties of Germans who crossed the river at night. The flat, uninteresting country inland was patrolled by both Germans and British. It was necessary to escort Harrier to the boat in darkness with sufficient troops to protect us if we met the enemy.

Harrier was excitable and romantic, qualities often necessary in underground war.[1] He fancied himself as a secret agent, for which he had no training. But I was anxious to set the 'Windmill' escape line in motion. Within a week, I was regretting my choice.

At this time, the 101st American airborne division was stationed near Nijmegen and a young American paratrooper volunteered to accompany him. Both men were told that their mission would last only for a few days. They were to make contact with addresses given us by Dick Kragt and recruit guides from Ede to Tiel. Messages from Fabian of S.A.S. and Ham showed that the 1st Airborne survivors hiding round Ede must be got back as soon as possible.

I fixed the night of October 11th/12th as the date for them to cross and that evening, with a small patrol of the Highland Light Infantry, Fraser, Lieut. Koch of the Dutch Intelligence Bureau and I accompanied Harrier with his American companion over the farmland, divided by dykes, which led to the bank of the Waal. In the darkness there was hardly a landmark, only an occasional

[1] He has since died but in view of what happened I prefer not to give his name.

farmhouse and a single haystack. We marched in silence for half an hour till we were within a few hundred yards of the river. Harrier whispered excitedly:

"Airey, I can't go on."

"What on earth do you mean?" I asked. "Don't make so much noise. There are plenty of Germans around here."

"I am not going on, because there are thirteen in the party."

I was dumbfounded. I had not had much regard for this particular superstition. Counting the men, I found that with the Highland troops and their officer, a 2nd Lieutenant, there were in fact thirteen. But it was better to reassure Harrier and at this moment, I saw the outline of the haystack. Angry at the interruption, I ordered the 2nd Lieutenant to remain there and wait for us. We marched on towards the river without further conversation. Harrier was no coward and his fear of the number thirteen was sincere. But this precaution did not prevent the later tragedy.

At midnight, we were crouching in the grass where the waters of the Waal softly lapped the bank. It was a dark, still night and there was no sign of the enemy. For a long time, we could hear or see nothing. I began to wonder if the Dutchman with his passengers would appear. To the east towards Arnhem and Nijmegen I could see flashes of gunfire and hear the crash of shells, but opposite Tiel all was silence. Towards one o'clock, came a slight sound on the river and suddenly the shape of a boat was within a few feet of me. We moved forward and pulled it to the bank. The Dutchman was there with two figures in civilian clothes who hastily stepped out. Harrier and the American, fumbling in the darkness, got into the boat and, within half a minute, it had disappeared towards Tiel as we began to withdraw silently to the haystack.

At the haystack, it was safe to whisper to the 'V.I.P.s' who had come from occupied Holland. One of them, a dark, thickset man in an overcoat, told me that he must reach Prince Bernhardt's headquarters with a message for the Dutch Government. He was Herman Van Roijen, now Netherlands Ambassador in London.[1] We still had a long journey in the darkness to find our transport, with every risk of running into German patrols. Each dyke and road looked the same, and it was more than an hour before we reached a shell-torn village of Afferden where I.S.9. (W.E.A.) had one of

[1] H. E. Dr. Jan Herman Van Roijen, C.B.E.

their sections. Weary, and full of Army rum, we lay down un-comfortably on the floor of a school room. At dawn, I took Van Roijen to Nijmegen to deliver his message. He brought the exiled Dutch Government important information about occupied Holland and the sufferings of the people under the Germans. They had still six months to wait before their liberation in 1945.

In Nijmegen, 'Pegasus', the plan to bring 1st airborne survivors across the Rhine from near Wageningen, was the subject of further telephone conversations at the power station. Colonel Dobie was now in overall command of the crossing with Hugh Fraser and myself in charge of secret intelligence. A company of Royal Cana-dian Army Engineers were found to row across in assault boats, escorted by troops from the 101st American airborne division. I was expecting that at least 100 survivors would come down from Ede.

On October 18th, the project received an unpleasant setback. There had been no news of Harrier except that he had arrived safely and was in the house of the Ebbens family at Tiel. But during the night a Dutchman crossed the Waal, reached our lines and was driven at high speed to Nijmegen, arriving at two o'clock in the morning. He brought this message.

"Harrier and the American were seen by a quisling in civilian clothes in daylight. Later the Germans arrested them in bed and both have been shot."

I took the Dutchman back in the darkness and he crossed to Tiel again before it was dawn. I had to take the chance that he had not been sent by the Germans and asked him to return next night. He reappeared with better news. Harrier and the American were alive and imprisoned in the schoolhouse at Tiel. The Germans had searched them and found their uniforms and military identity cards, which gave ground for hope that they would be treated as prisoners-of-war.

I was much relieved for I had given both of them a cover story, which was to say they had been cut off from their units and lost their way in the no-man's-land between the Waal and the Rhine. But for the Ebbens family the position appeared hopeless.

I reported this information to Langley in Brussels and M.I.9 in London began a lengthy inquest into the affair. There were shocked protests. I was held responsible for Harrier's safety and there was even talk of Questions in the House of Commons. But it soon became clear that both men had disobeyed a written order to stay in uniform and out of sight. Mr. and Mrs. Ebbens were subsequently shot by the Gestapo but Harrier was discovered in a prisoner-of-war camp. The American paratrooper, however, disappeared for good and no more was heard of him. This grim affair aroused much resentment among the Dutch Resistance after the war and was the subject of an enquiry. By their failure to obey a clear order both men had brought death to the Ebbens family, for they were seen in the street by daylight in civilian clothes. The ultimate responsibility must always remain with those in command but I had reason to feel that the tragedy was unnecessary.

Colonel Dobie was also furious at the incident. For twenty-four hours, worried by the news of the arrest and increased Gestapo activity at Tiel, he contemplated the postponement of 'Pegasus'. It might be better to wait for the excitement to subside. Then realising that paratroopers were assembling round Ede and it might be the only chance, he gave orders for the river crossing to take place, as planned, on October 22nd.

CHAPTER 24

Pegasus I and II

DOBIE had estimated that at least 200 men of 1st Airborne Division were still in hiding after Arnhem and, in the event, there were a great many more. Half were unwounded or sufficiently recovered by October to move across wooded country to the Rhine. In Ede alone, there were said to be a hundred and fifty on its outskirts. Their officers were in communication through youthful members of the Dutch Resistance who acted as courier.

After several visits to the Allied bank, a crossing-point was chosen near the village of Randwijk, opposite the town of Wageningen on the German side. A deserted farmhouse stood on low ground beside the river and a quarter of a mile inland was a dyke road which gave cover for our preparations. It was planned to carry boats over the dyke, launch them from the farmhouse and row across the river in darkness to collect the paratroops. Between Wageningen and Randwijk, the Rhine, in October, has a width from 150 to 200 yards.

Among the early problems was that of finding suitable craft. Fortunately, a company of Royal Canadian Engineers, stationed at Nijmegen, still had their assault boats. They had crossed and re-crossed the Rhine three weeks before, to evacuate 1st Airborne or what then remained of it, from Arnhem. Some of their boats—large dinghies rowed by engineers—had crossed more than a dozen times between midnight and dawn. In spite of terrific mortar and machine-gun fire only one of this company's boats had been sunk. This had been a classic operation, and I felt that we were lucky to have such experienced troops for a clandestine crossing. On October 18th, the assault boats were transported by road and hidden near Randwijk. They were then carried by night to the river bank and stored in a barn beside the farmhouse. There was little German activity along the river front, and British artillery had orders to remain quiet in the days preceding the operation.

Though 'Pegasus' resembled 'Sherwood' and the Forêt de Fréteval in its combination of military planning and secret intelligence, the Rhine crossing made it far more complex. Official histories do not disclose the part played by Room 900 and I.S.9 (W.E.A.). Feverish messages were passing through our various means of communication with enemy-occupied Holland. Up to the last minute, I continued to use the telephone at Nijmegen Power Station to talk to Ede. When I was told by the 'Voice' that it was proposed to bring some of the wounded down from Ede in cars and ambulances, I could hardly believe it. I was assured that there were very few Germans in the area since the battle of Arnhem and that this was quite possible. Kragt and Fabian of S.A.S., with whom we were in radio contact, reported that everything was ready for a crossing in the next few days. Brigadier Gerald Lathbury[1] would be with the party which would include a number of Dutchmen escaping from the Gestapo. But these messages arrived at Nijmegen, delayed by forty-eight hours. They had to be relayed from Room 900 in London and S.A.S. headquarters in Brussels. Without the indispensable direct line from the power station, things could easily have gone wrong.

The day before 'Pegasus' there was more bad news from Tiel. Alerted by the capture of Harrier, the Gestapo had arrived in Tiel and were said to have shot twenty members of the Resistance. It was said that after Harrier's arrest, the bodies of two German soldiers had been discovered in the garden of the Ebbens family and that their house had been burned to the ground. The Germans had obviously been watching the Waal at Tiel for some days but they had been unable to stop secret crossings. It was now reported that they were starting to evacuate all civilians from the riverside around Tiel, and on the Rhine as far inland as Ede. I began to fear that the whole operation at Randwijk might be hopelessly compromised, and in many quarters, the Harrier episode continued to be the subject of sharp comment. The return of the paratroops had the highest priority. Not only had they evaded capture, but they had vital information about the battle of Arnhem. Many important details of the fate of individual units were still needed.

On October 21st we were in a quandary about 'Pegasus' for a second time. Knowing that the Germans were watching for river

---

[1] General Sir Gerald Lathbury, G.C.B., D.S.O.

crossing by night, could we take the risk? The longer we waited, the more dangerous the situation would become, as the Germans evacuated civilians and increased their troops on the Rhine. This determined Colonel Dobie to make the attempt and on the night of October 21st I passed the final message by telephone to the 'Voice'. Lathbury and his party were to be on the German bank opposite the farmhouse at midnight. Most of them had kept their rifles or automatic weapons. Plans were already made for their escort by Dutch agents from Ede to the Rhine, a distance of about ten miles, and their commanders seemed to be in full control of the situation. I left the power station with a feeling of optimism.

To indicate the direction of the crossing point in the darkness, a Bofors gun half a mile behind the farmhouse would fire ten rounds of tracer across the river every quarter of an hour from eleven o'clock. Afterwards we felt that this signal made the operation too obvious to the enemy. Survivors gave interviews to the London press who published a full story, to the consternation of Crockatt and the War Office. Nonetheless the Bofors helped the men to identify their position as they crept through the dark countryside.

When they reached the river bank, they were to signal the letter 'V' on a torch with a red filter. The operation reminded me of Shelburne in Brittany, but the odds were much greater. If the Germans fired flares the party would come under heavy fire and the whole front would be ablaze. It was therefore agreed that, as a diversion, British artillery should shell the towns of Wageningen and Renkum on the German bank.

This scheme, one of the most interesting of its kind, combining the work of our own agents, S.A.S., and a mixed collection of forces, was in all respects an exercise in improvisation, since we were unprepared for the setback at Arnhem. In sending Kragt to Holland in 1943, I had only been concerned with airmen to be sent down the line to Spain, but the presence in Holland at the time of Arnhem of agents trained by Room 900 did much to make 'Pegasus' a success. The existence of secret communications with 1st Airborne survivors was of dramatic importance.

Throughout October 22nd, I remained at Nijmegen, still fearing that something else would go wrong; that more serious news of the Harrier affair would arrive from Tiel. No further reports arrived and by evening all was quiet on the Rhine. At eleven o'clock Dobie

Fraser and I were at the farmhouse near Randwijk which served as a command post for 'Pegasus'. The launching of the boats and the plans for the reception of the 'passengers' on arrival had been brilliantly organised by the American commander. From the river bank white tapes had been laid out through the fields to another farmhouse which was to serve as a first-aid post. Beside us in the darkness was the escort of thirty American paratroopers who were to cross in the assault boats and protect the operation. Dobie and a Canadian, Lieutenant Leo Heaps,[1] who made a spectacular escape from Arnhem after swimming the Rhine, were to accompany them as 'beachmasters' on the German bank. Fraser and I were beachmasters on the Allied bank, responsible for getting the men out of the boats and under cover as quickly as possible. It was an example of how British, Canadian and American troops of the highest quality and training could work together on such an intricate and dangerous scheme.

It had been raining the day before and the field around the farmhouse had become muddy from the passage of troops carrying the boats. Standing in the farmyard, I was startled by the sharp sound of the Bofors firing from behind me. Then came a tremendous barrage of artillery and mortar fire from our side. In the bright flash of bursting shells, I could see the houses of Renkum and soon large fires had started. On the Rhine all remained calm and there was no answering fire from the Germans.

The Bofors continued to fire at intervals. At midnight, there was a movement among the dark shapes around me and I could hear light splashes as the boats were launched. As they were lifted from the barn, there was the squeal of little pigs, for in the darkness someone had trodden on a litter. I could feel the men around me grow tense because such sounds would carry far across the river. But nothing happened. There was no fire from enemy machine guns in position near Wageningen. I strained my eyes for the 'V' sign in Morse by torch. Half an hour passed as the Bofors fired its signal above us at regular intervals, the tracer shells reflected in the dark river. From the enemy came the red flash of six-barrelled mortars fired to our left which also illuminated the water, but opposite was no sound, no sign of life.

When I first saw the 'V' sign flashed, it was 400 yards to the right

[1] M.C. He joined I.S.9 (W.E.A.) and took part in many other rescue operations.

of where we expected it. There were whispered orders and the Americans entered the boats which, with a splash of oars, began to move off. The scraping noise of their rowlocks seemed uncomfortably loud. On our bank, I suddenly felt everyone shudder as a short uncertain burst of rifle fire was heard on the far bank. Had the party from Ede run into a German patrol? But it did not continue. Twenty minutes passed and then the boats appeared out of the darkness, returning smoothly over the Rhine and, one by one, they touched down against the muddy bank. My duty was to count the men as they arrived. First of all loomed the tall figure of Lathbury in civilian clothes, and then came officers and men, some badly wounded, following the white tapes laid by the Americans across the field to the first-aid post. When all were safe, Fraser and I silently shook hands with the American Commander and Dobie. I had counted 138 including several Dutchmen. We followed the survivors back to the first-aid post and there, to my surprise, were two Dutch naval officers who had escaped from Colditz after my own success in 1942. They had made their way to Holland and been in hiding ever since. I soon recognised the 'Voice', the officer who had spoken to me on the Power Station line from Nijmegen to Ede. This was Major Digby Tatham-Warter,[1] to whose calm and ingenuity the success of 'Pegasus' owed much.

It was interesting to hear what those who had been in hiding on the other side of the river thought about 'Pegasus'. Early in October, when the men had first collected round Ede, there had been plans to reform the remnants of the division since they were still in possession of machine-guns and anti-tank weapons which could be used if the British 2nd Army crossed the Rhine and formed a bridgehead.[2] They had then discussed the 'Windmill' line to Tiel. This had the disadvantage that two rivers had to be negotiated and the men could only travel across country in small parties.

It soon became obvious that, with such large numbers, a major crossing must be risked and they had accepted the plan for 'Pegasus'. Talking to them in the first-aid post, I was amazed at the ease which they had come down through enemy territory. The only mishap had been the firing near the crossing-place which no one seemed able to explain.

[1] D.S.O.
[2] Major-General R. E. Urquhart; *Arnhem*, Cassell, 1958.

The Dutch Resistance in Ede, under the command of a burly schoolmaster known as 'Big Bill' Wildeboer had brought off a magnificent coup. They had many narrow escapes. The Germans, increasingly suspicious of what was happening in the town, sent an S.S. detachment only two days before. I was told by the survivors that another hundred and fifty men were still in the area. Some of them had been seriously wounded but would be fit to move in a fortnight or three weeks. I was urged on all sides to mount a second operation over the Rhine at the earliest opportunity.

Fraser and I left Randwijk with the men, many of them weak and ill, and drove to Nijmegen and the town hospital, now a casualty clearing station. It was only then, about two in the morning, that the Germans began to shell us. One jeep was destroyed and a rescued officer badly wounded in the arm. I was able to revive him in hospital with champagne sent by M.I.9 at Beaconsfield. 'Pegasus I', as it was now called, had been a striking, indeed memorable performance, thought by Langley to be the best in which I.S.9 (W.E.A.) ever took part. Not only had it recovered highly trained airborne troops, but they brought with them important information about the battle of Arnhem, and ideas for organising new escapes for those who remained in occupied Holland.

Next day, I began plans for 'Pegasus II'. I had no doubt that this would be even more difficult. The Germans would surely discover what had happened and reinforce their strength on the opposite bank. The publicity given to 'Pegasus I' when the survivors reached London would also help them. A new attempt must be made soon, for it was the last week in October and the river was rising.

In a few days, the situation was further altered by the replacement of 30th British Corps by 2nd Canadian Corps at Nijmegen, and I had to begin plans with a new staff. The 101st American airborne division and the Royal Canadian Engineers fortunately remained in position. On October 24th, Fraser and I made a reconnaissance of the river bank to find a new crossing place. We selected a point at the tiny village of Heteren, four miles east of Randwijk in territory held by an American parachute regiment. Numerous secret organisations were now using the power station telephone at Nijmegen and a special officer was appointed to conduct conversations with Ede. For 'Pegasus II' we again relied on Fabian who was in direct contact with S.A.S. Messages from Kragt and Ham still had to be relayed from London with a delay of twenty-four hours, a most clumsy arrangement. Three weeks at least would be required to prepare 'Pegasus II' and I fixed a preliminary date for November 16th, 1944. This message was passed to Major Hugh Maguire, the intelligence staff officer of the division, who was in command of the second party of about 140 men.[1]

By the middle of November the river would be too high and fast for rowing boats and suitable craft had to be found to cross it under their own power. It was decided to use flat-bottomed 'storm boats' fitted with outboard-engines to which primitive silencers were later added. This would not have been possible had I not succeeded in gaining the support of General Simonds, the Canadian Corps Commander.[2] He gave immediate orders for a dozen of these boats to be collected.

On November 16th Ham reported that the assembly of the survivors for 'Pegasus II' was going well. But the Rhine, rising rapidly, was already at five knots. There was some doubt whether storm boats, even with their own power, would be able to manage the crossing which this time might well have to be carried out under fire. The Germans had greatly reinforced their line between Renkum and Arnhem.

On November 18th I wrote to Langley in Brussels that, though the situation was critical, I had sent a message that we would be waiting at Heteren from November 22nd at midnight for three nights. The party were to show the morse signal 'B' on a red torch from the opposite bank. The Bofors signal would only be used every half-hour and there would be another big artillery barrage as a diversion.

I was uncertain whether 'Pegasus II' ought to be undertaken. It involved the possibility of serious casualties among men who were already wounded and who might be killed instead of spending the rest of the war in prison-camps. I was also nervous about the security of the operation. Every day, Dutchmen were crossing the Rhine and the Waal whom it was impossible to check. It was probable that German agents were working in the area between Nijmegen and Arnhem known as 'The Island'. But once having agreed to a plan, the hopes of the men who had waited so long could not be

[1] Graeme Warrack, *Travel by Dark after Arnhem*, Harvill Press, 1963.
[2] Lieut.-General G. G. Simonds, C.B., C.B.E., D.S.O.

dashed. I still had with me, besides Hugh Fraser, Leo Heaps and several excellent S.A.S. and 1st Airborne officers seconded to I.S.9 (W.E.A.). We had daily conferences with the American parachute company at Heteren which had orders to work with us. By November 20th we had decided to take the chance, and the message that we would be ready at midnight on November 22nd for three nights was confirmed through Ham and the telephone to Ede.

The night was very dark, with a high wind, as we moved into the empty village, where a small house dangerously exposed above the level of the dyke had a cellar which served as a command post. The storm boats were already stored in the village beside a ruined church and ready to be launched. We were heavily shelled as we arrived and one of the Canadian officers was badly wounded. As the wind rose on the river, I realised that it would help to hide the sound of the outboard motors, but reaching the bank, I could see that the current was swift and treacherous. We should be lucky to avoid what I had described in my letter to Langley of November 18th as 'an extremely cold death'. On the first night, we watched until dawn through a slit in the brickwork of the cellar. The wind lashed the river and it was impossible to see across. Had we missed the Morse signal in the darkness and rain? At dawn, we were again shelled from Arnhem, and gingerly crept inland to plan another night of watching on the Rhine.

On the afternoon of November 23rd, the weather had brightened and the wind had gone down. There seemed no reason to think that the enemy had noticed our activities, but were shelling Heteren to destroy the church tower and prevent its use for artillery observation. We returned to the village and its silent houses at dusk.

At three o'clock next morning, American paratroopers along our bank reported hearing 'an Irish voice' calling across the river. A storm boat was quickly launched and returned safely with three men in civilian clothes who were brought to the cellar of the house by the dyke. They were wet and shivering and barely able to speak. After they had drunk liberally from a jar of rum, they proved to be an R.A.F. sergeant, with a strong Irish accent named O'Casey, and two Dutchmen. They came from a party of 120 men, mostly from 1st Airborne, who had set out on the evening of 22nd from north of Ede, a distance of twenty miles from the river, accompanied by a doctor and a nurse. Ahead they could see Bofors tracer signal marking the crossing place. At the Ede-Arnhem road, they were challenged, flares went up, and they were fired on. The party was obliged to scatter, several were killed and the rest taken prisoner. Only seven escaped.[1] Many of the men had walked in their stockinged feet, their boots having been removed by Germans at Arnhem and from whom they had escaped into the hands of Resistance. Others were too weak for such a long night march.

I was deeply depressed at this news. It seemed to end all hope of bringing out those still hidden in occupied Holland, until the spring. As I was consoling myself with the rum, reports came of another voice calling across the river. There was a hurried conference. The American Commander was reluctant to send another storm boat across, for by now the wind had risen again and the Germans were firing flares. A tall American Lieutenant intervened and volunteered to cross with another soldier in one of the canoes stored in the village for taking patrols across the river at night. He was a native of Florida named Dixon, used to navigating rivers in fast currents. At first the Commander ordered him not to go. But again came the despairing cry for help. The canoe was launched with the two men who took with them a walkie-talkie set. We waited, staring into the darkness until, listening on our side, Leo Heaps heard the Lieutenant say, "I have found a British paratrooper and an airman and am bringing him across."

We heard no more of him or his canoe. There was no further sound save that of the waves against the dyke. Half an hour later came reports of cries for help down-stream. Many weeks afterwards, the Dutch Resistance at Dordrecht reported that a body had been washed ashore in American uniform. It seems likely that the canoe had overturned and the men had clung to it, but were swept away in the strong current. At dawn, we moved sadly from Heteren again under heavy shell fire from the heights of Arnhem. I reported the disaster in a disconsolate letter to Langley, but told him that I still believed that well-led parties could cross the river further down. The struggle to recover the men would have to last throughout the winter of 1944 and into 1945 for I knew that there were many still at large and in contact with Kragt. But it was the end of large scale rescue operations.

Ten days later, Crockatt decided that Room 900, in danger of

[1] Urquhart, *Arnhem*.

extinction by the War Office, should be the base for new operations in conjunction with I.S.9 (W.E.A.) at Nijmegen. Leaving Fraser in charge, I returned to London in December with instructions to organise the supply of canoes and other craft for individual crossings in Western Holland at the Biesbosch or mouth of the Waal. My other duty was to hasten the dropping of supplies to Kragt and Ham whose arrest was reported shortly after I returned to Room 900.

'Pegasus II' had been a grim disappointment, but on reflection only a miracle could have prevented disaster. It was clear that a strong force of Germans was waiting for the escapers, and this has since been attributed to the detailed newspaper stories which appeared in London after 'Pegasus I'.

The two 'Pegasus' operations had been mainly military in character, but after November 1944, I.S.9 (W.E.A.) at Nijmegen under Fraser reverted to its clandestine role and began new operations on the Rhine and the Waal. For the next few months, Fraser employed agents along the German bank of the Rhine using radio telephones to aircraft. He was assisted by Captain Maurice Macmillan.[1] Fraser created an excellent communications network with the Dutch Resistance and supplied British and Canadian forces with military intelligence. This was not the accepted function of I.S.9 (W.E.A.) and the War Office would have protested had they known about it. It nonetheless contributed to the success of our artillery and airforce by providing targets.

Escape operations were resumed by contact between Room 900 and Kragt. Routes to the Biesbosch were created through a maze of waterways and over thirty officers and men of the 1st Airborne Division were brought out by canoe before April 1945. Kragt, in spite of an unfortunate disagreement with S.A.S. had a special success in helping Brigadier Hackett[2] to escape in February 1945. Hackett had been severely wounded at Arnhem when in command of the 4th Parachute Brigade. Though still badly injured, he left hospital with the help of young Dutch guides and hid for several months in the care of four old ladies at Ede. He had not sufficiently recovered to take part in either 'Pegasus I' or 'Pegasus II' but, by Christmas 1944, I was receiving impatient messages from Kragt to assist in his escape. One suggestion was that he should be picked

[1] Mr. Maurice Macmillan, M.P.
[2] General Sir John Hackett, K.C.B., C.B.E., D.S.O., M.C.

up by a light aeroplane on a main road. The Air Ministry would not consider the proposal. In view of the numbers already arriving by canoe, it seemed safer to entrust Hackett to the river line.

The canoes, paddled by Dutch guides in Kragt's service, embarked on the lower reaches of the Waal and keeping close to the northern bank swung across the river, reaching the British lines with very few casualties. In this way Hackett reached an outpost of the 11th Hussars and made contact with I.S.9 (W.E.A.). He was greatly impressed by Kragt and critical of the failure of Room 900 to supply him with more wireless sets. His comments came at a time when Room 900 needed resuscitation, and they proved useful in my efforts to make it more effective. I was able to parachute two more wireless sets and other supplies to Kragt in March. With his Dutch supporters, he had a difficult and frustrating experience after the failure of 'Pegasus II'. As in France, the Gestapo became vindictive and brutal and many of them were arrested.

At least fifty 1st Airborne survivors and a number of airmen were still in hiding. In supplying Fraser with canoes, radio telephones and other equipment, I hoped to make our escape organisation on the Waal more effective. But the war was nearly over, and, with it, the need for rescue operations. All available aircraft were needed to drop food to the starving Dutch. As the Allies advanced into Germany, Crockatt discussed an abortive plan to parachute special teams to prisoner-of-war camps, including Colditz, and save the inmates from massacre. I imagined myself landing in the courtyard of the Castle which I had left in 1942. Wisely, the scheme was abandoned for it would certainly have endangered the lives of the prisoners.

In the first week in April I returned to Holland. As the Germans withdrew from Arnhem, I crossed the bridge over the Rhine for which so many lives had been sacrificed in September 1944. With Hackett and Fraser, I walked through the rubble of the town to find the headquarters of 1st Airborne Division. After this pilgrimage, we moved westwards as the Germans retreated and at Barneveld were reunited with Kragt who had survived two precarious years in occupied Holland. Forty-eight hours before the official announcement of V.E. Day, I was given permission to cross the German lines, established after the armistice signed at Wageningen, and drove to Amsterdam and the Hague.

The Dutch thronged the streets in a frenzy of welcome and rejoicing and it was hours before I could reach the addresses of our helpers. A week after the end of hostilities I was ordered by Crockatt to set up an Awards Bureau, with·Windham-Wright, in the Hague to recommend honours for those who had worked for us. This congenial task kept me in Holland until the end of August, when I was sent to Nuremburg as an official of the International Military Tribunal for the trial of Goering and other principal Nazi war criminals. This was the close of my service at Room 900 which had begun three years before, with my escape from Germany.

PART VIII

AFTERMATH

CHAPTER 25

The Traitors

I RETURNED to Germany by the same route from the port of Emmerich on the Rhine that I had followed as a half-starved prisoner in 1940. At first, it was as a prosecutor and collector of evidence against the Krupp armament firm at Essen. I was deeply embittered against the Nazis, not on my own account, but for those who had died for the escape organisations. In October, I was the official of the International Military Tribunal who served copies of the indictment on Hitler's chief lieutenants in the Nuremburg prison. At the beginning of 1946, I became Chief Commissioner for Criminal Organisations. This awe-inspiring title indicated my responsibility for hearing evidence on commission on behalf of those organs of Nazi Government declared to be criminal. They included the S.S., the Abwehr, the Gestapo and S.D., as well as the web of Security Police units. These were the chief enemies in occupied territory of Room 900.

In the summer of 1946 the Commission heard 100 witnesses for the defence and reported on their evidence to the Tribunal.[1] I was thus able to picture Himmler's complex security system, both political and military. To give a full description of it would be an exercise beyond my powers. The witnesses claimed not to understand it themselves. It was nonetheless possible to see the outline of the organisation which had infiltrated the escape lines and brought about the deaths of over 500 people. I was able to confirm that Hitler and Goering attached importance to smashing the escape lines. They realised the impact on the Allied war effort of hundreds of trained airmen slipping through their hands. This accounted for the employment of the Secret Police of the Luftwaffe, of which Goering was the Commander in Chief. The brutality displayed by their secret police

[1] *Trial of the Major War Criminals:* Volume XLII, pp. 1–153. The author's report is dated August 1946.

to those who helped Allied airmen was a disgrace to an otherwise honourable Air Force. In Brussels and Paris they collaborated with their political enemies in the Gestapo and S.D.[1]

As Commissioner, it was my duty to hear evidence of responsibility for the savage 'commando order' issued by Hitler on October 14th, 1942.[2] This laid down that all sabotage parties, in or out of uniform, who fell into German hands were to be shot. Six of Hasler's party on the Bordeaux raid were executed under this order, which stated that those arrested by local police were to be handed over to the S.D.[3] At a later stage of the war, several groups of S.A.S. were summarily murdered on this authority by S.S. troops.

The 'defence' of the S.D. to the charges of being concerned in carrying out the order was unconvincing. I quoted from my own report to the Tribunal. S.S. Standartenführer Dr. Knochen, chief of the Security Police and S.D. in France from 1942 to 1944, stated: "The execution of this order did not belong to the tasks of the S.D. in France." He also said that the expression 'handing over to the S.D.' which appeared in the Commando Order meant 'handing over to Department 4 of the Security Police'.[4] Since the Security police comprised the criminal police in Germany[5] and the secret state police, better known as the Gestapo,[6] the answer to the charge was singularly unimpressive. The Allied judges declared both the Gestapo and S.D. to be criminal organisations. The witnesses for the S.S. made similar denials especially with regard to concentration camps. According to S.S. Oberführer and Judge Gunther Reinecke, of the S.S. legal department, whose evidence is summarised in my report, members of the staff of concentration camps were under the jurisdiction of the S.S. and police courts. When cross-examined he said that atrocities 'could only have taken place within the sphere of administration of concentration camps . . . and it was impossible to penetrate the secrecy surrounding them'. He had never 'heard any of the guards mention atrocities' and 'the reports received by the S.S. were carefully and expertly drawn up'.

[1] Though they seem to have quarrelled over Dédée.
[2] Document 498–P.S., U.S.A.–501.
[3] See Chapter 16.
[4] *Trial of Major War Criminals*, Vol. XLII, p. 105. The security police were Sicherheitspolizei or Sipo.
[5] Kriminalpolizei or Kripo.
[6] Geheimestaatspolizei or Gestapo.

These statements, like many others, demonstrate the cynicism and cowardice of our secret police opponents. I quote them only as illustrations of the Nazi mind. There is no doubt that Himmler's security system was designed to conceal as much of the terrible truth as possible. After the war, especially at Nuremburg, some, but not all, of it was admitted. Other witnesses sought, by stressing the obscurity of its structure, to deny knowledge of any crimes whatever.

At Nuremburg, it was also possible for me to study the German security services in occupied France, Belgium and Holland which had combatted the escape lines with such severity. The term usually applied to all anti-resistance organisations was the Gestapo. At the beginning of the Occupation, there were, in fact, two distinct branches which were in conflict with each other, both in Western Europe and Germany. The Military Counter-Espionage Service, which was responsible for destroying many escape circuits, was the Abwehr under Admiral Canaris. The Abwehr consisted of the Field Police (Feldgendarmerie) and the Secret Field Police (G.F.P.). These Field Police organisations frequently invaded the homes of our helpers in the dead of night and carried them off for interrogation. In general, they behaved rather less unpleasantly than their rivals in the Gestapo. Himmler and the Gestapo achieved complete control over the Abwehr, which disappeared on June 1st, 1944. Canaris was executed for his part in the attempt to murder Hitler in July 1944.

The political or Nazi Party Security Service under Himmler-generally known as the Gestapo, consisted of the Geheimestaats, polizei and the S.D. or Sicherheitsdieust. For all practical purposes the Gestapo and S.D. were indistinguishable. At the end of the war, all security police organisations were administered from the Reich Security Headquarters in Berlin. When the Abwehr disappeared, the English traitor Harold Cole, who had been recruited by it in 1941, was transferred to the S.D. in Paris to betray escape workers as late as July 1944. The use of such traitors was a feature of the opposition to all subversive organisations. They were used by both the Abwehr and the Gestapo. The escape lines with their chains of 'safe houses' stretching from the Hague to the Pyrenees, and un-trained workers suffered especially from them.

In unoccupied France, the position was complicated by the use of Vichy security services as well as undercover Gestapo agents. The Vichy government created its own police force, the Milice, to which reference has already been made. The Milice were informers and particularly dangerous to Garrow and O'Leary. In contrast, there are very few instances of gendarmes of the civil police betraying the escape lines. After the occupation of the whole of France, the Gestapo quickly assumed control.

Traitors and informers of 'V' men constituted the Gestapo's chief weapons against escape organisations. After the war, it became possible to discover the fate of those who did the greatest damage.

Our worst enemies were: Roger Leneveu (Roger le Légionnaire), Prosper Desitter ('the man with the missing finger'), Jacques Desoubrie (Jean Masson or Pierre Boulain) and Harold Cole (Paul). Of the end of Roger Leneveu who betrayed O'Leary, Louis Nouveau, the Comtesse de Mauduit and many others, there is little information. He was one of several Frenchmen who were blackmailed or bribed to work against his own countrymen. After the arrest of O'Leary, he was transferred to the Gestapo at Rennes to break up 'Shelburne' in Brittany. Things became hot for him and he does not appear to have done much damage in that region after 1943, though he was apparently trying to penetrate routes to Spain as late as June 1944. He was liquidated by the maquis at the liberation of France.

Prosper Desitter and his mistress, Flore Dings, worked with Jacques Desoubrie to destroy Comet in Paris in 1943 and 1944. Desitter and the girl were frequently seen in the company of Desoubrie which suggests a lack of security. The absence of one of his fingers also made it easy to identify him. Room 900, who had a complete file on his activities, were able to warn other organisations against him. With Flore Dings, he was executed for treason at the end of the war. Before he was shot, he was heard howling with terror in his cell.

Jacques Desoubrie was an electrician from Tourcoing on the Belgian frontier. Except for Cole, he was the most successful of our enemies and certainly responsible for the arrest of fifty French and Belgians. His particular task was the penetration of Comet in June 1943. He worked mainly in France, the destruction of the Jean Greindl organisation at the Swedish Canteen at Brussels being carried out by Germans of the Abwehr disguised as American pilots, which precipitated the Maréchal affair in November 1942. Desoubrie was the illegitimate son of a Belgian doctor and had been abandoned by his mother at an early age. He was eighteen at the outbreak of war and was quickly inspired by Nazi propaganda.

His most dramatic coup was the arrest of Dédée's father, Frédéric de Jongh, with virtually the whole Paris organisation in June 1943, and his behaviour on this occasion demonstrated him to be a complete fanatic. Realising that he would be in danger after the arrest of Frédéric de Jongh, the Germans kept him under cover till the end of 1943. He then dropped the pseudonym of Jean Masson after having brought about thirty arrests. In January 1944 he reappeared under the name of Pierre Boulain, claiming not only to have worked for Frédéric de Jongh but also that he was charged with the duty of liquidating Jean Masson.

Desoubrie was responsible with Desitter for the arrest of Nothomb and Legrelle in Paris and possibly for the tragedy of Capitaine Potier. He was tried and executed at Lille in 1945. At his trial, at which Nothomb and other members of Comet gave evidence, he proclaimed himself to be a National Socialist. It was established that he had received substantial sums from Comet to help airmen, which he had handed over to the Gestapo. Like Desitter, he was a greedy character with a love of money. In his last hours, his conduct, though less craven than his fellow-traitor Desitter, was in contrast with the extreme bravery of many of his victims.

Harold Cole was at once the most interesting and dangerous of our particular opponents. Deputy Commander Reginald Spooner of Scotland Yard regarded him as the worst traitor of the war.[1] Nor only did he betray his own country but more that 150 French people who worked for the Allies. It is believed that fifty of them lost their lives, most of them members of the O'Leary organisation. He was the most callous of German agents, actually helping the Gestapo to torture those he had given away.

Cole was born on January 24th, 1903, and christened Harold, though he used the name Paul in France. He trained as an engineer. By the time he was in his twenties he had a record of convictions at Scotland Yard for housebreaking and false pretences. He was also a 'con-man' with a military moustache, smartly dressed with a regimental tie. Before the war he constantly used such expressions as 'old man' or 'old boy' to ingratiate himself, which he also did in France. He joined the Army in 1939 and became a sergeant. In April 1940, before the invasion of France, he disappeared with the Sergeants' Mess funds of which he was in charge. When France was

[1] Iain Adamson. *The Great Detective.*

occupied Cole was living in Lille declaring himself to be a 'Captain in the British Secret Service'. He spoke French with a pronounced British accent and when questioned by Germans would produce a letter certifying that he was 'deaf and dumb'. He pretended to use sign language to be understood. Before his quarrel with O'Leary in Marseille in 1941, he organised a genuine escape line from Lille and there are many examples of his audacity while escorting soldiers and airmen during that period.

In September 1941 Garrow sent a pretty young French girl to work with Cole as a guide. In the next three months they took thirty-five evaders from Paris over the demarcation line. Late in December 1941 they went through a form of religious marriage in Paris, after Cole had forged a certificate for a civil marriage. After the scene with O'Leary in Dr. Rodocanachi's flat in Marseille, Cole returned to Lille where he was arrested by the Germans on December 6th, 1941. Only two days later, he appeared in Abbeville and betrayed the Abbé Carpentier and Monsieur Duprez. There is no firm evidence as to his agreement to work for the Germans, probably he was 'persuaded' to do so by the Sonderführer Richard Christmann of the Abwehr. Christmann had penetrated several S.O.E. circuits in France using a bogus escape line. He also worked on the 'North Pole' deception under Colonel Giskes, head of the Abwehr in Holland.[1]

At the time of Cole's arrest and treason in December 1941, the Abwehr was in charge of counter-espionage in France against 'British agents', while the Gestapo and S.D. concentrated on French Resistance groups. By 1944, when the Gestapo was the ultimate police authority in France, Cole worked under the direction of S.S. Sturmbannführer Kieffer, head of the S.D. in Paris, with whom he fled to Germany at the liberation. With the exception of O'Leary and Darling few of his fellow escape workers suspected Cole. Why did he go over to the Germans? He was probably threatened with execution and worked with them to save his own skin. He has been described as having a 'yellow streak'. He is known to have given the Gestapo in Lille a complete statement of all he knew about the O'Leary line. After his marriage, he continued to betray his former colleagues in Paris, and deceived his wife by sending her on false errands to collect airmen. He later crowned his infamous career

[1] E. H. Cookridge. *Inside S.O.E.*, Arthur Barker, 1966.

by denouncing her elderly aunts, who had hidden airmen, and stealing their jewellery.

The first details of his treachery appeared in a letter smuggled from the prison at Loos by the Abbé Carpentier which reached O'Leary several months later and was sent to Room 900. The Abbé revealed that Cole's statement to the Gestapo comprised thirty type-written pages in which he gave every name and address known to him in the organisation. Early in 1942, Cole pursued his stratagem of appearing to rebuild a genuine escape line for O'Leary. He even obtained new clothes and identity papers for escapers, provided by the Germans.

Cole and his wife crossed the demarcation line in April 1942 and were arrested at the Hotel D'Angleterre in Lyon. The arrest was the subject of speculation for a long time. It was carried out on the orders of Monsieur Louis Triffe, head of the Direction de Surveillance du Territoire for Lyon. Although Triffe was working for the Vichy Government, he was strongly pro-Allied. He had heard of Cole's treachery and decided that Resistance organisations in the Unoccupied Zone must be protected. With other members of his staff, he tried to convince Cole's wife that he was a traitor. She refused to believe him until, during an interrogation, a Vichy French detective struck Cole in the face. Cole then fell to his knees and began to weep.

"It's true," he confessed, "I am a traitor, I don't know why I did it".[1]

The scene is reminiscent of the episode in Dr Rodocanachi's flat a few months before.

Cole and his wife were tried by court-martial at Montluc in the Unoccupied Zone on charges of espionage and 'delivering French citizens into the hands of the Germans'. Cole was convicted and sentenced to death but on the evidence of Monsieur Triffe, the girl was acquitted. In August 1942 she returned to Marseille and made contact with O'Leary after writing a bitter letter to Cole. On October 30th she had a son who died on January 23rd, 1943, in miserable conditions at a hotel in Marseille. She was again arrested after the Germans occupied the whole of France, for she had renewed her underground activities. The Gestapo used every device to make her betray the O'Leary organisation, without success, and she was imprisoned at Castres but escaped to Paris on September 16th, 1943.

[1] Gordon Young, *In Trust and Treason*, Edward Hulton, 1959.

She was now in mortal danger from Cole who, having denounced her to the Germans, was released to search for her in the winter of 1943. It is terrible to think what might have happened had he found her, but, on April 14th, 1944, she was taken off by the Navy from Brittany and arrived in England where she went into training with S.O.E. Her extraordinary courage and steadfastness were rewarded and she is now happily married and living in England.

After the Allied invasion of France in June 1944 the Gestapo and S.D., realising they had lost the war, rounded up, shot or deported to concentration camps hundreds of Resistance workers. Cole played his part in this and betrayed several more French people who had hidden airmen, most of whom were tortured or executed. When I arrived in Paris, I was told that he had left, dressed as a German officer, on August 17th 1944. It was evident that he was by now regarded as a trusted agent by the Germans.

His movements are not known until the spring of 1945 when he walked into the headquarters of an American Cavalry Regiment in south Germany, as 'Captain Mason', a British Secret Agent. He was accompanied by his crony S.S. Sturmbannführer Kieffer of the S.D. He told the Americans that Kieffer had been very useful to him and asked for a safe conduct. The unsuspecting Americans gave Cole a Captain's uniform and a job in their Counter Intelligence Corps where he was employed on interrogation. This gave him the opportunity to denounce his former Gestapo and S.D. associates to the Allies. But the Security Service and Scotland Yard were at last on his trail.

Realising that Cole might contact friends in Paris, especially women, Commander Spooner had their letters and postcards intercepted. But his whereabouts seem to have been discovered by chance. In the later summer of 1945, a girl came to see Darling, by now head of the M.I.9 Awards Bureau in Paris. She had been one of Cole's mistresses and believed in him, for she said to Darling:

"I know what you think about Harold Cole and what everybody has been saying, but you see you are wrong and he is an Intelligence Officer in the Army."

She showed Darling a pencilled note.

"Chérie. You see I am safe and well and hope soon to see you again. Much love Sonny Boy."

"Sonny Boy," she said. "I always used to call him that!"

While her attention was distracted, Darling copied the address on the postcard and telephoned Major Peter Hope of the Security Service and Lefort of the B.C.R.A. Hope and a French detective then hurried to the American Army Zone, where they discovered Cole acting as host at a cocktail party at the headquarters where he was 'stationed'. They arrested him and took him to Paris where he was detained in the S.H.A.E.F. military prison. He was there identified by the Reverend Donald Caskie, though Cole maintained that they had never met.

Cole had lost nothing of his capacity for deception. He seems to have persuaded the American guards at the prison that he should write his 'memoirs' in the guardroom. He escaped without difficulty by taking an American Sergeant's uniform jacket which had been left hanging in the room. For some weeks he hid above Billy's Bar in the Rue de Grenelle in Paris. He had won the confidence of the proprietress, a widow, saying that he was 'Sergeant Carpenter' awaiting demobilisation.

During the next few weeks the B.C.R.A. were searching Paris for him but he was finally caught by two gendarmes looking for deserters. They had been warned that a man was hiding above Billy's Bar.[1] They knocked on his door and Cole appeared brandishing a pistol.

"We have come to arrest you," said one of the gendarmes, seeing the pistol.

Cole fired three times, wounding one of them, but they returned the fire and shot him dead. There is an unconfirmed report that he hesitated in a 'last gesture of chivalry' because the proprietress was in the line of fire. His body was identified by O'Leary, recently released from his imprisonment in Dachau.

It is fashionable today to analyse the motives of traitors and even to find excuses for their actions. What can be said of Cole? He was exceptionally attractive to women and in many cases did not betray those whom he liked. His unstable temperament and absence of any moral or patriotic feeling probably derived from a broken home. No one really knows, but I have met people, even in 1968, who believe him to have been the victim of circumstances. Even if this be true, he was among the most selfish and callous traitors who ever served the enemy in time of war.

[1] Accounts of the end of Cole differ. This is based on private information from Mr. Darling who believes that the gendarmes did not know that the man was Cole. They were not connected with the search by the B.C.R.A.

CHAPTER 26

In Retrospect

THE episodes in this book were chosen from a multitude of incidents covering the whole of the war. They illustrate the objectives of Room 900, and through them, the programme of escape and evasion training of M.I.9. They emphasise the different features and personalities in an ever changing process. From the shambles of Dunkirk arose the need for organisation and funds. With the increase in air operations over Europe came the more specialised techniques of rescue linked to the provision of escape aids and lectures. The local Resistance leaders are gradually replaced by trained secret agents, able to mount evacuations by sea and air. Finally, when the Allies land on French soil, extempore armed Units are devised to extricate survivors. Here and there can be found glimpses of individual servicemen but these are less important than the ingenuity and calibre of their friends in need. Many who got home have written their personal accounts. These pay admiring tributes to their helpers, but I have sought to show the intricate texture of the underground service which stood behind them.

My purpose has been to relate, in a personal context, the history of this service in occupied countries. Many people in Europe and the United States know of its existence, but how it emerged after the Occupation and how M.I.9 and Room 900 came into being is not widely understood. Many even in the Armed Forces suppose that, briefed by M.I.9, large numbers of servicemen returned by their unaided efforts. Only the minority were genuine 'lone' escapers from France, Belgium or Holland whether they had been shot down or broke out of prison camps. The interrogation reports confirmed that the majority received help to return to Britain.

That the nature of this basically unprofessional movement should be obscure is hardly surprising. Only from Room 900 could it be viewed as a whole. Many of its former beneficiaries know nothing except the names—true or disguised—of those who helped them. Servicemen who received training and lectures from M.I.9 were only told how to approach the population for help if they were in danger of capture. They were not given details of the methods or even the localities in which our agents operated, with the exception of the Marine Commandos and the Mary Lindell organisation at Ruffec in 1942. When they came into the hands of guides and travelled long distances by train they learned very little. Guides were obliged to be uncommunicative, and after the arrests of O'Leary and Dédée it was rare that servicemen met the leaders. Even whose who returned from Brittany by sea seemed puzzled. They had been told by M.I.9 to surrender themselves and be treated as 'parcels' or 'bodies'. They were to ask no questions. Hence the mystique and the loyalty which persists today. Their memories are of ordinary people, like themselves, who saved them.

Why did people in France, Belgium and Holland run these enormous risks? All resistance to tyranny and oppression is inspired by a sense of outrage. Escape workers added the stimulus of compassion and fellow feeling for the lost and stranded. The stories of Dédée and her father and of Louis and Renée Nouveau, imbued with their hatred of injustice, and their impulse to contribute to Nazi defeat, best express the philosophy that guided them to the bitter end. They were joined by others, mostly young people, often in defiance of their parents, who set out on this dangerous course which often led to torture and death. Their counterparts can be found today all over the world, especially among the opponents of Soviet imperialism. Their unity of purpose, sharpened by the reality of military occupation, cuts right across religion, race and politics as it did in the nineteen-forties.

No one of any consequence in the escape lines was taking these risks for money or personal glory. If that had been their motive, they would have collaborated with the enemy and betrayed their friends. What does the story reveal in terms of human character? The evaders showed determination at a time when it would have been easier to have spent the war in the relative security of a prison camp. But they were soldiers. The Resistance Movement in occupied Europe, especially in escape work, was largely civilian and exposed to graver penalties. In each struggle against military occupation and

Secret Police there will always be the few who stand out through their independence and magnetism. They are the kind of men and women described in this book. They were the exceptional people, and the natural leaders. They had in common the ideal of service to humanity. It is therefore not surprising to find that they have continued to pursue this aim in their personal lives.

O'Leary always dominates the scene. After he was liberated from Dachau, he ceased to be 'Lieutenant Commander Patrick Albert O'Leary, R.N.' of H.M.S. *Fidelity*, though it was in this name that he was awarded the George Cross. As Capitaine Guèrisse he rejoined the Belgian 1st Lancers as medical officer. In 1951 he was Chief of Medical Service to the Belgian Volunteer Battalion in Korea and, at one time, was medical officer of the 29th British Brigade. During this campaign he climbed out of a tank under fire to rescue a wounded man. For this characteristic action he was again decorated and has thirty-two ribbons on his uniform. He is now a Major-General in the Belgian Army and Director of Medical Service to the Belgian Forces in Germany at the age of fifty-seven.

Dédée, now fifty-three, was seriously ill after her experiences in Ravensbrück. When she had recovered, she trained as a nurse and was for many years a sister in a leper hospital in the Congo. When the Congo became independent of Belgium and civil war broke out, she was obliged to leave after the hospital had been looted and later destroyed. Undeterred by the sight of suffering and persecution, she is now matron of a hospital at Addis Ababa. She has lost none of her charm and independence. These two life stories demonstrate why both O'Leary and Dédée had so strong a hold on their followers. Nothomb, another dedicated leader, who refused to give up his mission in the face of certain arrest, became a worker-priest among the Indians in Venezuela. These three, and many others, were undeterred by the horror of concentration camps which would have destroyed lesser characters.

Louis Nouveau, too, was among those who met the challenge with extraordinary fearlessness and self-reliance. It is a miracle that he survived the tortures of Buchenwald for he had been badly gassed in 1917. It has been said that those who came out alive from Nazi imprisonment did so by their determination and will to live. Nouveau was certainly such a man. He had formidable presence, a ready wit and a sharp tongue. Aeftr he had received his George

Medal and many other decorations he went back to Marseille and made a considerable success in business.

I saw him last in 1961 when he was suffering from the illness which killed him five years later. He was essentially a Frenchman, sometimes sardonic, but a true friend of freedom. He owed his great achievements as a secret organiser to his strong personality and passion for the Allied cause. In this valiant episode he was supported by his wife. At her villa near Aix-en-Provence she remains the shrewd and generous Frenchwoman of a generation ago at the flat on the Quai Rive Neuve.

No one who visits Monsieur and Madame Coache at their unpretentious home in Asnières, unchanged since they were hiding airmen, can mistake the true meaning of courage. They fought the Nazis with few advantages except their own faith, and expected little in return. Like other leaders who emerged under the challenge of war, they had their moments of greatness. History has produced others like them in the past, and in this lies hope for the future of liberty.

It has been impossible to name the many thousands of helpers, recognised and unrecognised, past and present. The figure of 12,000 was only an estimate based on M.I.9 reports at the end of the war. Despite careful enquiries by the Awards Bureaux, there must be many who are unknown to us. They formed an essential link in the whole machinery of escape and without them these achievements would not have been possible. I can only give them anonymous mention in this book. I never knew the name of 'the girl who looked like Joan of Arc' at Annemasse, who first discovered for me the meaning of the French Resistance Movement. In Holland, too, the story of the young Dutch people who brought the airborne survivors through the enemy lines has the same pattern. The orderly persistence of their efforts until the end of the war saved many lives.

In recent years, attempts by professional historians in Britain to describe the actions and errors of men and women who fought the Nazis underground have assumed an unpleasant air of disdain. Academic writers have attempted to belittle their contribution to the war. That they would not have written in this vein had they taken part themselves is self-evident. No one who saw secret agents actually leave for occupied territory could afford such arrogance.

Historical analysis of this kind is highly misleading and belies the true atmosphere of those times, which was one of mutual sacrifice not easily assessed in scholar's language. In the case of the escape lines, the achievement can be measured in the return of the men, all lives of great value to the Allied cause.

How would the British have behaved under German occupation? I believe that they would have acted like the people of occupied Europe. The younger generation in Britain may find this difficult to grasp. They have to express their feelings by demonstration and irreverence to authority. Those who worked in the escape lines had the same passions. They were shared by the young Czechs who chalked swastikas on tanks in defiance of Soviet Occupation. The difference is that, in war, these emotions have to be organised.

Britain had prepared a Resistance Movement in the event of invasion by the Nazis and Mr. David Lampe has given a fascinating description of the auxillary units which would have formed it, in his book *The Last Ditch*.[1] Had Britain been occupied, she would have been subject to the same terror. There would have been those who defied the Germans just as there might well have been traitors, and collaborators with the enemy. There would certainly have been a Jean Greindl and a Mary Lindell, though geography would have made it impossible to run an escape organisation in Britain, such as that which existed across the Channel. No German prisoner-of-war escaped from Britain itself and got back. Despite many attempts, the only successful escape was from Canada, to America, then neutral, in 1941.[2]

I have tried to show in this book, how escape training by M.I.9 and its American counterpart M.I.S.X. played a part in the restoration of thousands of men to action against the enemy. In the Second World War, each branch of the services had its own intelligence department. Foreshadowing an integrated Ministry of Defence and Military Intelligence, M.I.9 worked for the Navy, Army and Air Force. There is some reason to think that old prejudices are now forgotten, and that the technique of escape and combat survival will remain part of military training. The recovery of highly trained men will be more important than ever in the future. There is the tangible reason that the cost of training a pilot and other specialists

[1] Cassell, 1968.
[2] Kendal Burt and James Leasor, *The One That Got Away*, Collins, 1956.

is now ten times higher than it was in the Second World War. More important than these material standards is the effect on the morale and character of the individual. Escape and evasion are not only tests of nerve and endurance. They enrich the understanding of human values in time of danger. Twenty-five years ago in occupied Europe, thousands of servicemen were brought in touch with the charity and sacrifice of ordinary people.

After the war, I was in command, until 1951, of the successor to I.S.9 known as I.S.9 (T.A.)[1] which continued to study the subject. Training in combat survival remains the subject of the strictest secrecy and under the present rules no account of it can be published until the year 1998. It is to be hoped nonetheless that the lessons of Room 900 have been learned. The highest priority should be given to the recovery of those with the best military training and skills who are in danger of capture by the enemy. Not only are they of value as combatants but they are an important source of military information.

The struggle of Room 900 for recognition should not be necessary in the future. As time passes, it may no longer be possible to recruit former escapers to operate such a service. It was no coincidence that Crockatt selected Langley, Garrow and myself to work in Room 900. He believed that we could picture the emotions and problems of those who were hidden in occupied territory. In spite of our mistakes, which are frankly recorded in this book, we could claim a special experience.

The aftermath of resistance to the Nazis has brought painful human problems and I cannot end this book without remarking on British official attitudes to them. Over the years the spirit of those times has often been sadly forgotten. Though this may not be true of the Armed Forces, there has been a reluctance by British governments to press the claims of those who endured so much in their service. I have already described how the Foreign Office, after years of continuous pressure in Parliament, finally exerted themselves to obtain compensation for British inmates of concentration camps.[2] Their interpretation of the agreement with the Germans, in a particular case, led to a finding of maladministration against them, three

---

[1] Later 23 S.A.S. Regiment (T.A.).
[2] See Chapter 1. Under the Anglo-German Agreement, over a thousand received compensation, among them Mary Lindell and Tom Groome.

years later.[1] Whatever the true explanation for the conduct of ministers and officials in the Sachsenhausen case, these reports reveal a disquieting and insensitive obstinacy. Another example has been the unwillingness of British governments, until the delegation to Dachau in September 1968, to contribute to memorial ceremonies for those who suffered in concentration camps.

In writing this story of M.I.9 and Room 900, and their friends and enemies, I have tried to picture their role in the struggle for liberty. The qualities displayed by the escape lines a generation ago are those of which Britain and the world will always be in need.

---

[1] Third Report of the Parliamentary Commissioner for Administration, December 20th, 1967, and First Report of the Select Committee on the Parliamentary Commissioner for Administration, May 16th, 1968, on Sachsenhausen Concentration Camp.

ACKNOWLEDGEMENTS

I wish to express my thanks for permission to use material from the following books:

The Harvill Press, for *Travel by Dark After Arnhem,* by Graeme Warrack.

Arthur Barker, for *No Drums No Trumpets,* by Barry Wynne.

Frederick Muller, for *The Great Detective,* by Iain Adamson.

Hutchinson, for *Pantaraxia,* by Nubar Gulbenkian.

Cassell, for *The Way Back,* by Vincent Brome.

Heinemann, for *Cockleshell Heroes,* by C. E. Lucas-Phillips.

Studio Vista, formerly Edward Hulton, and the Estate of the late Gordon Young, for *In Trust and Treason,* by Gordon Young.

INDEX

Abwehr (German counter espionage), 84, 100, 146, 175, 206, 207, 208, 210, 211, 303, 305, 306, 308

Aircraft 'pickups', 16, 23 244–6

Ancia, Albert ('Daniel Mouton'), 243, 250, 252–4, 264, 278

Annemasse, author in, 45–7; mentioned, 177, 202, 315

Anse Cochat Bay (Brittany), escapes from, 220, 222, 223, 227 et seq., 237

Ardennes, proposed escape camps in the, 241, 243, 250, 278

Arnhem, rescue operations around, 28, 280, 281 et seq., 289–99; see also Pegasus I and II

Augustus the Strong, elector of Saxony, 34

Aylé, Robert, 136, 168–9, 170

'Bacon' (Dutch agent), 281

Baillet-Latour, Count, 139

Bailey (valet), 76–7

Baker, Captain Peter, 268, 275, 276

Barcelona, British Consulate at, 71, 75, 76, 78, 79, 86, 111, 115, 116, 183

Barnet, Flight-Lieutenant, 99

Baverstock, Flight-Sergeant, 134

Bayonne, 131, 135, 137, 157, 159, 160, 161, 256

Beaconsfield (principal headquarters of M.I.9), 55, 64 et seq., 79, 110, 172, 201, 230, 294

Belgium, escapes from, 16, 18, 19, 20, 22, 23, 62, 69–70, 127 et seq., 205–6, 241 et seq., 312, 313; see also Brussels and Comet Line

Bernhard, prince of the Netherlands, 286

Bernardo (contact man in Spain), 143

Best, Captain Payne, 205

Biarritz, 138, 160, 204

Bidoul, Gaston, 172

Bilbao, British consulate at, 128, 129, 132, 172, 179

Bismarck, Count von, 185, 187, 188

Blanchain, Francis (guide), 54, 92, 112, 117

Blum, Léon, 50

Blum, Sous-Lieutenant, 50

'Boeuf, Lieutenant', 156, 162–3

Bonaparte operation, 229–38

Bordeaux, commando raid on, 197–9; mentioned, 137, 160, 161, 223, 237

Bougaiev, see Ivan

Boulain, Pierre (Gestapo agent), 249–50, 253–4, 261, 306; see also Desoubrie and Masson

Bouryschkine, Vladimir; see Williams, Val

Boussa, Squadron-Leader Lucien ('Belgrave'), 243, 250–5, 257, 265, 267–8, 270–1

Bouteloupt, Madeleine, 168–9

Brauchitsch, Field Marshal Walter von, 77

Brégi, Philippe, 115

Britanny, naval escape operations in, 23, 102, 109, 128, 172, 217–38, 251, 264, 266, 291, 310, 313; see also 'Shelburne'

Brome, Vincent, 18

Broussine, Georges ('Burgundy'), 226, 236

Brusselmans, Anne, 278 n.

Brussels, escape organisation in, 18, 23, 69, 71, 128–35, 144–50, 151–7, 160, 162–5, 166–7, 170–2, 180, 206, 208, 223, 242–3, 247–8, 253; see also Comet Line

Buchenwald Concentration Camp, 27, 122, 314

Burgundy line, 226, 236

Calais, author's capture at, 26–7; mentioned, 30, 50, 52, 53, 59, 60

Camors, Jean-Claude ('Bordeaux'), 226

Campinchi, François, 222, 225, 229, 233, 234

Canaris, Admiral Wilhelm, 305

Canet-Plage (Perpignan), escapes from, 87–8, 104–6, 108, 218, 219, 227

Carpentier, Abbé, 84, 98, 100, 308, 309

Cartwright, Colonel Henry (British military attaché in Berne), 33, 37, 39–42, 46, 60, 192, 201, 202, 203

Caskie, the Reverend Donald, 91, 218, 277, 311

Cavell, Edith, 19, 69–70, 132, 147, 172, 190

Charles II, king of England, 58

Châteaudun, 186, 237, 241, 250, 252, 254, 255, 259, 265, 275

Châtelaudren, 234, 238

Cheramy family, 117, 118

Christmann, Sonderführer Richard, 308

Churchill, Lieut.-Colonel Jack, 24

Churchill, Winston, 44, 45, 61

Cloyes, 186, 250, 252, 254 et seq., 268, 270, 271

Coache, Raymonde, 136–7, 168, 315

Coache, René ('Dover'), 136–7, 168, 192, 264, 279, 315

Codrington, Colonel, 175

Colditz, author's escape from, mentioned, 21 n., 33, 39, 46, 50, 52, 53, 55, 56, 57, 58, 59, 63, 82, 89, 95, 112, 114, 194, 231, 283, 293, 299

Cole, Harold, his treachery, 23, 82–5, 86, 91–2, 97, 98, 99–100, 106, 109, 110, 116, 119, 126, 127, 145–6, 305, 306; his career and death, 307–11

Comet line (escape route to Spain), 18–19, 23, 128–80, 192, 208, 221, 223, 243, 244, 247, 249 n., 252, 253, 254, 256, 257, 259, 264, 271, 277, 278, 279, 306, 307

Commando raids on French coast, 194–204, 313

Compton, Sir Edmund, 25

Concentration camps, see Buchenwald, Dachau, Mauthausen, Natzweiler, Ravensbrück and Sachsenhausen

Cortes, Fabien de, 120, 121

Crockatt, Brigadier Norman (organiser of M.I.9), 19, 60–2, 68, 70, 87, 93, 107, 110, 111, 152, 170, 174, 201, 202, 221, 231, 236, 238, 242, 262, 278, 291, 297, 299, 300, 317

Dachau Concentration Camp, 110, 122, 311, 314, 318

Darling, Donald ('Sunday'), M.I.9 agent at Gibraltar, 55, 56, 69, 71, 75–8, 79, 82, 86, 87, 88, 95, 96, 99, 108, 109, 127, 129, 140 n., 153, 167, 172, 173, 175, 177, 178, 218, 230–1; takes over Room 900, 262–3, 266, 270

Dassié, Jean, 159, 160, 161

Dawson, Flight-Lieutenant, 203

Day, Group-Captain, 24, 25 n.

de Blommaert, Baron Jean (Rutland), 243, 246, 249, 250, 252–7, 259, 265, 268, 269, 270, 271, 275, 276

Debreuil, Armand, 200

Decat, Sergeant Henri ('Lieutenant Drew'), 145, 153, 156, 162–3, 164, 178

Dédée (Andrée de Jongh), founder of Comet line, 18, 62, 70, 128–58; her arrest and imprisonment, 159–64, 165, 166, 167, 170–1; her postwar life, 314; mentioned, 176, 177, 179, 193, 206, 207, 243, 307, 313

de Greef, see Greef

de Jongh, see Jongh

Delloye, Commandant Jean, 145

Derksema, Dr., 205

Desitter, Prosper (Gestapo agent), 250, 253, 261, 306, 307

Desoubrie, Jacques (Gestapo agent), 180, 254, 261, 306, 307; see also Boulain and Masson

Dings, Flore, 306

Dissart, Françoise, 115, 117, 118, 120, 121, 123–4, 151, 249

Dobie, Colonel David, 284–5, 287, 288, 289, 291, 292, 293

Dorré, Monsieur, 230

Dowding, Bruce, 84, 98

Dowling, Corporal, 28

Dowse, Sydney, 24

Dubois, Madame, 225

Dumais, Sergeant-Major (now Capitaine) Lucien, 106, 109, 225, 227–38, 243, 244, 256, 264

Dumon, Andrée (Nadine), 133, 135, 156

Dumon, Micheline ('Michou'), 135, 138, 247–8, 249, 250, 253

Dunkirk, 17, 20, 21, 26, 27, 46, 61, 67, 75, 76, 83, 110, 124, 218, 256, 259, 312

Duprez, Monsieur, 83, 84, 98, 308

Duvillard, Monsieur, (French Ministre des Ancièns Combatants), 271

Ebbens family, 285, 287, 288, 290

Eisenhower, General Dwight D., 278

Escape lines, see Burgundy, Comet, O'Leary

Escape routes: for Air see Aircraft 'pickups'; for Land see Escape lines; for Sea, 94–109, 217–38

Evans, A. J., 19 n.

'Fabian' (Belgian S.A.S. commander), 283, 285, 290, 294

'Ferière' (radio operator), 85

Fidelity, H.M.S., 80, 314

Fiocca, Nancy, 112
Florentino (guide), 131, 136, 138–9, 140–3, 157, 158–9, 164, 166
Forbes, Flying Officer Norman, his escape and recapture, 30–4
Fort de la Revère (near Monte Carlo), 46, 87, 93, 99, 102, 103–4, 111, 218, 223
Fort Meauzac (Dordogne), 78, 93, 110–111, 112, 120
Fort St. Hippolyte (near Nîmes), 46, 80, 87, 91
Fouquerel, Aimable, 136
France, escape organisations in, see Bayonne, Brittany, Marseille, Paris, Perpignan, Ruffec, St. Jean de Luz, Toulouse
Franco, General, 75, 172
Frankton operation, 197 et seq., 203
Fraser, Major Hugh, 284, 287, 292, 293, 296, 298, 299
Fresnes prison, 27, 97, 98, 167, 170, 187, 191, 249, 261
Fréteval, Forêt de, camp for airmen in, 237, 241, 246, 250–60; their rescue, 265–71, 275–6
Friend, Tony, 102, 103, 223
Furness, Viscount and Viscountess, 187

Garrow, Captain (later Lieut-Colonel) Ian, organiser escape routes in South of France, 18, 78–9, 80, 86, 124; arrested, 83, 91, 93, 110–11; rescued, 111–16, 120, 121; mentioned, 306, 317
Gaulle, General Charles de, 54, 113
Gestapo, 16, 17, 18, 23, 24, 25, 27, 28, 31–4, 38, 39, 41, 42, 46, 50, 51, 52, 57–81, 64, 65, 71, 86, 88, 91, 94, 95, 97–8, 110, 111, 112, 116, 117–19, 121, 123, 127, 128, 133, 135, 138, 149–50, 151, 152, 154–5, 158, 159, 160, 161, 164–5, 167, 169, 170, 171, 173, 175, 180, 187, 189, 191, 196, 203, 204, 213, 222, 223, 224, 225, 233, 234, 242, 245, 247, 249, 250, 253, 254, 260, 261, 271, 277, 279, 288, 290, 299, 303 et seq.
Gibraltar, 40, 46, 50, 52, 54–5, 56, 71, 75, 79, 82, 85, 86, 87, 88, 93, 94, 95, 98, 99, 107, 108, 109, 145, 162–78, 218, 260
Giocoechea, see Florentino
Giquel family, 232
Giskes, Colonel (head of Abwehr in Holland), 206, 209, 211, 308
Goering, Hermann, 15, 99, 150, 167, 171, 300, 303
Gosling, Mr., 86

Gramman, Monsignor, 172
Graudenz aerodrome, 31, 32, 33
Greef, Madame Elvire de, 137–8, 140, 143, 151, 157, 158–9, 160, 161, 165, 167, 179, 252, 253, 264
Greef, Fernand de, 137, 158
Greef, Frederic de, 137–8
Greef, Janine de, 138, 140
Greindl, Baron Albert, 135, 164–5, 171, 247, 277
Greindl, Baroness Bernadette, 154, 164, 165 and note, 171
Greindl, Baron Jean ('Nemo'), his work for Brussels escape line, 134–5, 142 n., 143, 144, 145, 146, 147, 148, 149, 150, 151, 152–6, 162; his arrest, 163–5; his death, 171–2; mentioned, 178, 193, 206, 244, 277, 306, 316
Greville-Bell, Captain Anthony, 266
Groome, Thomas, his work for O'Leary line, 111–19, 122–3, 127, 192, 202, 317 n.
Guérisse, Major-General A. M., see O'Leary, P. A.
Gulbenkian, Calouste, 76
Gulbenkian, Nubar, 76–7
Guillot, Pierre ('Pernod'), 226

Hackett, Brigadier (later General Sir John,) 298–9
'Ham' (Dutch agent), 281, 285, 294–5, 298
Hamilton, Second Officer Marie, 202
Harcourt, Pierre d', 27, 53
'Harrier' (M.I.9 agent), 285–8, 290, 291
Hasler, Major (now Lieut.-Colonel), H. G., 197–203, 304
Hawkins, Flight-Lieutenant, 99, 103
Heaps, Leo, 292, 296, 297
Henaff, Yves de ('Curacao'), 226
Hickey, Flight Sergeant, 99
Higginson, Squadron Leader, 93, 99–109, 218
Himmler, Heinrich, 29, 303, 305
Hiscocks, Charles, 63
Hitler, Adolf, 15, 18, 26, 37, 47, 51, 57, 96, 106, 199, 203, 303, 304
Holland, escape and rescue work in, 16, 19, 20, 23, 205–13, 275–99, 312, 313, 315
Hope, Major Peter, 311
Horrocks, General Sir Brian, 284
'Horse' (cover name of M.I.9 agent in Barcelona), 71, 79
Horsely, Pilot Officer, 134
Hovelacque, Lieutenant Patrick ('Kummel'), 260, 277

Howard, Leslie, 173
Huet (guide), 234
Hyde-Thompson, Lieutenant John, 36

Ingels, Jean, 135, 172
I.S.9(d)—Intelligence School No. 9 (D)
  —19, 28, 33, 60, 61, 62, 64 et seq., 68,
  317; see also Room 900
I.S.9 (Western European Area), 241, 260,
  261 et seq., 277, 278, 283, 284, 286, 290,
  292 n., 294, 296, 298, 299
Ivan (Ivan Bougaiev), 224, 232, 233

Johnson, Albert Edward ('B'), 139, 140,
  160, 161, 165, 166
Joly, Private, 219
Jones, Robert Roberts, 172
Jongh, Andrée de, see Dedée
Jongh, Frédéric de, his work for Comet
  line in Brussels, 18, 128–9, 132–3, and
  in France, 134, 135–6, 143, 144, 152,
  157–8, 162, 166–8; his arrest and fate,
  169–71, 176, 247, 307, 313
Jongh, Suzanne de, see Wittek, S.
Jubault, Omer, 255, 270, 271

Keitel, Field Marshal Wilhelm, 51, 203
Kelly, Sir David and Lady, 38
Kerambrun, François, 234, 235–6
Kieffer, S.S. Sturmbannführer, 308, 310
King, Flight Sergeant, 134
Kipling, Rudyard, 190
Knochen, S.S. Standartenführer, 304
Koch, Lieutenant (Dutch intelligence
  officer), 285
Kragt, Dignus ('Frans Hals'), 279–83,
  285, 290, 291, 294, 297, 298, 299

Labrosse, Ray, (now Lieut–Colonel)
  220–2, 225, 226–7, 229–30, 236–8, 256
Lafleur, Corporal Conrad ('Charles'),
  219, 243–6
Lake, Philippe d'Albert 254, 256,
  259, 260
Lake, Virginia d'Albert 259–60
Lampe, David, 316
Langley, Captain (now Lieut.-Colonel)
  J. M. ('Jimmy'), his work in charge of
  I.S.9(d), 59–62, 68, 69, 71, 79, 82–3,
  86, 88, 91, 92–3, 103, 104, 106, 110,
  111, 116, 121–2, 144, 151, 153, 162,
  172, 183, 187–8, 191, 194, 203, 217,
  219, 220, 221, 223, 226, 230–1; his
  work as joint commander I.S.9
  (Western European Area), 241, 260,

262, 263, 277, 278, 283, 285, 287, 294,
  295, 296, 297, 317
Lapeyre, Robert and Yvonne, 161
Last, Dirk ('Zwarte Kees'), 281
Lathbury, General Sir Gerald, 290, 293
Laver, Corporal, 198, 199
Le Balch, Doctor, 229
Lebreton, Madame, 104
Le Calvez, Marie-Thérèse, 233
Le Cornec, François, 217, 220, 222, 226,
  230, 232–3, 235–6, 237–8
Lefort, Capitaine Gilles, 264, 265
Legrelle, Count Jacques, 145, 177, 178–
  180, 243, 244, 307
le Légionnaire, Roger, see le Neveu, R.
Lemaître ('London') (radio operator),
  243, 246, 247, 256
le Neveu, Roger (Gestapo agent), 119–
  121, 128, 220, 222, 234, 306
Lille, 27, 28, 59, 83, 84, 86, 100, 102, 168,
  169, 180, 184, 254, 307, 308
Lindell, Mary (Countess de Milleville),
  her early escape work in France and
  her enrolment as M.I.9 agent in
  London, 183–93; her return to
  France and her organisation there,
  194–203; her arrest, 204; mentioned,
  19, 221, 234, 255, 313, 316
Livry-Level, Colonel Philippe, 221
Luteyn, Lieutenant, escapes from Colditz,
  35–7, 58
Lyon, 187, 191, 200, 201, 202, 309

Macmillan, Captain Maurice, 298
Madrid, 71, 79, 86, 131, 143, 157, 166,
  172, 175, 177, 178
Maguire, Major Hugh, 295
Mallet, Jean Pierre, 249 n.
Mannerheim, General Baron Gustaf,
  167, 171
Manser, Pilot Officer, 134
Marathon operation (rescue of Allied
  airmen), 172, 241 et seq., 278
Maréchal, Albert, 147, 172
Maréchal family (Elsie, Georges and
  Madame), 147–50
Maréchal Affair, 146–50, 151, 154–6,
  164, 170, 208, 242, 306
Marseille, escape organisation at, 17, 18,
  43, 48 et seq., 62, 68, 69, 76, 78 et seq.,
  82, 83–4, 85, 86, 87, 88, 91–3, 96 et
  seq., 103, 110, 111, 119, 187, 218, 308,
  309
Martel, Simon ('Brandy'), 226
Martinez, Dr., 196
Martineau (guide), 202

Mason-MacFarlane, Lieut.-General Sir Noel, governor of Gibraltar, 175–6

Masson, Jean (Gestapo agent), 167–9, 180, 244, 247, 249, 250, 254, 261, 306–7; see also Boulain and Desobrie

Mauduit, Comte de, 222

Mauduit, Comtesse Betty de, 222, 223, 227, 234, 307

Mauthausen concentration camp, 122, 153, 212

Menten de Hornes, Eric de, 172

Merode, Prince Werner de, 203

M.I.9, 15, 16, 38, 40, 41, 42, 44, 54, 55, 57 et seq., 64 et seq., 75 et seq., 85, 86, 88, 92, 93, 100, 110, 123, 129, 131, 135, 143, 167, 168, 172, 174, 179, 185, 188, 193, 197, 199, 202, 206, 207, 224, 230, 231, 232, 233, 237, 238, 242, 262, 263, 271, 287, 294, 312–13, 315–18

Michiels, Josée, 154, 155

Michiels, Victor, 149, 154, 155

Michiels, Yvon ('Jean Serment'), 252

Milleville, Comtesse de, see Lindell, Mary

Milleville, Maurice de, 197, 200, 204

Mills, Flight Lieutenant, 134

Mills, Marine, 199

'Mithridate' (agents in Paris), 222–3

'Monday' (M.I.9 agent at Madrid), 71, 79, 82, 86, 87, 127, 129, 131, 133, 138, 143, 144, 145 n., 151, 157, 162, 166, 172, 173, 175, 177, 178, 179, 222, 247, 264

Mongelard, Madame, 117, 118

Montet, Maurice, see Martell, Simon

Montgomery of Alamein, Field Marshal Viscount, 261

Morelle, Elvire, 135, 136, 149–50, 154, 155, 170

Morris, John (later Lord Morris of Borth-y-Guest), 63

Mott, Flight Lieutenant, 86–7

Mountbatten, Lord Louis (later Earl Mountbatten of Burma), 197

Myrda, Father, 102, 103, 218

Nabarro, Flight Sergeant, 99

Natzweiler concentration camp, 122

Neave, Airey ('Saturday')—the author— captured at Calais, 26–7; at Spangenburg, 29; at Thorn 30; his escape and recapture, 30–4; at Colditz, 34; his escape, 35–7; in Switzerland, 38–45; journey to England via Marseille and Gibraltar, 48–55; works for M.I.9, 56 et seq.; attends meeting at Gibraltar, 170, 172–7; refused permission to go to Brittany, 230–1; in charge of Room 900, 241 et seq.; lands in Normandy, 260–1; takes part in Sherwood operation, 261–76; in Paris, 277; in Brussels, 278; takes part in rescue operations (Pegasus I and II) after Arnhem, 283–300; member of International Military Tribunal Nuremburg 303 et seq.

Négre, Gaston, 104

Nelson, Lieut.-Colonel Richard, (U.S. Army) 241, 262

Neybergh, Ghislain, 172

Nitelet, Jean (radio operator), 86, 87, 92, 93, 99, 102, 103, 104, 106

Nosek, S.S. Gruppenführer, 97–8

Nothomb, Baron Jean-François ('Franco')—head of Comet line— 140, 151, 160, 161, 165, 166, 167, 168, 170, 171, 172, 173, 176–9; his arrest, 180; mentioned, 221, 223, 243, 244, 247, 279, 308

Nouveau, Louis, his work for O'Leary line, 49–54, 61, 78, 82, 86, 88, 96, 97, 103, 107, 110, 111, 112, 119; his arrest, 120–2; mentioned, 127, 151, 217, 220, 222, 306, 307, 313, 314–15

Nouveau, Renée, 51, 52, 53–4, 56, 78, 110, 111, 112, 121, 313, 315

Oaktree operation, 220 et seq., 229

O'Casey, Sergeant, 296

O'Leary, Pat—organises O'Leary escape line in South of France, 18, 51, 58, 61, 70, 75, 79–81, 82–6, 87, 88, 90, 91–3, 96–9, 102–9, 110–19; his arrest, 120–3; his release, 313–14; mentioned, 127, 128, 144, 146, 151, 173, 187, 202, 218, 219, 222, 226, 243, 249, 306, 308, 309, 311, 313

O'Leary escape line, 23, 51, 75–124, 146, 217, 219, 220, 307

Ollard, Richard, quoted, 58

Operations, see Bonaparte, Marathon, Oaktree, Pegasus I and II, Shelburne and Sherwood

Oultremont, Count Edouard d', 135, 152–3, 155, 156, 163, 208

Oultremont, Count Georges d' ('Ormond'), 135, 152–3, 155, 156, 163, 192, 208, 242–7, 263, 277

Paris, escape organisation in, 18, 83, 85, 86, 89–90, 119–20, 121, 135, 136–7, 144, 145, 146, 149, 152, 156, 157, 161, 162, 163, 164 5, 166 7, 168–70, 179– 180, 184–5, 187, 189–91, 192, 204, 219,

Paris—*cont.*
    222–3, 230, 231, 238, 244, 245, 247,
    249, 250, 252, 253, 256, 259, 260, 265,
    268, 275–8, 305, 306–7, 308, 309, 310,
    311
'Parker', 77, 79
Patton, Lieut.-General G. S., 264–5
Pegasus I and II operations, 284, 285,
    289–300
Perpignan, 76, 77, 87, 88, 104, 202, 219,
    230; *see also* Canet-Plage
Pétain, Philippe, marshal of France, 17,
    112, 113
'Pierre', 112–13, 114
Plastiras, General, 97
Plock (Poland), author interrogated by
    Gestapo at, 31–3
Plouha (Brittany), escapes from, 217,
    220, 222, 227 *et seq.*, 264; *see also*
    Anse Cochat Bay
Potier, Captaine Dominique-Edgar, 243,
    246, 261, 307
Prassinos, Mario, 54, 68, 78, 84, 88, 97,
    104, 107 and note
Priem, Captain, 53
Pyrenees escape route, 23, 54, 75, 85, 91,
    128, 131, 136, 138–9, 140–3, 144, 157–
    159, 164, 166, 200, 203, 247, 264, 305

Rait, Colonel Cecil, 172–3
Rasquin, Henri, 172
Ravensbrück concentration camp, 117,
    135, 140, 153, 168 *n.*, 204, 212, 222,
    260, 314
Reddé, Madamoiselle, 117–19
Reinecke, Judge Gunther, 304
Rémy, General Louis, 18, 93, 95
Rennes, 222, 233, 234, 241, 264, 306
Rodocanachi, Dr., 83–4, 91, 92, 99, 200,
    308, 309
Roger, Max, 166, 170, 177
Roger, *see* de Neveu, R.
Room 900 (headquarters of organisation
    to recover Allied servicemen in
    occupied territories), 19, 25, 64 *et seq.*,
    75, 78, 79, 80, 82, 83, 87, 88, 91, 93, 95,
    99, 102, 104, 107, 108, 112, 115, 118,
    120, 121, 123, 127, 131, 135, 144, 145,
    146, 151–2, 162, 172, 173–4, 175, 179,
    183, 191, 192–3, 195, 198, 201, 202,
    203, 205, 212, 213, 217, 218, 219, 220,
    222, 223, 226, 227, 229, 230, 231, 232,
    238, 241 *et seq.*, 256, 260, 263, 277, 279,
    281, 297–8, 300, 312, 317–18
Ruffec, Mary Lindell's organisation in,
    187, 191–204, 313

R.V.P.S. (Royal Victoria Patriotic Asy-
    lum for the Orphan Daughters of
    Soldiers and Sailors killed in the
    Crimean War)—interrogating centre
    for non-British arrivals in U.K.—
    94–6, 98, 164

Sachsenhausen concentration camp, 24,
    25 *n.*
St. Jean de Luz, escape route through,
    23, 128–9, 131, 137–9, 140–1, 144,
    158–9, 165, 252
St. Valery, survivors from, 21, 78, 110,
    128
San Sebastian, 23, 129, 131, 136, 143, 157,
    178–9
Savinos, Leoni, 87–8, 94, 96–8
Savinos, Madame, 87–8, 94, 96–8
'Saturday' (author's cover name), 71
Schreieder, S.S. Sturmbannführer, 206,
    211–12
S.D. (Sicherheitsdienst) German Se-
    curity Service—175, 203, 204, 207,
    211, 212, 303, 304
Shaw, Colonel Cecil, 184, 185, 189
Shelburne operation—sea escapes from
    Brittany—172, 226–38, 243, 256, 264,
    277, 306
Sherwood operation, 249–71, 275, 290
Sillars, Major Ronald, 202
Simon, Louis, 45–7
Simonds, Lieut.-General G. G., 295
Smit, (M.I.9 agent at the Hague) 207,
    209, 210, 212
Snoy et d'Oppuers, Baron Jean-Charles,
    171 *n.*
S.O.E. (Special Operations Executive)—
    sabotage organisation—68–9, 80, 98 *n.*,
    107 *n.*, 112 *n.*, 194–6, 204, 205–12,
    245, 279, 310
Somer, Dr. J. M., 280
Spain, 18, 19, 20, 21, 22–3, 38, 40, 46, 50,
    51, 53–4, 55, 59, 61, 70–1, 75 *passim*,
    180, 183, 187, 191, 193, 202, 205, 217,
    223, 225, 226, 227, 230, 234, 236, 241,
    242, 243, 247, 254, 257, 259, 277, 279,
    306
Spangenburg (Oflag IXa), the author at,
    29–30
Sparks, Marine, 197, 198, 199, 200, 201,
    202, 203
Spooner, Commander Reginald, 307,
    310
Spriewald, Paula, 99, 104, 106–9, 112 *n.*
Stevens, Colonel, 205

Straight, Squadron Leader Whitney, 87–92, 94, 99, 102, 104, 112
Switzerland, 15, 19, 21, 37–45, 48, 58, 60, 124, 167, 200, 201–3, 204, 212

Tarana sea rescue operations, 87–8, 99, 104–9, 110, 111, 218, 227
Tatham-Warner, Major Digby, 293
Temmerman ('Timon'), 281
Terwindt, Beatrice, *see* Trix
Thorn (Stalag XXa), 30 *et seq.*, 57
Thornton, Major James, (U.S. Army) 264, 265
Toulouse, escape organisation at, 78, 79, 110, 111, 113, 115, 116, 117–21, 123–4
Toussaint ('Taylor'), radio operator 252, 254–5, 256–7
Triffe, Louis, 309
Trix (Beatrice Terwindt) ('Felix'), 205–213, 234, 279

Ulmann, Paul, 113, 120
Ursel, Count Antoine d', 142 *n.*
Usandizaga, Francia, 140, 141, 158–9

van den Boogert, J. J. ('Koos'), 281
Vanier, Private, 219
van Lier, Peggy, 135, 152–3, 163, 208
van Roijen, Jan Herman, 286–7
Venlo incident, 205
'Victor' (M.I.9 agent in Geneva), 42, 43–4, 46, 52, 120, 121, 167, 192, 201, 204
Viron, Monsieur, 256, 267, 268, 269

Westminster, Hugh Grosvenor, 2nd Duke of, 18
Wildeboer, 'Big Bill', 294
Williams, Val (Vladimir Bouryschkine), 102, 217–25, 226, 227, 229, 232–4
Windham-Wright, Patrick, 174, 229, 231, 235, 237, 238, 300
Windsor-Lewis, Captain (later Brigadier) James, 183–7, 188, 189, 191, 204, 255
Wittek, Suzanne, 132, 133, 136, 167
Woollatt, Captain Hugh, escapes from Germany, 41–55; mentioned, 59, 75, 92, 96, 98, 117
Wynne, Barry, 19